STS

山田社

STS

山田社

3 及時複習法—保持單字長期記憶的秘訣，一舉公開！

▲每課學習計畫，以「艾賓浩司遺忘曲線」告訴你如何背單字不易忘。

▲每週學習計畫：「學習→複習」隨時鞏固記憶。

　全書學時共6週30課，週一到週五一天一課，週六到週日，鞏固複習。

　「艾賓浩司遺忘曲線」來自德國學者艾賓浩司，他將人的記憶分為：很快就被遺忘的暫態記憶（幾秒）、短時記憶（幾分鐘），和不容易忘記的長時記憶（1小時甚至幾個月）。所以，我們不應該等到記憶徹底消失後再重新記憶，而是應該在暫態記憶和短時記憶還沒有消失時，及時加深印象。所以，要想保持長期記憶的秘訣就是：在你忘記之前，「及時複習」它，並記住它。

　結合「及時複習法」的規律原理，我們總結了一套抗遺忘記憶法。每課單字我們進行科學分組、分塊。**每課4組(Group)**，每組再分**4塊**，每塊**5個單字**，指導讀者學習與複習，能最大限度地克服遺忘。

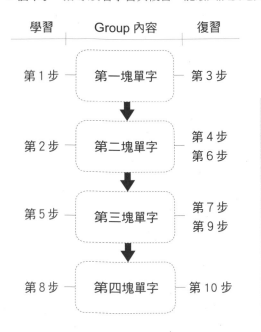

學習	Group 內容	複習
第1步	第一塊單字	第3步
第2步	第二塊單字	第4步 第6步
第5步	第三塊單字	第7步 第9步
第8步	第四塊單字	第10步

第1步：學習第一塊
第2步：學習第二塊
第3步：複習第一塊
第4步：複習第二塊
第5步：學習第三塊
第6步：複習第二塊
第7步：複習第三塊
第8步：學習第四塊
第9步：複習第三塊
第10步：複習第四塊

字根字首 巧記法

中學英語
單字大全
贈MP3

General English Proficiency TEST

星火記憶研究所　馬德高　著　**Spark**®星火英語

山田社
San Tian She

有人說：想要成功，學會英語可以省下 10 年功。

想知道老外都在想什麼？
想得到外國的技術支援，
學測想加分，想加薪，
想看懂原文書、電影、影集、雜誌，從中找 know how，
國外旅行，讚嘆度 UP!UP!

《心智圖 完全攻略 中學英語大全》出新版了！
全新最好背、好讀的萬用單字書《字根字首巧記法！中學英語大全》，
您還在等什麼？趕快來去考英檢吧！

■ 英語考試權威助陣，權威單字，就是這麼威！
■ 打造背英文單字 10 倍記憶的「星火燎原單字巧記法」。
■ 及時複習法—保持單字長期記憶的秘訣，一舉公開！
■ 片語就是記憶鉤，掌握中學必考片語，就是初級英檢高分的關鍵！
■ 聲音穿腦法—以實戰朗讀光碟，熟悉美籍老師語調及速度，聽力訓練，最佳武器。
■ 輕鬆取得加薪證照，搶百萬年薪！

書中，收錄了語言訓練中心所公布的全民英檢初級必備單字 2260 個，還有中學必考片語。

1 英語考試權威助陣，權威單字，就是這麼威！

▲ 單字附音標、詞性、單字意義，另額外補充同、反義字、片語跟衍生字，讓你精確掌握單字各層面的字義，活用的領域更加廣泛！

▲ 單字附例句，例句不僅配合初級文法，內容還非常實際有用。當你的大腦對一種內容感到興趣，就會積極配合，幫助你記住，而且會想要儘快運用。例句特別以套色方式標示，從例句來記單字，有了例句當背景，就更能「心神會」單字的意思，很自然就能記在腦中，不容易忘記。這對根據上下文適切語彙的題型，更是大有幫助，同時也紮實了文法及聽說讀寫的超強實力。

2 片語就是記憶鉤，掌握中學必考片語，就是初級英檢高分的關鍵！

▲ 短句裡經常有片語，長句就更不用說了，長句一般都是由短句跟片語所組。因此，**想提升英語實力，提高溝通能力，掌握片語就是掌握記憶英語的關鍵**。要快速累積英語的聽力跟口說能力，就要大量聽、說、練片語。以強化語的節奏感，培養你的英語語感！

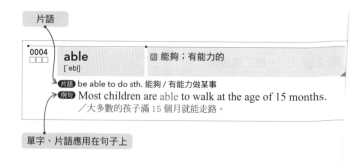

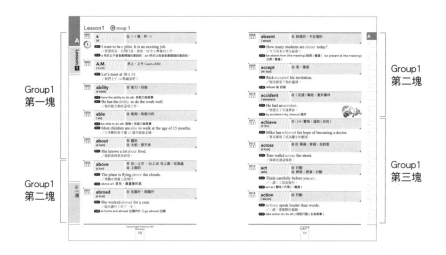

Group1
第一塊

Group1
第二塊

Group1
第二塊

Group1
第三塊

「及時複習法」強化記憶的方法是「**重複、重複、再重複**」。強化單字背誦能力的方法也是「**重複、重複、再重複**」。所謂「熟能生巧」，一再地「重複、重複、再重複」，不但不容易忘記，而且在考試時能更具有信心。

▲每組學習計畫——「魔術之七原理」的應用。

美國心理學家 G. 米勒通過大量實驗發現：人的記憶廣度平均數為 7，即大多數一次最多只能記憶 7 個獨立的「塊」。這就是人們所說的「魔術之七」，我們利用這一規律，**將短時記憶量控制在 7 個之內，每塊包括 5 個單字，從而科學使用大腦，是記憶穩步推進。**

4 打造背英文單字 10 倍記憶的「星火燎原單字巧記法」。

詞根＋聯想式記憶 ＋ 圖解記憶 ＋ 語境記憶 ＝ 單字 10 倍記憶法

▲詞根＋聯想式記憶——追根溯源，星火燎原單字聯想

　　書中採用，「**星火式記憶法**」充分挖掘並利用了英語詞彙之間的內在聯繫，由少數熟悉的單字，迅速記憶多數生詞，使星星之火迅速蔓延成為燎原之勢。

　　詞根記憶以單字的「根頭尾」為工具，剖析單字結構，如同庖丁解牛，讓你從深層次上把握單字記憶的方法。聯想是記憶的橋樑，通過中學熟悉的單字聯想記憶詞根，中學生詞，使記憶效果事半功倍。

字根＋聯想式記憶

0347
childhood
['tʃaɪld,hʊd]
图 童年，幼年（時代）

巧記 -hood 加在名詞後構成名詞，表示「時期」：babyhood（嬰兒時期）；childhood（童年時代）；girlhood（少女時代）；boyhood（少年時代）。

例句 She was lovely in her childhood.
／她小時候很可愛。

▲圖解記憶——千言萬語不如看一張圖

抽象的語言描述與活潑的插圖解釋，哪個效果更好？結果不言而喻。本書收錄了漫畫圖片，不管是幫助記憶單字，或記憶一詞多義，還是進行近義辨析，說明都妙趣橫生，一目了然，增強記憶效果。

圖解記憶

0312
catch
[kætʃ]
動[及物]（caught, caught）抓住，接住；趕上（車輛）；患（傳染病等）

巧記 圖解 catch 的一詞多義：

catch the fish
抓魚

catch the ball
接球

catch a bus
趕公車

catch (a) cold
著涼，感冒

例句 You'll catch a cold if you don't put a coat on.
／你要是不穿外套就會感冒。

▲語境記憶——Know the Word

　　有位外國人在評價我們的學生單字水準時，說「just recognize, never know」。不帶語境的單字，只會使你 recognize，只有在語境中，我們才能 know the word，才會使用。

因此，本書精選模考例句，佳句和實用、經典美句，讓您追趕最 in 的時尚潮流，同時擴充單字量，自信備考。

5 聲音穿腦法—以實戰朗讀光碟，熟悉美籍老師語調及速度，聽力訓練最佳武器。

隨書附贈光碟，讓你可以利用零碎的時間，例如搭捷運、坐公車、散步或運動，用聽的就能輕鬆記住單字。同時提升聽說讀寫能力，是一次考上英檢的好幫手。

本書也是考高中、托福、多益必考的中學程度單字及片語書。

符號說明

1 詞性符號語略語

詞性	呈現	詞性	呈現
名詞	名	冠詞	冠
動詞（及物＋不及物）	動	代詞	代
及物動詞	動 [及物]	副詞	副
不及物動詞	動 [不及物]	介詞	介
助動詞	助	連詞	連
形容詞	形	感嘆詞	感
數詞	數		

sb.=somebody 某人　　　　sth.=something 某物

2 文法符號

(sing.) 單數名詞　　　　　　(常 sing.) 常用單數
(pl.) 複數名詞　　　　　　　(常 pl.) 常用複數
(sing. 同 pl.) 單複數同形
不規則變化的動詞過去式、過去分詞用括號標注，

如：bind [baɪnd] 動 [及物](bound; bound)

目錄

GEPT
Elementary

Week 1

第一週

A

Lesson 1

0001
☐☐☐
a
[ə]

冠 一（個，件⋯）

例句 I want to be a pilot. It is an exciting job.
／我想成為一名飛行員。那是一份令人興奮的工作。
用法 a 用於以子音音素開頭的單詞前；an 用於以母音音素開頭的單詞前。

0002
☐☐☐
A.M.
[`e`ɛm]

副 早上，上午 (=a.m.=AM)

例句 Let's meet at 10 A.M.
／我們上午 10 點碰面吧！

0003
☐☐☐
ability
[ə`bɪlətɪ]

名 能力；技能

片語 have the ability to do sth. 有能力做某事
例句 He has the ability to do the work well.
／他有能力做好這項工作。

0004
☐☐☐
able
[`ebl]

形 能夠；有能力的

片語 be able to do sth. 能夠 / 有能力做某事
例句 Most children are able to walk at the age of 15 months.
／大多數的孩子滿 15 個月就能走路。

0005
☐☐☐
about
[ə`baʊt]

介 關於
副 大約，差不多

例句 She knows a lot about food.
／她對食物很有研究。

0006
☐☐☐
above
[ə`bʌv]

介 在⋯上方 ，以上 副 在上面；在高處
形 上面的

例句 The plane is flying above the clouds.
／飛機在雲層上面飛行。
片語 above all 首先，最重要的是

第一週

0007
☐☐☐
abroad
[ə`brɔd]

副 在國外，到國外

例句 She worked abroad for a year.
／她在國外工作了一年。
片語 at home and abroad 在國內外 ‖ go abroad 出國

0008 ☐☐☐

absent
[`æbsn̩t]

彤 缺席的，不在場的

例句 How many students are absent today?
／今天有多少學生缺席？

片語 be absent from (the meeting) 缺席（會議） be present at (the meeting) 出席（會議）

0009 ☐☐☐

accept
[ək`sɛpt]

動 收，接受

例句 Rick accepted his invitation.
／瑞克接受了他的邀請。

反義 refuse 動 拒絕

0010 ☐☐☐

accident
[`æksədənt]

名（交通）事故；意外事件

例句 He had an accident.
／他發生了交通事故。

片語 by accident (=by chance) 偶然

0011 ☐☐☐

achieve
[ə`tʃiv]

動〔及物〕實現；達到（目的）

例句 Mike has achieved his hope of becoming a doctor.
／麥克實現了成為醫生的願望。

0012 ☐☐☐

across
[ə`krɔs]

介副 橫過，穿過；在對面

例句 Tom walkd across the street.
／湯姆走過這條街。

0013 ☐☐☐

act
[ækt]

名 行動
動 表現；表演；行動

例句 Think carefully before you act.
／〔諺〕三思而後行。

片語 act as（暫時）代理（…職務）

0014 ☐☐☐

action
[`ækʃən]

名 行動

例句 Actions speak louder than words.
／〔諺〕事實勝於雄辯。

片語 take action (to do sth.) 採取行動（去做某事）

0015 ☐☐☐

active
[`æktɪv]

形 積極的；活潑的

例句 Tony is a quiet student, but he is active in class.
／東尼是個沈默寡言的學生，但他在課堂上很活躍。

片語 be active in 在…方面積極 ‖ take an active part in 積極參加…

0016 ☐☐☐

activity
[æk`tɪvətɪ]

名 活動；生氣，朝氣

例句 We should take an active part in outdoor activities.
／我們應該積極參加戶外活動。

0017 ☐☐☐

actor
[`æktɚ]

名 (男) 演員

巧記 〔熟〕act 表演 → 〔生〕actor；actress 女演員
例句 Her son wants to be an actor. ／她兒子想成為一名演員。

0018 ☐☐☐

actress
[`æktrɪs]

名 女演員

例句 The actress is always the focus of attention.
／那位女演員永遠是眾人注目的焦點。

0019 ☐☐☐

actually
[`æktʃʊəlɪ]

副 實際上，事實上

例句 Actually, the earth is getting warmer.
／實際上，地球正逐漸變熱。

Group 2

0020 ☐☐☐

track 2

add
[æd]

動 加；增加，添加；補充

片語 add to 添加，增添 ‖ add...to... 把…加到…上 ‖ add up to 合計達
例句 Every failure one meets will add to one's experience.
／〔諺〕不經一事，不長一智。

0021 ☐☐☐

addition
[ə`dɪʃən]

名 加，加法；添加，增加的人 (或物)

片語 in addition (=as well) 另外 ‖ in addition to (=besides，相當於介系詞)
除…之外 (還)
例句 There was a new addition to our family.
／我們家新添了人丁。
例句 What did Mozart write in addition to operas?
／除了歌劇，莫札特還寫了什麼？

0022 ☐☐☐ **address** [ə`drɛs]
名 地址；演說
動 [及物] 發表演說

例句 Please write your name and address on the postcard.
／請把你的姓名和地址寫在明信片上。

0023 ☐☐☐ **admire** [əd`maɪr]
動 [及物] 欽佩，羨慕

例句 I admire John for his courage.
／我欽佩約翰的勇氣。

衍生 admiring 形 令人佩服的

0024 ☐☐☐ **admit** [əd`mɪt]
動 [及物] 允許…進入；承認，供認
動 [不及物] 承認

巧記 圖解 admit 的一詞多義：

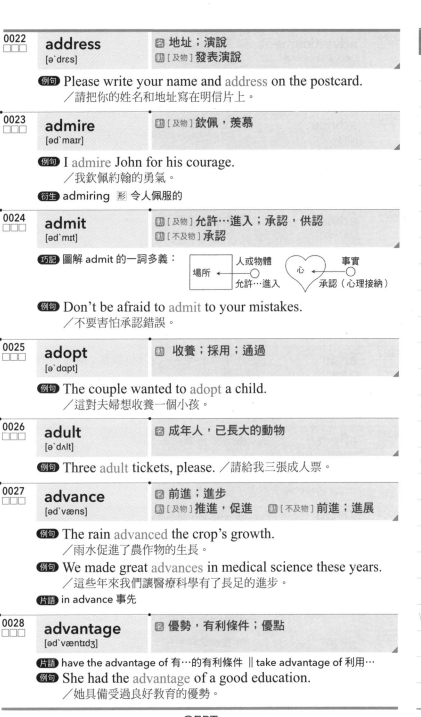

人或物體　　　　　　　　　　　事實

場所　　　　　　　　　　心　　

允許…進入　　　　承認（心理接納）

例句 Don't be afraid to admit to your mistakes.
／不要害怕承認錯誤。

0025 ☐☐☐ **adopt** [ə`dɑpt]
動 收養；採用；通過

例句 The couple wanted to adopt a child.
／這對夫婦想收養一個小孩。

0026 ☐☐☐ **adult** [ə`dʌlt]
名 成年人，已長大的動物

例句 Three adult tickets, please. ／請給我三張成人票。

0027 ☐☐☐ **advance** [əd`væns]
名 前進；進步
動 [及物] 推進，促進　　動 [不及物] 前進；進展

例句 The rain advanced the crop's growth.
／雨水促進了農作物的生長。

例句 We made great advances in medical science these years.
／這些年來我們讓醫療科學有了長足的進步。

片語 in advance 事先

0028 ☐☐☐ **advantage** [əd`væntɪdʒ]
名 優勢，有利條件；優點

片語 have the advantage of 有…的有利條件 ‖ take advantage of 利用…

例句 She had the advantage of a good education.
／她具備受過良好教育的優勢。

0029 ☐☐☐
advertisement
[ˌædvə-ˈtaɪzmənt]
名 廣告

例句 The newspapers are full of advertisements for cars.
／報紙上全是汽車廣告。

0030 ☐☐☐
advice
[ədˈvaɪs]
名 忠告；建議

例句 Let me give you a piece of advice.
／讓我給你一點建議吧。
用法 advice 是不可數名詞，表示數量時，需借助單位詞 piece。

0031 ☐☐☐
advise
[ədˈvaɪz]
動 勸告；建議

片語 advise (doing) sth. 建議 (做) 某事 ‖ advise sb. to do sth. 建議 / 勸告某人做某事 ‖ advise that one (should) do sth. 建議 / 勸告某人做某事〔子句用虛擬語氣〕
例句 I advised him to stop smoking. ／ I advised him that he (should) stop smoking.
／我勸他戒煙。

0032 ☐☐☐
affair
[əˈfɛr]
名 事情，事件；(常 pl.) 事務，事態；(個人的) 事

例句 I am not concerned with the affair.
／這件事與我無關。

0033 ☐☐☐
affect
[əˈfɛkt]
動 [及物] 影響

例句 The noise here affected my sleep.
／這裡的噪音影響了我的睡眠。

0034 ☐☐☐
afraid
[əˈfred]
形 害怕的；擔心的

片語 be afraid to do sth. 不敢做某事 ‖ be afraid of doing sth. 擔心 / 害怕做某事
例句 Mr. Black was afraid to climb the tree, because he was afraid of falling down from it.
／布雷克先生不敢爬樹，因為他怕從樹上掉下來。

0035 ☐☐☐
after
[ˈæftə-]
介 在⋯之後，在⋯後面
連 在⋯之後

例句 After the movie they fell asleep. ／看完電影以後，他們睡著了。

第一週

例句 After a few days he came back, but he said he would leave again in a few days.
／幾天後他回來了，可是他說他將在幾天後再度離開。

片語 look after 照顧

用法 「after+ 一段時間」通常與過去時態連用；「in+ 一段時間」通常與未來時態 (一般未來式和過去未來式) 連用。

| 0036 □□□ | **afternoon** [`æftɚˈnun] | 名 下午，午後 |

例句 I want to play badminton in the afternoon.
／我下午想去打羽毛球。

| 0037 □□□ | **again** [əˈɡɛn] | 副 又，再一次 |

例句 Say it again, please. ／請再說一遍。
片語 again and again 再三地，反複地 ‖ once again 再一次

| 0038 □□□ | **against** [əˈɡɛnst] | 介 反對；倚靠 |

例句 We are against war. ／我們反對作戰。

Group 3

| 0039 □□□ 3 | **age** [edʒ] | 名 年齡，年紀；時代 |

例句 At what age do children start school in your country?
／你們國家的小孩幾歲上學？

| 0040 □□□ | **ago** [əˈɡo] | 副 以前 |

例句 Two days ago I went to visit him, but his wife said that he had left four days before.
／兩天前，我去拜訪他，可是他的妻子說他在四天前就走了。

辨析 ago, before
(1) ago 指從現在算起若干時間以前，與動詞的一般過去式連用。
(2) before 指從過去算起的某個時間之前，用於過去完成式。

| 0041 □□□ | **agree** [əˈɡri] | 動 同意；贊成 |

片語 agree to (do) sth. 贊成 (做) 某事 ‖ agree with sb. 同意某人的意見

例句 He has no ideas of his own, so he always agrees with his friends about everything.
／他沒有自己的主見，所以他總是以他朋友的意見為意見。

衍生 agreement 名 協定；同意

0042 □□□	**ahead** [əˋhɛd]	副 在前面；向前；事前，預先 形 前面的

例句 The school is two kilometers ahead.
／學校在前方兩公里處。

片語 ahead of 比…提前，比…更早 ‖ go ahead ①進行 ②取得進展 ③先走

0043 □□□	**aid** [ed]	名 幫助；援助；助手 動 [及物] 幫助

片語 aid sb. with sth. 在 (某方面) 幫助某人 ‖ first aid 急救
例句 Thank you for aiding me with the work.
／謝謝你幫我做這個工作。

0044 □□□	**AIDS** [edz]	名 愛滋病

巧記 諧音：〔英〕AIDS 一音譯→〔漢〕愛滋
例句 AIDS is a fatal disease.
／愛滋病是絕症。

0045 □□□	**aim** [em]	動 瞄準，對準；致力 名 目標，目的

片語 aim at ①向…瞄準 ②以…為目的，針對 ‖ without aim 漫無目的地
例句 He aimed at the bird. ／他瞄準小鳥。
例句 She always aims for perfection.
／追求完美一直都是她的目標。

衍生 aimless 形 無目的的，無目標的

0046 □□□	**air** [ɛr]	名 空氣；大氣；天空

例句 Let's go outside and get some fresh air.
／讓我們出去呼吸些新鮮空氣吧。
片語 by air 搭乘飛機 ‖ in the open air 在戶外

0047 □□□	**aircraft** [ˋɛrˌkræft]	名 飛機

例句 Aircraft sometimes fuels in the air.
／飛機有時會在空中加油。

0048 □□□ **airline** [ˋɛr͵laɪn]　　名 航空公司

例句 He spent ten years as an airline pilot.
／他在航空公司當了 10 年的飛行員。

0049 □□□ **airplane** [ˋɛr͵plen]　　名 飛機

例句 The pilot landed the airplane.
／飛行員讓飛機降落。

同義 plane 名 飛機

0050 □□□ **airport** [ˋɛr͵port]　　名 航空站，飛機場

例句 I'm going to meet Lily at the airport tomorrow.
／我明天要去機場接莉莉。

0051 □□□ **alarm** [əˋlɑrm]　　名 警報器，警報；鬧鐘；驚慌

例句 The fire alarm sounded.
／防火警報器響了。

0052 □□□ **album** [ˋælbəm]　　名 相簿；唱片專輯

例句 I presented a photograph album to her.
／我送給她一本相簿。

0053 □□□ **alike** [əˋlaɪk]　　形〔作主詞補語〕相像的
副 相像地，相似地；一樣地

例句 Great minds think alike.
／〔諺〕英雄所見略同。

0054 □□□ **alive** [əˋlaɪv]　　形 活著的；現存的

例句 We don't know whether he is alive or dead.
／我們不知道他是生還是死。

0055 □□□ **all** [ɔl]　　形 全部的，所有的
副 完全地；都；很　代 全部，全體

例句 They all respect him. ／他們都很尊敬他。

例句 All the money was spent on clothes. ／所有的錢都花在買衣服上。

片語 after all 畢竟 ‖ all right 好，可以 ‖ at all〔常用於否定句、條件句以加強語氣〕根本，絲毫 ‖ in all 總共，總計

0056 □□□
allow
[əˋlaʊ]
動[及物]**允許，准許**

片語 allow doing sth. 允許做某事 ‖ allow sb. to do sth. 允許某人做某事 ‖ be allowed to do sth. 被允許做某事

例句 My parents didn't allow me to go to the party.
／我爸媽不准我去參加派對。

0057 □□□
almost
[ˋɔl͵most]
副 幾乎，差不多

例句 Almost all the students passed the exam.
／幾乎所有的學生都通過了考試。

G roup 4

0058 □□□

alone
[əˋlon]
形 單獨的，孤獨的；只有
副 單獨地；孤獨地

例句 You shouldn't leave a child alone in the house.
／你不該讓小孩獨自留在家裡。

0059 □□□
along
[əˋlɔŋ]
副 向前；一起；來到
介 沿著

例句 We went for a walk along the road. ／我們沿著公路散步。
片語 along with 與…一道 ‖ get along with ①進行，進展 ②相處

0060 □□□
aloud
[əˋlaʊd]
副 大聲地，出聲地

例句 What about reading aloud to practice pronunciation?
／大聲朗讀來練習發音好嗎？
例句 Read the dialogue aloud with your teacher.
／跟著你的老師大聲朗讀。

同義 loudly **副** 大聲地

0061 □□□
alphabet
[ˋælfə͵bɛt]
名 字母表

巧記 早已會讀 α 和 β，何須死記 alphabet?
▲詞源：正如同 ABC 是取英文字母表前三個字母代替全體字母一樣，alphabet 是取希臘文前兩個字母 α (alpha) 和 β (beta) 代指全體字母。
例句 There are twenty-six letters in the English alphabet.
／英語字母表中共有 26 個字母。

0062 already
[ɔl`rɛdɪ]
圖 已經，早已

例句 We got there early but Mike had already left.
／我們很早就到了那裡，但是麥克已經離開了。

0063 also
[`ɔlso]
圖 也；而且

例句 He is also very famous in Taiwan.
／他在台灣也是很有名氣。

例句 I also have many other duties.
／我也有很多其他的任務。

0064 although
[ɔl`ðo]
連 雖然；但是

例句 Although the girl is only nine, she takes care of her younger brother every day.
／雖然這個女孩只有 9 歲，但她每天都負起照顧弟弟之責。

用法 在英語裡，although/though 和 but 不能同時使用。

0065 altogether
[ˌɔltə`gɛðə]
圖 合計，總共

例句 How much will the cost be altogether?
／成本總共是多少？

0066 always
[`ɔlwez]
圖 總是，始終；永遠

例句 I will always love you.
／我會永遠愛你。

用法 always 是頻度副詞，一般置於行為動詞之前，助動詞、情態動詞或系動詞之後；always 與 not 連用，表示部分否定，意為「不總是，有時」。

0067 am
[əm／（重讀）æm]
動 [不及物] 是

例句 I am a model.
／我是一個模特兒。

0068 ambulance
[`æmbjələns]
名 救護車

例句 The wounded injured were taken to hospital by ambulance.
／受傷者被救護車送往醫院。

0069
☐☐☐
America
[ə`mɛrɪkə]

名 美國；美洲

例句 I have been to America many times.
／我去過美國很多次了。

0070
☐☐☐
American
[ə`mɛrɪkən]

形 美國的，美國人的
名 美國人

例句 He attended a lecture on American literature yesterday.
／他昨天參加了一個關於美國文學的講座。

0071
☐☐☐
among
[ə`mʌŋ]

介（通常指三者或三者以上）在…之中；在…中間

例句 His grade in the exam put him among the top students in his class.
／這次的考試成績使他進入班級資優生的行列。

0072
☐☐☐
amount
[ə`maʊnt]

名 數量，數額

片語 a large amount of〔與不可數名詞連用〕大量
例句 A large amount of money is spent on tobacco every year.
／每年都花費大量的金錢在香菸上。

0073
☐☐☐
ancient
[`enʃənt]

形 古代的；古老的

例句 He got an ancient coin. ／他得到了一枚古幣。

0074
☐☐☐
and
[ənd ／（重讀）ænd]

連 和，又；然後

例句 These apples are big and delicious.
／這些蘋果又大又好吃。
片語 and so on 等等 ‖ and then 然後

0075
☐☐☐
angel
[`endʒl]

名 天使，安琪兒

例句 My little daughter is as lovely as an angel.
／我的小女兒像天使一樣可愛。

0076
☐☐☐
anger
[`æŋgɚ]

名 生氣，憤怒

例句 They were filled with anger at the news.
／聽了這消息，他們滿腔怒火。

0077
□□□
🔊5

angry
[`æŋgrɪ]

形 生氣的，憤怒的

片語 be angry at/about sth. 因某事生氣 ‖ be/get angry with sb. 對某人生氣
例句 If you tell him the truth, he'll be angry with you.
／如果你告訴他實情，他會很生你的氣。

0078
□□□

animal
[`ænəml]

名 動物，野獸，牲畜

例句 This animal lives in water.
／這種動物生活在水中。

0079
□□□

ankle
[`æŋkl]

名（腳）踝，踝關節

例句 She fell and hurt her ankle.
／她摔倒並扭傷了腳踝。

0080
□□□

another
[ə`nʌðɚ]

形 再一；另一個

例句 I've had an apple, but I'd like another.
／我已經吃了一個蘋果，但我想再吃一個。
片語 one after another 一個接一個
用法 another+ 可數名詞單數：another day 另一天；another+ 數詞 + 可數
名詞複數：another ten days 又 10 天。

0081
□□□

answer
[`ænsɚ]

動 回答，答覆
名 答案；回答，答覆

例句 Give me your answer tomorrow.
／明天給我答覆。
片語 answer a question 回答問題 ‖ an answer to a question 問題的答案

0082
□□□

ant
[ænt]

名 螞蟻

例句 The ant is a social insect.
／螞蟻是群居昆蟲。

0083
□□□

any
[`ɛnɪ]

形 任何的，任一的
代 任何人，任何一個（些）

例句 Any of them can apply for the job.
／他們誰都可以申請這份工作。

0084 □□□
anybody
[ˈɛnɪˌbɑdɪ]

代 誰，任何人

例句 Anybody can do it.
／誰都能做這件事。

0085 □□□
anyone
[ˈɛnɪˌwʌn]

代 任何人，每個人

例句 Is there anyone at home?
／家裡有人嗎？

辨析 anyone, any one
(1) anyone 只能指人，後面不接 of 短語。
(2) any one 既指人又指物，後面可接 of 短語。

0086 □□□
anything
[ˈɛnɪˌθɪŋ]

代 任何事，無論何事

例句 Is there anything special you want to do in Taiwan?
／你在台灣有什麼特別想做的事情嗎？

用法 something, anything, everything, nothing 等不定代詞如有形容詞修飾時，形容詞要後置。

0087 □□□
anyway
[ˈɛnɪˌwe]

副 無論如何；至少

例句 I will go anyway, no matter what you say.
／不管你說什麼，我還是要去。

同義 anyhow 副 無論如何

0088 □□□
anywhere
[ˈɛnɪˌhwɛr]

副 任何地方，哪裡

例句 I can sleep anywhere.
／在任何地方我都能睡覺。

同義 anyplace 副 任何地方

0089 □□□
apartment
[əˈpɑrtmənt]

名 〔美〕（一戶）公寓房間

例句 He works very hard so that he can buy his own apartment.
／他努力工作，為的是能買一間自己的公寓。

同義 flat 名 〔英〕（一戶）公寓

0090 □□□
apologize
[əˈpɑləˌdʒaɪz]

動 [不及物] 道歉，謝罪

例句 I apologized to her for coming late.
／我因遲到而向她道歉。

0091 □□□
appear
[ə`pɪr]

動 [不及物] 出現；看起來；上市

例句 The stars appear at night.
／星星在夜間出現。

用法 appear作「看起來」講時，後面可以接形容詞、名詞或不定式作主詞補語。
例如：He appears honest. 他看起來很誠實。

反義 disappear 動 [不及物] 消失

0092 □□□
appearance
[ə`pɪrəns]

名 外觀，外貌；出現，露面

例句 Judging from his appearance, he may be sick.
／從他的外表來看，他或許生病了。

例句 Many museums have changed in appearance.
／許多博物館在外觀上有了變化。

0093 □□□
apple
[`æpl]

名 蘋果（樹）

例句 An apple a day keeps the doctor away.
／〔諺〕一天一蘋果，醫生遠離我。

0094 □□□
apply
[ə`plaɪ]

動 [不及物] 申請，請求
動 [及物] 應用，運用

片語 apply...to 把…應用於，運用 ‖ apply to 適用於 ‖ apply (to sb.) for (向某人)申請，請求

例句 You have to apply for a passport in advance.
／你必須提前申請護照。

衍生 applied 形 應用的 ;application 名 申請

0095 □□□
appreciate
[ə`priʃɪˌet]

動 [及物] 感謝，感激；欣賞

例句 I deeply appreciate your help.
／我很感謝你的幫忙。

Group 2

0096 □□□
April
[`eprəl]

名 四月 (=Apr.)

6

例句 I'm going to England next April.
／我明年 4 月份去英國。

用法 表示「在四月」，其前用介系詞 in；若表示在四月的某一日，則用介系詞 on，如 on April 25 在 4 月 25 日。其他表示月份的名詞也是這種用法。

0097 are
[ɚ/（重讀）ɑr]

動 是

例句 You are a student, aren't you?
／你是學生，不是嗎？

0098 area
[`ɛrɪə]

名 面積；區域，地區

例句 What is the area of Taiwan?
／臺灣的面積有多大？

0099 argue
[`ɑrgjʊ]

動 [不及物] 爭吵；爭辯

例句 He and his wife are always arguing about money.
／他跟她的妻子總是為錢爭吵。

片語 argue against/ argue for 反對 / 贊成

0100 arm
[ɑrm]

名 手臂；（椅子等的）扶手

例句 My arm is hurting badly.
／我的手臂痛得很厲害。

片語 arm in arm （指兩人）手挽著手

0101 armchair
[`ɑrm,tʃɛr]

名 扶手椅

例句 The old man is sitting in an armchair.
／那位老人坐在扶手椅上。

0102 army
[`ɑrmɪ]

名 軍隊

例句 Almost every family in the village has a man in the army.
／這個村子幾乎家家都有一名男子從軍。

片語 join the army 參軍

0103 around
[ə`raʊnd]

介 圍繞；在…四處
副 附近；到處；向相反方向；大約

例句 There are many trees around the house.
／房子的四周有許多樹。

片語 all around 四周，到處

0104 □□□

arrange
[əˋrendʒ]

勔 安排，準備；整理

例句 The meeting was arranged for Sunday.
／會議定在星期天召開。

0105 □□□

arrest
[əˋrɛst]

勔[及物] 逮捕，拘留
名 逮捕，拘留

例句 He was arrested for murder.
／他因為殺人而被警察逮捕了。

0106 □□□

arrive
[əˋraɪv]

勔[不及物] 到達，抵達；來臨

片語 arrive at/in 到達
例句 Connie arrived at the village on a snowy night.
／康妮在一個下雪的晚上到達村莊。
用法 arrive 後面的介系詞，按到達地點的大小來決定：at 用於較小的場所，如鎮、家、店等；in 用於較大的地方，如國家、大都市等。

0107 □□□

art
[ɑrt]

名 藝術，美術；技術，技藝

例句 The vase is a work of art.
／這個花瓶是件藝術品。

0108 □□□

article
[ˋɑrtɪk!]

名 文章；冠詞

例句 It is an interesting article on education.
／這是一篇關於教育的有趣文章。

0109 □□□

artist
[ˋɑrtɪst]

名 藝術家，美術家，（尤指）畫家

例句 I want to be an artist.
／我想成為一名藝術家。

0110 □□□

as
[əz／（重讀）æz]

連 像…一樣；當…的時候；因為
介 作為

片語 as...as 像，如同 ‖ as...as possible 盡可能…地 ‖ as if 好像 ‖ as long as 只要 ‖ as soon as 一…就… ‖ as well as 也，又
例句 I play basketball every day because I want to play as well as Jeremy Shu-How Lin.
／我每天都打籃球，因為我想打得和林書豪一樣好。

0111 □□□
Asia
[ˋeʃə]

名 亞洲

例句 The Indian Ocean is on the south of Asia.
／印度洋位於亞洲南部。

0112 □□□
Asian
[ˋeʃən]

形 亞洲的，亞洲人的
名 亞洲人

例句 Many of the shops were run by Asians.
／許多商店都是亞洲人經營的。

0113 □□□
ask
[æsk]

動 問，詢問；要求，請求

例句 May I ask you a question?
／我可以問你一個問題嗎？
片語 ask for 請求，要求 ‖ ask sb. about sth. 詢問某人有關某事的情況 ‖ ask sb. for sth. 向某人討要某物

0114 □□□
asleep
[əˋslip]

形 睡著的

片語 fall asleep 睡著，入睡
例句 While I was reading, I fell asleep.
／當我在看書的時候，不知不覺就睡著了。
用法 asleep 不用 very 修飾，而常用 fast/sound 修飾：be fast/sound asleep 熟睡。
反義 awake 形 醒著的

Ⓖroup 3

0115 □□□
assistant
[əˋsɪstənt]

名 助手，助理

⑦
例句 She has long been hoping to become the assistant manager.
／她很久以前就想當經理助理。
片語 an assistant to... …的助理

0116 □□□
assume
[əˋsjum]

動 [及物] 以為，假定；假裝

巧記 趣味記憶：Never assume, for it makes an ASS out of U and ME. 永遠不要去主觀的判斷，因為那會使你我成為笨蛋。
片語 assuming/assume that...(=supposing/suppose that...) 假定…
例句 I assume that it is true.
／我假定那是真的。

0117 ☐☐☐

at
[ət／(重讀) æt]

介〔表示地點、位置〕在…；〔表示時間〕在…時間(刻)；〔表示動作的目標和方向〕向…

例句 The party begins at five.
／宴會 5 點開始。

0118 ☐☐☐

attack
[ə`tæk]

名 動 攻擊，抨擊；(疾病) 侵襲

例句 We attacked the enemy.
／我們攻擊了敵人。

0119 ☐☐☐

attend
[ə`tɛnd]

動 [及物] 出席，參加；看護

例句 Only five people attended the meeting.
／只有 5 個人出席了會議。

0120 ☐☐☐

attention
[ə`tɛnʃən]

名 注意，專心，留心

片語 pay attention to 注意〔to 為介系詞〕

例句 You'd better pay more attention to the way you speak when having a discussion.
／討論的時候你最好多注意一下你的說話方式。

0121 ☐☐☐

audience
[`ɔdɪəns]

名 聽眾，觀眾

例句 There was a large audience in the theatre.
／劇院裡有很多觀眾。

用法 audience 側重指整體時，用作單數；側重指各個成員時，用作複數。

0122 ☐☐☐

August
[ɔ`gəst]

名 八月 (=Aug.)

例句 It happened sometime in August.
／這事發生在八月的某個時候。

0123 ☐☐☐

aunt
[ænt]

名 姨，姑，嬸，伯母，舅母 (=auntie=aunty)

例句 My aunt gave me a book for my birthday.
／我生日時姨媽送了一本書給我。

0124 □□□
Australia
[ɔ`streljə]

名 澳洲，澳洲大陸

例句 Could you tell us if it snows in winter in Australia?
／你能告訴我們澳洲冬天會下雪嗎？

0125 □□□
Australian
[ɔ`streljən]

形 澳洲人的，澳洲的
名 澳洲人

例句 The Australian team will appear.
／澳洲隊將會出場。

0126 □□□
autumn
[`ɔtəm]

名 秋天，秋季

例句 The weather is cool in autumn. ／秋天，天氣涼爽。
同義 fall 名〔美〕秋天

0127 □□□
available
[ə`veləbl]

形 可利用的；有空的

例句 Are you available on Tuesday?
／你星期二有空嗎？

0128 □□□
avoid
[ə`vɔɪd]

動〔及物〕避免，防止；避開

例句 You can't escape punishment this time, but you can avoid making mistakes next time.
／你這次不能逃避懲罰，但你下次可以避免犯錯。
用法 avoid 後常接動詞 -ing 形式，不接 to do 結構作受詞。

0129 □□□
aware
[ə`wɛr]

形〔作主詞補語〕意識到的，知道的

片語 be aware of 意識到
例句 I was aware of that fact.
／我知道了那個真相。
例句 To identify risks, we need to know the rules and be aware of the facts.
／為了辨識風險，我們需要瞭解規則，認清事實。

0130 □□□
away
[ə`we]

副 離開；向遠處；向另一方向

片語 be away from 離⋯⋯一段距離 ‖ far away 遙遠，遠離
例句 My home is 1,000 meters away from here.
／我家離這裡有 1,000 公尺遠。

0131 □□□ **baby** [`bebɪ]　图 嬰兒；幼獸

例句 Our baby is at the walking stage.
／我們的孩子正在學步階段。

0132 □□□ **back** [bæk]　图 背部；後面　副 回原處；向後　形 後面的

例句 There's a park at the back of his house.
／他家後面有個公園。
片語 back to back 背靠背

0133 □□□ **backward** [`bækwə-d]　副〔美〕向後，朝反方向；倒退地

例句 He made a backward step.
／他向後退了一步。
片語 backward and forward 來回地，忽前忽後地
同義 backwards 副〔英〕向後；倒退地

Group 4

0134 □□□ **bad** [bæd]　形 (worse, worst) 壞的；不擅長的；嚴重的；可惜

Track 8

片語 be bad for 對…有害 ‖ go bad (食物) 變壞 ‖ not bad〔口〕不錯
例句 Smoking is bad for your health.
／抽煙有害健康。

0135 □□□ **badminton** [`bædmɪntən]　图 羽毛球

例句 I want to play badminton in the afternoon.
／下午我想去打羽毛球。

0136 □□□ **bag** [bæg]　图 袋，包；手提包

例句 Open the bag and put the money in.
／打開手提包，把錢放進去。

0137 □□□ **bake** [bek]　動 烘，烤，焙

例句 Mary is baking a cake.
／瑪麗正在烤蛋糕。

0138 □□□
bakery
[`bekərɪ]

名 麵包店

例句 The boy bought a piece of cake at the bakery.
／那個男孩在麵包店買了一塊蛋糕。

0139 □□□
balcony
[`bælkənɪ]

名 陽台

例句 Juliet spoke to Romeo from the balcony.
／茱麗葉在陽臺上對著羅密歐說話。

0140 □□□
ball
[bɔl]

名 球，球狀物

例句 Are there any balls here?
／這裡有球嗎？

0141 □□□
balloon
[bə`lun]

名 氣球

例句 The balloon burst.
／氣球爆炸了。

0142 □□□
banana
[bə`nænə]

名 香蕉

例句 Apples, bananas and strawberries are my favorite fruits.
／蘋果、香蕉和草莓是我最喜歡吃的水果。

0143 □□□
band
[bænd]

名 帶（狀物）；橡皮圈；樂團

例句 The band finished with a few slow dances.
／樂隊以幾支節奏緩慢的舞曲來結束表演。

0144 □□□
bank
[bæŋk]

名 銀行

例句 Could you tell me how to get to the bank?
／可否請你告訴我銀行怎麼走？
片語 bank account 銀行帳戶

0145 □□□
banker
[`bæŋkɚ]

名 銀行家

例句 I am a banker.
／我是銀行家。

0146 ☐☐☐
bar
[bɑr]

名 酒吧，櫃檯

例句 Tom is at the bar.
／湯姆在酒吧。

0147 ☐☐☐
barbecue
[`bɑrbɪˌkju]

名 烤肉野餐〔從烤肉的「橫木」(bar) 而來〕

例句 We'll have a barbecue this Friday.
／這個星期五我們要辦烤肉野餐。

用法 barbecue 在廣告之類的地方，通常寫成 B.B.Ques 或 Bar.B.Q. 有時，也簡單地寫成 B.B.Q。

barbecue

0148 ☐☐☐
barber
[`bɑrbɚ]

名（為男子服務的）理髮師

例句 I had my hair cut at the barber's.
／我在理容院理了頭髮。

0149 ☐☐☐
bark
[bɑrk]

動 [不及物] 吠叫
名 吠聲，（狗等的）叫聲

例句 The dog barked at the strange man.
／那隻狗對著陌生人吠叫。

0150 ☐☐☐
base
[bes]

名 根基，底座；基礎，根據；（棒球）壘

片語 base...on/upon... 以…為基礎，以…為根據
例句 This story is based on facts.
／這個故事是真人真事。

0151 ☐☐☐
baseball
[`besˌbɔl]

名 棒球運動；棒球

巧記 base(壘)+ball(球)
例句 My brother is a baseball fan.
／我的弟弟是個棒球迷。

0152 ☐☐☐
basement
[`besmənt]

名 地下室

例句 He lives in the basement of the apartment.
／他住在公寓的地下室裡。

B

Lesson **3**

0153
☐☐☐
9

basic
[`besɪk]

形 基礎的；初級的

例句 That game is easy, once you learn the basic rules.
／一旦你學會基本規則，這遊戲就很簡單了。

0154
☐☐☐

basis
[`besɪs]

名 基礎；根據 (pl. bases)

例句 His theory has a solid basis in fact.
／他的理論是以可靠的事實作為根據的。
片語 on the basis of 在…的基礎上

0155
☐☐☐

basket
[`bæskɪt]

名 籃子；(籃球比賽中的) 球籃

例句 Let's pick out the bad potatoes from the basket.
／讓我們把壞掉的花生從籃子裡挑出來吧。

0156
☐☐☐

basketball
[`bæskɪt͵bɔl]

名 籃球；籃球運動

例句 All of my brothers like basketball.
／我的兄弟們都喜歡打籃球。
片語 basketball game 籃球賽 ‖ play basketball 打籃球

0157
☐☐☐

bat
[bæt]

名 (棒球) 球棒；蝙蝠

例句 A bat isn't a bird. ／蝙蝠不是鳥。

0158
☐☐☐

bath
[bæθ]

名 洗澡；浴室；浴缸

片語 have/take a bath 洗澡
例句 He took a bath and shaved before dinner.
／晚餐前他洗了澡，刮了臉。

0159
☐☐☐

bathroom
[`bæθ͵rum]

名 浴室，盥洗室

例句 She went into the bathroom and took a shower.
／她到浴室去淋浴。

0160
☐☐☐

be
[bi]

動 (was/were, been) 是；成為

例句 He was to become a teacher.
／他即將成為一名教師。

第一週

用法 「be+ 動詞不定式」表示計畫做某事；be 與 arrive, come, go, leave 等動詞的 -ing 形式連用表示將來。

0161
☐☐☐
beach
[bitʃ]

名 海灘，沙灘

例句 In summer people often go to the beach and swim.
／夏天人們常到海灘游泳。

0162
☐☐☐
bean
[bin]

名 豆，豆科植物

例句 Please buy a bag of beans for me.
／請幫我買一袋豆子。

0163
☐☐☐
bear
[bɛr]

名 熊

例句 He took aim at the bear.
／他瞄準了那隻熊。

片語 polar bear 北極熊 ‖ teddy bear 泰迪熊

0164
☐☐☐
bear
[bɛr]

動 [及物] (bore, born/borne) 忍受，忍耐；運送

例句 I can't bear this pain.
／我無法忍受這種痛苦。

同義 stand 動 [及物] 忍受

0165
☐☐☐
beard
[bɪrd]

名 (下巴上的) 鬍鬚

例句 Do you know the man with a long beard?
／你認識那個留著長鬍子的人嗎？

0166
☐☐☐
beat
[bit]

動 (beat, beaten)(心臟等) 跳動；敲打；(多次) 擊打 名 (心臟等的) 跳動 (聲)；(音樂的) 節拍

巧記 圖解 beat 的一詞多義：

敲　　　　　　心跳　　　　　　擊打

例句 My heart is beating fast.
／我的心臟跳得很快。

0167 □□□
beautiful
[`bjutəfəl]

形 美好的，美麗的

例句 Amy is wearing a beautiful yellow blouse.
／艾咪穿了一件漂亮的黃色襯衣。

反義 ugly 形 醜陋的

0168 □□□
because
[bɪ`kɔz]

連 因為

例句 He didn't go to school because he was ill.
／他因為生病而沒有去上學。

片語 because of 因為，由於

0169 □□□
become
[bɪ`kʌm]

動 (became, become) 變得；成為

例句 Danny becomes quiet.
／丹尼安靜下來了。

用法 become 作系動詞「變得」講時，其後可以跟形容詞作主詞補語；
become 是暫態性動詞，在完成時態中不能與表示一段時間的副詞連用。

0170 □□□
bed
[bɛd]

名 床

例句 It's time for bed now, honeys!
／寶貝們，睡覺時間到了！

片語 go to bed 去睡覺 ‖ keep one's bed 臥病在床 ‖ make the bed 鋪床

0171 □□□
bedroom
[`bɛd͵rʊm]

名 臥室

例句 I could hear him walking back and forth in his bedroom.
／我聽到他在臥室裡來回走動著。

Ｇroup 2

0172 □□□
bee
[bi]

名 蜂，蜜蜂

片語 as busy as a bee 非常忙碌
例句 She is always as busy as a bee in the morning.
／早上她總是忙得團團轉。

0173 □□□

beef
[bif]

名 牛肉

例句 Which do you like better, beef or pork?
／牛肉和豬肉，你比較喜歡哪一種？

0174 □□□

beer
[bɪr]

名 啤酒

例句 This bottle contains two glasses of beer.
／這個瓶子可以裝兩杯啤酒。

0175 □□□

before
[bɪˋfor]

介 副 連 在…之前；以前；在…前面

例句 Before long he had to return to the village where he once lived long before.
／不久以後，他得回到他很久以前住過的那個村子。

辨析 before long, long before
(1) before long 意為「不久後」，後面不可接任何詞語，表示將來或過去。
(2) long before 意為「很久以前」，表示過去，可以單獨作副詞，後面還可以接子句或名詞。

0176 □□□

begin
[bɪˋgɪn]

動 (began, begun) 開始

例句 Well begun is half done.
／〔諺〕好的開始是成功的一半。

片語 begin with 從…開始
反義 end 動 [不及物] 結束；finish 動 [不及物] 結束

0177 □□□

beginner
[bɪˋgɪnɚ]

名 初學者；生手，新手

例句 He's a beginner in French.
／他是個初學法語的人。

0178 □□□

beginning
[bɪˋgɪnɪŋ]

名 開始
形 初級的

例句 This is the beginning of the garden tour.
／參觀花園就從這兒開始。

片語 at/in the beginning 起初 ‖ at the beginning of 在…之初 ‖ from beginning to end 自始至終，從頭到尾

0179 ☐☐☐
behave
[bɪ`hev]

動 [不及物] 表現；舉止

例句 You two should stop fighting and behave like gentlemen!
／你們兩個應該停止打鬥，表現出應有的紳士的風度！

0180 ☐☐☐
behind
[bɪ`haɪnd]

介 副 在…之後

例句 The gym is behind the science labs.
／體育館在實驗室後面。
片語 fall behind 落後
反義 before 代 副 在…之前

0181 ☐☐☐
belief
[bɪ`lif]

名 信任，信賴；信念；信仰

例句 My belief is that he will win.
／我相信他會贏。
片語 beyond belief 難以置信的
反義 doubt 名 懷疑

0182 ☐☐☐
believe
[bɪ`liv]

動 相信；認為

例句 I believe in you, so I believe what you said.
／我信任你，因此我相信你說的話。
用法 believe 後接表示否定意義的受詞子句時，需要將否定前移，例如不能說 I believe he can't... ，而要用 I don't believe he can... 。
辨析 believe, believe in
(1) believe 表示相信某人的話、相信某事等。
(2) believe in 常表示「信任」，多指品德上的相信。

0183 ☐☐☐
bell
[bɛl]

名 鐘，鈴

例句 There goes the bell.
／鈴聲響了。

0184 ☐☐☐
belong
[bə`lɔŋ]

動 [不及物] 屬於，附屬

片語 belong to 屬於〔▲不用於被動語態〕
例句 This book belongs to Dan.
／這本書是丹的。

0185 □□□
below
[bə`lo]

副 在下面；向下
介 在…以下

例句 I heard a noise from the room below.
／我聽到樓下房間有吵鬧聲。
反義 above 副 介 在（…）上方

0186 □□□
belt
[bɛlt]

名 皮帶，腰帶

例句 He wore a nice leather belt yesterday.
／他昨天繫了一條漂亮的皮腰帶。

0187 □□□
bench
[bɛntʃ]

名 長凳，長椅

例句 I sat on a park bench.
／我坐在公園的一張長椅上。

0188 □□□
beside
[bɪ`saɪd]

介 在…旁邊

例句 He sat beside his mother all night.
／整個晚上他都坐在母親身旁。

0189 □□□
besides
[bɪ`saɪdz]

介 除…之外（還有）
副 此外（還）；而且

例句 I don't really want to go. Besides, it's too late now.
／我並不是真的想去。而且現在也太晚了。

0190 □□□
best
[bɛst]

形 副 最好的（地）

例句 What do you like best?
／你最喜歡什麼？
片語 all the best 萬事如意 ‖ best of all 更好的是 ‖ do one's best 盡某人最大的努力

Group 3

0191 □□□
better
[`bɛtɚ]

形 副 更好的（地）

Track **11**

片語 had better do sth. 最好做某事
例句 You look quite tired. You'd better stop to have a good rest.
／你看起來很累，最好停下來好好休息一下。

0192 □□□
between
[bɪ`twin]

介 介於…之間

片語 between...and... 在…與…之間

例句 John is standing between Gina and Jim.
／約翰正站在吉娜和吉姆之間。

辨析 between, among
(1) between 一般表示「在兩者之間」。
(2) among 表示「在三者或三者以上之中」。

0193 □□□
beyond
[bɪ`jɑnd]

介〔表示位置〕在…那邊;〔表示範圍、限度〕超出　**副** 在那邊

例句 We saw a light beyond the river.
／我們看到燈光在河的那邊。

0194 □□□
bicycle
[`baɪsɪkl]

名 自行車

例句 In Britain, you can't ride your bicycle on the pavement.
／在英國,你不可以在人行道上騎車。

同義 bike 名 自行車

0195 □□□
big
[bɪg]

形 大的;重要的

例句 This shirt isn't big enough.
／這件襯衫不夠大。

反義 small 形 小的

0196 □□□
bill
[bɪl]

名 帳單;鈔票

例句 The bill for the repairs came to $500.
／修理費用共計 500 美元。

0197 □□□
biology
[baɪ`ɑlədʒɪ]

名 生物學

巧記 bio(=life)+-logy(…學)

例句 He is interested in biology.
／他對生物學感興趣。

0198 □□□
bird
[bɝd]

名 鳥,禽

例句 Some kinds of birds can't fly.
／有些鳥不會飛。

第一週

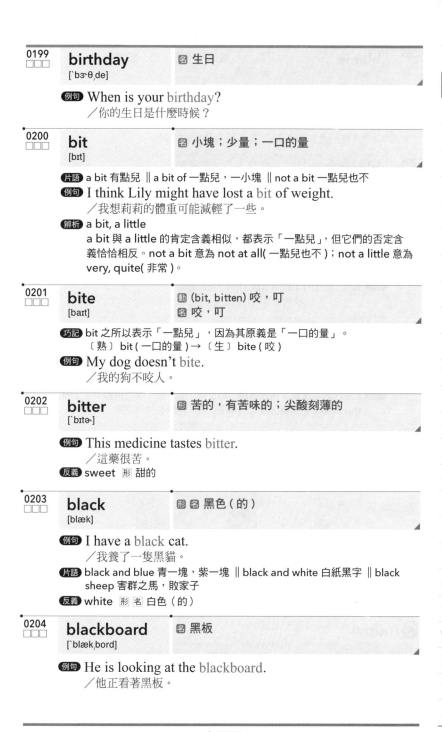

0199 □□□ **birthday**
[ˋbɝθˏde]

名 生日

例句 When is your birthday?
／你的生日是什麼時候？

0200 □□□ **bit**
[bɪt]

名 小塊；少量；一口的量

片語 a bit 有點兒 ‖ a bit of 一點兒，一小塊 ‖ not a bit 一點兒也不
例句 I think Lily might have lost a bit of weight.
／我想莉莉的體重可能減輕了一些。
辨析 a bit, a little
a bit 與 a little 的肯定含義相似，都表示「一點兒」，但它們的否定含義恰恰相反。not a bit 意為 not at all(一點兒也不)；not a little 意為 very, quite(非常)。

0201 □□□ **bite**
[baɪt]

動 (bit, bitten) 咬，叮
名 咬，叮

巧記 bit 之所以表示「一點兒」，因為其原義是「一口的量」。
〔熟〕bit (一口的量) → 〔生〕bite (咬)
例句 My dog doesn't bite.
／我的狗不咬人。

0202 □□□ **bitter**
[ˋbɪtɚ]

形 苦的，有苦味的；尖酸刻薄的

例句 This medicine tastes bitter.
／這藥很苦。
反義 sweet 形 甜的

0203 □□□ **black**
[blæk]

形 名 黑色 (的)

例句 I have a black cat.
／我養了一隻黑貓。
片語 black and blue 青一塊，紫一塊 ‖ black and white 白紙黑字 ‖ black sheep 害群之馬，敗家子
反義 white 形 名 白色 (的)

0204 □□□ **blackboard**
[ˋblækˏbord]

名 黑板

例句 He is looking at the blackboard.
／他正看著黑板。

A
B
C
D
E
F
G
H
I
J
K
L
M
N
O
P
Q
R
S
T
U
V
W
X
Y
Z

0205
☐☐☐

blame
[blem]

* 動 [及物] 責備，指責；把…歸咎於
* 名 罪過

片語 put the blame on... 把責任推給… ‖ take the blame for... 對…負責 ‖ (be) to blame (for sth.) (對壞事) 負有責任的

例句 He put the blame for his failure in the exam on his teacher.
　　／他把考試不及格的責任歸咎於他的老師。

0206
☐☐☐

blank
[blæŋk]

* 形 空白的，空著的
* 名 空白處；(記憶中) 空白，遺忘

例句 Leave the last page blank.
　　／最後一頁留白。

0207
☐☐☐

blanket
[ˋblæŋkɪt]

* 名 羊毛毯，毯子

例句 It's cold; I need another blanket.
　　／太冷了。我需要再加一條毯子。

0208
☐☐☐

blind
[blaɪnd]

* 形 瞎的，盲的

例句 He is blind in the left eye. ／他左眼失明。
片語 go blind 失明 ‖ turn a blind eye (to) (對…) 視而不見
用法 blind 的主詞是人而非眼睛。中文說「眼」瞎，英語則說「人」blind。the blind 〔總稱〕盲人，作主詞時，述語動詞用複數。

0209
☐☐☐

block
[blɑk]

* 名 (木、石等的) 塊；街區
* 動 [及物] 阻止，妨礙

巧記 圖解 block 的一詞多義：

a block of rock
一塊岩石

one block
一個街區

traffic block
交通阻塞

例句 Walk two blocks, and you'll find the store at the corner.
　　／走過兩個街區，你就會在拐角處找到那家店。

Group 4

0210
☐☐☐

blood
[blʌd]

* 名 血，血液

12

例句 Blood is thicker than water.
　　／〔諺〕血濃於水。

0211 ☐☐☐
blouse
[blaʊz]

名 (女式)襯衫，短上衣；罩衫

例句 She has a white blouse on.
／她穿著一件白色襯衫。
【同義】shirt (男式)襯衫

0212 ☐☐☐
blow
[blo]

動 (blew, blown) 吹；爆炸

例句 The wind is blowing from the north.
／風從北邊吹來。
片語 blow out 吹滅 (火焰等)

0213 ☐☐☐
blue
[blu]

形 藍色的；沮喪的，憂鬱的

例句 I felt blue at the news. ／我聽到這消息感到很沮喪。

0214 ☐☐☐
board
[bord]

名 木板；牌子；甲板

巧記 〔熟〕blackboard 黑板 → 〔生〕board 〔根義〕板 → 〔多義〕木板；牌子；甲板
片語 on board 在船 (車、飛機)上
例句 A few passengers went on board the plane.
／數名乘客上了飛機。
例句 There are 20 children on board the ship.
／船上有 20 名兒童。

木板

甲板

0215 ☐☐☐
board
[bord]

動 上船 (車、飛機)

例句 Please board the plane immediately.
／請立刻登機。

0216 ☐☐☐
boat
[bot]

名 船，小船

片語 by boat 乘船 ‖ take a boat 上船，乘船
例句 The best way to visit the place is by boat.
／遊覽那個地方的最好方式是坐船。

0217 ☐☐☐
body
[ˋbɑdɪ]

名 身體，軀體

例句 You need to eat more vegetables for a healthy body.
／為了身體健康，你要多吃蔬菜。

0218 ☐☐☐
boil
[bɔɪl]
動 [不及物] 沸騰
動 [及物] 煮，煮沸

例句 Water boils at 100℃ .
／水在 100℃沸騰。

0219 ☐☐☐
bomb
[bɑm]
名 炸彈
動 [及物] 轟炸

例句 The bomb went off at 12:00 in the night.
／炸彈在夜裡 12 點爆炸了。

0220 ☐☐☐
bone
[bon]
名 骨，骨頭

例句 I broke a bone in my foot while running.
／我的腿因為跑步而骨折。

片語 all skin and bone 皮包骨頭的，極瘦的

0221 ☐☐☐
book
[bʊk]
名 書；本子

例句 I am reading a book on Shakespeare.
／我正在讀一本關於莎士比亞的書。

0222 ☐☐☐
book
[bʊk]
動 預訂 (車票、座位、房間等)

例句 I want to book two adult tickets.
／我想預訂兩張大人的票。

0223 ☐☐☐
bookcase
[`bʊkˌkes]
名 書架，書櫃

例句 Put the books back into the bookcase.
／把書放回書櫃裡。

0224 ☐☐☐
bored
[bord]
形 感到厭煩的，覺得無聊的

例句 People would not like to do such jobs and would get bored.
／人們不喜歡這樣的工作，並且感覺枯燥乏味。

0225 ☐☐☐
boring
[`borɪŋ]
形 令人厭煩的，無聊的

例句 I found the talk very boring.
／我覺得這個談話很無聊。

辨析 bored, boring
(1) bored 指人「覺得煩的，無聊的」。
(2) boring 指事物「令人厭煩的，無聊的」。

0226
born
[bɔrn]

形 出生的；天生的
動 出生

例句 I was born in a small village.
／我出生在一個小村莊裡。

0227
borrow
[`baro]

動 [及物] (向別人) 借，借用

例句 Can I borrow your pen for a minute?
／我可以借你的筆用一下嗎？

0228
boss
[bɔs]

名 老闆

例句 I'll have to ask my boss for a day off.
／我得向老闆請一天假。

B

Lesson **4**

0229
☐☐☐
13

both
[boθ]

形 副 兩者，兩者都
代 兩者，雙方

片語 both... and... ①兩者都 ②既…又…

例句 Both my mom and dad are movie lovers.
／爸爸和媽媽都是電影愛好者。

辨析 both, all
(1) both 用於兩者，其全部否定意義的詞為 neither。
(2) all 用於三者或三者以上，其全部否定意義的詞為 none。

0230
☐☐☐

bother
[`baðɚ]

動 [及物] 騷擾，煩擾

例句 Don't bother your father now; he's very tired.
／現在別去打擾你父親，他很累。

0231
☐☐☐

bottle
[`batl]

名 瓶子；一瓶之量

例句 Six bottles of water should be enough.
／六瓶水應該夠了。

0232
☐☐☐

bottom
[`batəm]

名 底部；末端
形 底部的；最末的

片語 at the bottom of 在…的底部或末端 ‖ from the bottom of one's heart 從某人心底裡

例句 Please write your name at the bottom of this paper.
／請在這張紙的最底部，寫上你的名字。

反義 top 名 頂部 形 頂端的

各種 bottoms

0233
☐☐☐

bow
[baʊ／(指「弓」時) bo]

名 鞠躬，點頭；弓
動 低(頭)；(使)彎曲

例句 The actor bowed to the audience.
／演員向觀眾鞠躬。

0234
☐☐☐

bowl
[bol]

名 碗；一碗的容量

例句 There are some plates and bowls on the table.
／桌子上有些盤子和碗。

0235 ☐☐☐
bowling
[ˋbolɪŋ]
图 保齡球運動

例句 Do you want to go bowling with us on Sunday?
／星期天你想和我們一起去打保齡球嗎？

0236 ☐☐☐
box
[bɑks]
图 盒，箱；一盒（箱）之量

例句 They sat on wooden boxes.
／他們坐在木箱子上。

0237 ☐☐☐
boy
[bɔɪ]
图 男孩；兒子

例句 You are a good boy.
／你是個好男孩。

0238 ☐☐☐
brain
[bren]
图 大腦；（常 pl.) 智力

例句 If you had any brains, you'd know what I meant.
／如果你有點腦子，你就會明白我的意思。

0239 ☐☐☐
branch
[bræntʃ]
图（樹）枝；（機構的）分部，分店

巧記 圖解 branch 的一詞多義：

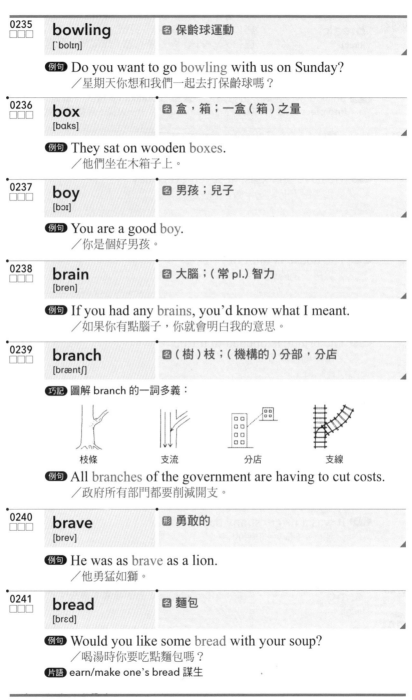

枝條　　支流　　分店　　支線

例句 All branches of the government are having to cut costs.
／政府所有部門都要削減開支。

0240 ☐☐☐
brave
[brev]
形 勇敢的

例句 He was as brave as a lion.
／他勇猛如獅。

0241 ☐☐☐
bread
[brɛd]
图 麵包

例句 Would you like some bread with your soup?
／喝湯時你要吃點麵包嗎？
片語 earn/make one's bread 謀生

0242 break
[brek]

動 [及物] (broke, broken) 打破；違背
動 [不及物] 打破了，壞了 名 (課間等) 休息時間

例句 He worked for five hours without a break.
／他連續工作了五個小時，中間沒有休息。

片語 break down 毀壞，出毛病，不運轉 ‖ break into 闖入，潛入 ‖ break into pieces (使) 成為碎片 ‖ break out (戰爭、火災、疾病等) 突然爆發

0243 breakfast
[`brɛkfəst]

名 早餐

例句 We have breakfast at seven every day.
／我們每天七點吃早飯。

0244 brick
[brɪk]

名 磚，磚塊

例句 The house is built of bricks.
／這房子是磚砌的。

0245 bridge
[brɪdʒ]

名 橋，橋樑

例句 The bridge is opened to traffic.
／這座橋通車了。

0246 brief
[brif]

形 短暫的；簡潔的，簡短的

例句 My father is now on a brief visit to Canada.
／我父親目前正在加拿大作短時間的訪問。

片語 in brief 簡單地說，簡言之 ‖ to be brief 〔用作插入語〕簡單地說，一句話

0247 bright
[braɪt]

形 明亮的，發亮的

例句 It was a bright sunny day.
／那是一個陽光明媚的日子。

Ｇroup 2

0248 bring
[brɪŋ]

14

動 [及物] (brought, brought) 帶來；拿來；取來

例句 Bring me some sugar. /Bring some sugar for me.
／給我拿些糖來。

片語 bring in ①使賺到，使掙得 ②引進 ‖ bring up 養育，撫養

0249 □□□
Britain
[`brɪtən]

名 英國，不列顛

例句 Rabbits and foxes are common in Britain.
／兔子和狐狸在英國很常見。

0250 □□□
British
[`brɪtɪʃ]

形 英國的，英國人的
名 (the～) 英國人

例句 He was born in France but his parents are British.
／他出生於法國，但父母是英國人。

0251 □□□
broad
[brɔd]

形 寬的，寬闊的

例句 We went along a broad passage.
／我們走過一條寬闊的走廊。
辨析 broad, wide
(1) broad 側重于幅面的寬廣，如肩、背、胸、額等。
(2) wide 側重於兩線之間的寬，如兩岸間河寬、眼睛得大等。
反義 narrow 形 狹窄的

0252 □□□
broadcast
[`brɔdˌkæst]

名 廣播節目，電視節目
動 (broadcast, broadcast) 廣播，播放

例句 The interview was broadcast live across Europe.
／這次採訪以現場直播傳到全歐洲。

0253 □□□
brother
[`brʌðə]

名 兄弟

例句 My brother fell ill with a bad cold this week.
／這週我弟弟得了重感冒。

0254 □□□
brown
[braʊn]

名 形 褐色(的)，棕色(的)

例句 He has brown hair.
／他有一頭棕色頭髮。

0255 □□□
brunch
[brʌntʃ]

名 早午餐(午餐和早餐並作一頓)

巧記 breakfast(早餐)+lunch(午餐)
例句 What did you have for your brunch?
／你早午飯都吃了些什麼？

0256 brush
[brʌʃ]
名 刷子；畫筆
動 [及物] 刷

例句 He brushed his teeth and had a shower.
／他刷了牙並洗了個澡。

0257 bucket
[`bʌkɪt]
名 桶子；一桶之量

例句 We drew water in a bucket from the well.
／我們用水桶從井中取水。
同義 pail 名 桶；一桶之量

0258 buffet
[bʊ`fe]
名 自助餐

例句 The price includes morning coffee, buffet lunch, and afternoon tea.
／該價格包含早餐咖啡、自助午餐和下午茶。

0259 bug
[bʌg]
名 小蟲子；竊聽器；錯誤

例句 I love the outdoors, but I hate bugs.
／我喜歡戶外活動，但是我不喜歡小蟲子。
例句 There's a bug in the system. ／系統裡有一些毛病。

0260 build
[bɪld]
動 [及物] (built, built) 建造，建築
動 [不及物] 創（業）

例句 The house was built five years ago.
／這棟房子是五年前蓋的。

0261 building
[`bɪldɪŋ]
名 建築物，房屋

例句 The offices are on the top floor of the building.
／辦公室在建築物的最頂層。

0262 bun
[bʌn]
名 小圓麵包

例句 He can eat a bun in one bite. ／他能一口吃下一個小圓麵包。

0263 bundle
[`bʌndḷ]
名 捆，包，束

例句 He tied the firewood into large bundles.
／他把柴火捆成幾大捆。

0264 burn [bɝn]　勵 (burnt, burnt; burned, burned)（使）燃燒

例句 Dry wood burns easily.
／乾柴容易燃燒。

片語 burn down 把…燒毀，燒成平地 ‖ burn up 燒光

0265 burst [bɝst]　勵 (burst, burst)（使）爆炸
勵 [不及物] 沖，闖；充滿

例句 The gas containers burst at high pressure.
／這些煤氣罐遇到高壓就會爆炸。

片語 burst into ①闖入 ②突然…起來 ‖ burst out ①大聲喊叫 ②突然…起來
△ burst into+n.=burst out doing：

突然哭起來	突然笑起來
burst into tears	burst into laughter
burst out crying	burst out laughing

0266 bus [bʌs]　名 公共汽車

片語 by bus 乘公共汽車 ‖ get on/off the bus 上／下公共汽車
例句 Shall we walk or go by bus?
／我們是走路呢，還是坐公車呢？

Group 3

0267 business [ˋbɪznɪs]　名 商業，生意；出差

15 例句 It's a pleasure to do business with you.
／能與您做生意真是我的榮幸。

片語 business hours 營業時間 ‖ on business 因公出差

0268 businessman [ˋbɪznɪsˌmæn]　名 (pl.businessmen) 商人，企業家

例句 His grandfather was a businessman.
／他爺爺是個商人。

0269 busy [ˋbɪzɪ]　形 繁忙的，忙的，忙碌的

片語 be busy (in) doing sth. 忙於做某事 ‖ be busy with sth. 忙於某事
例句 He is busy (in) doing his homework. /He is busy with his homework.
／他正忙著做家庭作業。

0270 □□□

but
[bət／（重讀）bʌt]

連 但是
介 除…之外

例句 He wanted nothing but to play in the park.
／他只想在公園裡玩，別的什麼也不想做。

用法 but 作「除…之外」講時，若前面部分有 do(或 did, done)，but 之後
需接 do sth.，反之後接 to do sth.。

0271 □□□

butter
[`bʌtɚ]

名 奶油

例句 He spread butter on a slice of bread.
／他在一片麵包上塗上奶油。

0272 □□□

butterfly
[`bʌtɚ͵flaɪ]

名 蝴蝶；(the ～) 蝶泳

例句 I could never do the butterfly well.
／我永遠游不好蝶泳。

0273 □□□

button
[`bʌtn̩]

名 紐扣，扣子；按鈕 (開關)

例句 Button up your coat, it's cold outside.
／把大衣扣好，外面很冷。

0274 □□□

buy
[baɪ]

動 [及物] (bought, bought) 購買，買

例句 Money can't buy happiness.
／金錢買不到幸福。

片語 buy sb. sth.(=buy sth. for sb.) 給某人買某物

用法 buy 是暫態性動詞，在完成時態裡不與表示時間段的副詞連用。

反義 sell 動 賣，出售

0275 □□□

by
[baɪ]

介 在…旁邊，靠近；乘 (車、船等)；經過；靠

例句 His house is by the sea.
／他的房子在海邊。

0276 □□□

cabbage
[`kæbɪdʒ]

名 包心菜，洋白菜，高麗菜

例句 How much are the cabbages today?
／今天高麗菜是賣多少錢？

0277 □□□ **cabinet** [ˈkæbənɪt]

名 櫥子，貯藏櫥，陳列櫃

例句 Put the document in this file cabinet.
／把這些文件放在檔案櫃裡。

0278 □□□ **cable** [ˈkebl]

名 繩索；電纜；有線電視

例句 The boat was tied to the shore by a cable.
／這條小船用繩子綁在岸邊。

例句 I'll wait for the movie to come out on cable.
／我要等有線電視播出這部影片。

0279 □□□ **cafeteria** [ˌkæfəˈtɪrɪə]

名（學校、工廠等的）自助餐廳

例句 I have my meals in the cafeteria all along.
／我都是在自助餐廳吃飯。

0280 □□□ **cage** [kedʒ]

名 籠子，鳥籠

例句 There is a beautiful bird in the cage.
／鳥籠裡有一隻漂亮的鳥。

0281 □□□ **cake** [kek]

名 糕餅，蛋糕

例句 Jenny is making cakes for the party.
／珍妮正在為派對做蛋糕。

片語 a piece of cake 易如反掌

0282 □□□ **calendar** [ˈkæləndɚ]

名 日曆，月曆

例句 Do you have next year's calendar?
／你有明年的日曆嗎？

0283 □□□ **call** [kɔl]

動 把…叫作；拜訪；打電話
名 打電話

例句 His friends call him Bob.
／他的朋友叫他鮑勃。

片語 call back 回訪，回電話

用法 call 當「拜訪」講時，若訪問的是地方，用 at+ 地點；若訪問的是人，用 on+ 人。

0284
☐☐☐

calm
[kɑm]

形 鎮靜的，冷靜的
動 [不及物]（使）鎮定

片語 keep calm 保持冷靜 ‖ calm down 鎮定下來，平靜下來

例句 Calm down and tell me what happened.
／冷靜點，告訴我發生了什麼事。

0285
☐☐☐

camera
[ˋkæmərə]

名 照相機，（電視）攝影機

例句 How much does the camera cost? ／這台照相機多少錢？

Group 4

0286
☐☐☐

track **16**

camp
[kæmp]

名 營地
動 [不及物] 宿營，露營

例句 He camped near the top of the mountain.
／他在山頂附近露營。

片語 go camping 去露營 ‖ summer camp 夏令營

0287
☐☐☐

campus
[ˋkæmpəs]

名（大學）校園

例句 I take a walk on the campus every evening.
／我每天晚上都在校園裡散步。

0288
☐☐☐

can
[kæn]

助動 助 能，會；可以；可能
名 罐

例句 Can you help me lift the box?
／你能幫我抬起這個箱子嗎？

片語 as...as one can 盡可能…地 ‖ cannot help but do 不得不
辨析 be able to, can
　　(1) be able to 表示經過努力或克服困難達到目的，可用於多種時態。
　　(2) can 表示有能力做某事，僅用於一般現在時和一般過去式。

0289
☐☐☐

Canada
[ˋkænədə]

名 加拿大

例句 He will visit some place in Canada. ／他將訪問加拿大某地。

0290
☐☐☐

Canadian
[kəˋnedɪən]

形 加拿大的，加拿大人的
名 加拿大人

例句 The Canadian government is facing another political crisis.
／加拿大政府再次面臨另一場政治危機。

0291 cancel
[`kænsl]
動〔canceled, canceled〕取消，廢除；刪去，劃掉

例句 Mark canceled his order for a book.
／馬克取消了訂購一本書。

0292 cancer
[`kænsɚ]
名 癌，癌症

例句 The cancer cells have spread to her stomach.
／癌細胞已經擴散到她的胃部。

0293 candle
[`kændl]
名 蠟燭，燭形物

例句 The bedroom was lit by a single candle.
／一支蠟燭照亮了整個臥室。

0294 candy
[`kændɪ]
名〔美〕糖果，糖塊

例句 I used to eat candy all the time.
／我過經常吃糖。

同義 sweet 名 〔英〕糖果

0295 cap
[kæp]
名 帽子；瓶蓋

例句 Put the cap on the bottle.
／蓋上瓶蓋。

0296 captain
[`kæptɪn]
名 隊長；船長，機長

例句 Are we ready to sail, captain?
／船長，我們準備起航了嗎？

0297 car
[kɑr]
名 小汽車，轎車；車廂

例句 He goes to work by car.
／他開車去上班。

0298 card
[kɑrd]
名 紙牌；卡片，名片；明信片

例句 David sent us a card from Spain.
／大衛從西班牙給我們寄來一張明信片。

片語 play cards 玩紙牌

0299 ☐☐☐

care
[kɛr]

名 護理，照料；憂慮；注意
動 關心；在意

例句 I failed but I don't care.
／我失敗了，但我不在乎。

片語 care about 擔心，關心 ‖ care for 關懷，照顧 ‖ take care 當心
‖ take (good) care of (細心) 照顧，照看

0300 ☐☐☐

career
[kə`rɪr]

名 (終身) 職業，生涯

例句 My career as an English teacher didn't last long.
／我的英語教師職業沒有持續多久。

0301 ☐☐☐

careful
[`kɛrfəl]

形 小心的，仔細的

巧記 care(小心)+-ful(…的)

例句 He made a careful answer.
／他慎重地回答了。

片語 Be careful! 當心，小心 !

0302 ☐☐☐

careless
[`kɛrlɪs]

形 粗心的

巧記 care(仔細)+-less(不…的)；不仔細的 → 粗心的

例句 It was careless of me to leave the door open.
／都怪我粗心忘了關門。

0303 ☐☐☐

carpet
[`kɑrpɪt]

名 地毯

例句 He laid a red carpet on the floor.
／他在地板上鋪了一塊紅地毯。

0304 ☐☐☐

carrot
[`kærət]

名 胡蘿蔔

例句 You should eat more carrots.
／你應該多吃胡蘿蔔。

0305 □□□

🔊 **17**

carry
[`kærɪ]

🔰[及物] 運送；攜帶

例句 Please carry the desk upstairs.
／請把這桌子搬到樓上。

片語 carry away 運走，拿走 ‖ carry on 繼續下去，繼續開展 ‖ carry out ①執行，落實 (計畫、命令等) ②實現 (諾言等)

0306 □□□

cartoon
[kɑr`tun]

🔰 卡通，動畫片；漫畫

巧記 諧音：〔英〕cartoon 一音譯→〔漢〕卡通
例句 Children usually like cartoons.
／孩子們通常都喜歡卡通。

0307 □□□

case
[kes]

🔰 箱，盒；手提箱；情況；案例

例句 The price does not include the case.
／費用不包括盒子。

片語 in any case 無論如何 ‖ in case 免得，以防萬一 (發生某事)，假如 ‖ in case of 萬一發生…

0308 □□□

cash
[kæʃ]

🔰 錢，現金
🔰[及物] 兌付

例句 Please do not mail cash.
／請不要郵寄現金。

0309 □□□

cassette
[kə`sɛt]

🔰 盒式磁帶，盒式錄影帶

巧記 〔熟〕case 盒→〔生〕cassette 原義「小 (-ette) 盒 (case)」
例句 Put another cassette in the cassette recorder.
／請給盒式答錄機換一盤磁帶。

0310 □□□

castle
[`kæsḷ]

🔰 城堡

例句 We watched fireworks in front of the castle yesterday.
／我們昨天在城堡前看了煙火。

0311 □□□

cat
[kæt]

🔰 貓；貓科動物 (獅、虎、豹等)

例句 Care killed a cat.
／〔諺〕憂慮傷身。
片語 rain cats and dogs 下傾盆大雨

0312 ☐☐☐ **catch**
[kætʃ]

動 [及物] (caught, caught) 抓住，接住；趕上 (車輛)；患 (傳染病等)

巧記 圖解 catch 的一詞多義：

catch the fish
抓魚

catch the ball
接球

catch a bus
趕公車

catch (a) cold
著涼，感冒

例句 You'll catch a cold if you don't put a coat on.
／你要是不穿外套就會感冒。

片語 catch hold of 抓住，握住 ‖ catch up with 趕上

0313 ☐☐☐ **cause**
[kɔz]

動 [及物] 使發生；造成
名 原因

巧記 〔熟〕because 〔be(由於) + cause(原因)〕因為 → 〔生〕cause 原因

例句 The boy caused his teacher a lot of trouble.
／這男孩給他的老師帶來很多麻煩。

0314 ☐☐☐ **CD**
[`si`di]

名 光碟 (=compact disc)

例句 I lent him a CD. ／我借給他一張 CD。

0315 ☐☐☐ **ceiling**
[`silɪŋ]

名 天花板

例句 She lay on her back staring up at the ceiling.
／她仰臥著並凝視著天花板。

0316 ☐☐☐ **celebrate**
[`sɛləˌbret]

動 [及物] 慶祝

例句 People celebrate Halloween in many ways.
／人們用各種方式慶祝萬聖夜。

0317 ☐☐☐ **cell**
[sɛl]

名 細胞；牢房；(蜂巢中單個的) 巢室

巧記 圖解 cell 的一詞多義：

prison cell
單人牢房

cell 巢室

plant cell 植物細胞

例句 The prisoner was put in a cell. ／這囚犯被關進了牢房。

0318 ☐☐☐
cent
[sɛnt]

名（貨幣）分，美分

例句 Please stick an eight-cent stamp on the envelope.
／請貼一張 8 美分的郵票在這信封上。

0319 ☐☐☐
center
[`sɛntɚ]

名 中心，中央
動 [及物] 使集中（於一點）

例句 This school is in the center of the town.
／這所學校位於市中心。

0320 ☐☐☐
centimeter
[`sɛntə͵mitɚ]

名 釐米，公分 (=cm)

巧記 centi-(百分之一) + meter(米)
例句 The rope is 50 centimeters long. ／這條繩子長 50 公分。

0321 ☐☐☐
central
[`sɛntrəl]

形 中心的，中央的

例句 The city hall is in the central part of the town.
／市政府在城市的中心區域。

0322 ☐☐☐
century
[`sɛntʃʊrɪ]

名 世紀，百年

例句 The church was built in the eighties of the 20th century.
／這座教堂建於 20 世紀的 80 年代。

0323 ☐☐☐
cereal
[`sɪrɪəl]

名 穀類食物（如麥片等），麥片粥

例句 Cereal products are good for our health.
／穀物產品有益健康。

Ⓖroup 2

0324 ☐☐☐ **18**
certain
[`sɝtən]

形 某種；肯定的；無疑的

片語 be certain about/of 對…有把握 ‖ be certain to do sth. 一定會做某事 ‖ It is certain that... 一定會… ‖ make certain 弄清楚，確定
例句 He is certain to realize his dream. ／他肯定能實現夢想。

0325 ☐☐☐
certainly
[`sɝtənlɪ]

副 當然

例句 "Are you going with us?" "Certainly!"
／「你要跟我們一起去嗎？」「當然！」

0326 ☐☐☐ **chair**
[tʃɛr]

🔲 椅子；(the～) 主席席位

例句 He is sitting in a chair.
／他正坐在椅子上。

0327 ☐☐☐ **chairman**
[ˋtʃɛrmən]

🔲 (pl.chairmen) (會議的) 主席，主持人

例句 Mr. Brown is the chairman at the meeting.
／布朗先生是會議的主席。

0328 ☐☐☐ **chalk**
[tʃɔk]

🔲 粉筆

例句 My teacher bought a box of colored chalks.
／我老師買了一盒彩色粉筆。

0329 ☐☐☐ **chance**
[tʃæns]

🔲 機會；機遇

例句 Whenever you have a chance to speak English, you should take it.
／無論什麼時候只要你有機會說英語，你都應該多加利用。

片語 by chance (=by accident) 碰巧，偶然

0330 ☐☐☐ **change**
[tʃendʒ]

🔲 變化；零錢
🔲 改變；兌換

例句 The bad weather changed her plan.
／惡劣的天氣改變了她的計畫。

片語 change (...) into...(把…) 變成… ‖ change A for B 把 A 換成 B ‖ change from...to... 由…變為… ‖ change one's mind 改變某人的想法 / 主意

0331 ☐☐☐ **channel**
[ˋtʃænl]

🔲 水道，水渠；頻道；海峽

例句 Water runs along the channel to the fields.
／水順著水道流進田裡。

0332 ☐☐☐ **chapter**
[ˋtʃæptɚ]

🔲 (書的) 章，篇

例句 Study the next chapter.
／下一章請事先好好預習。

0333 □□□ **character**
[ˋkærɪktɚ]

名 性格；字，字體；人物，角色

例句 He has a strong character.
／他是個性格堅強的人。

片語 in character (與自身特性) 相符　out of character (與自身特性) 不相符

0334 □□□ **charge**
[tʃɑrdʒ]

動 對…收費，索價；將 (電池) 充電；起訴
名 價錢，費用；控告

例句 Do you charge for delivery?
／你們收運費嗎？

片語 charge (sb.) some money for sth. 為某物 (向某人) 要一些錢 ‖ charge sb. with... 指控某人有…罪 ‖ free of charge 免費

0335 □□□ **chart**
[tʃɑrt]

名 圖，圖表

例句 The chart shows our top 10 choices.
／該圖顯示出了我們的十大選擇。

0336 □□□ **chase**
[tʃes]

動 追趕，追逐，追捕

例句 This dog is chasing the boy.
／這隻狗正在追那個男孩。

0337 □□□ **cheap**
[tʃip]

形 便宜的

例句 It is too cheap to be good.
／便宜沒好貨。

用法 物品的「貴，賤」用 expensive, dear 或 cheap 表示；價格的「高，低」用 high 或 low 表示。

反義 dear 形 昂貴的；expensive 形 昂貴的

0338 □□□ **cheat**
[tʃit]

動 [及物] 欺騙，騙取
動 [不及物] 行騙，作弊

例句 He cheated her of her money. ／他騙取了她的錢。

0339 □□□ **check**
[tʃɛk]

動 檢查，核對
名 支票；(飯館等的) 帳單

例句 He was checking the traveler's luggage.
／他正在檢查旅客的行李。

片語 check in (在旅館、機場等) 登記，報到　check out 結帳離開 ‖ check up 核對，檢驗

0340
☐☐☐

cheer
[tʃɪr]

動（為…）歡呼，喝彩
名 歡呼，喝彩；愉快

例句 Let's give three cheers for our team—we've won!
／讓我們為我隊歡呼三聲——我們贏了！
片語 cheer up 使振作起來，使高興起來

0341
☐☐☐

cheese
[tʃiz]

名 乳酪，乾酪

例句 Cheese is made from milk.
／乳酪是用牛奶製成的。

Say "cheese!"   cheese

0342
☐☐☐

chemical
[ˋkɛmɪk!]

名 化學製品，化學藥品
形 化學的

例句 The same water was reused after chemical treatment.
／原來的水經過化學處理之後再度被使用。

Ⓖroup 3

0343
☐☐☐
19

chess
[tʃɛs]

名 棋，西洋棋

例句 I am good at playing chess.
／我擅長下棋。

0344
☐☐☐

chicken
[ˋtʃɪkɪn]

名 雞，（尤指）小雞；雞肉

例句 Don't count your chickens before
they are hatched.
／〔諺〕不要在還沒孵出小雞之前先數雞。
／別指望過早。／別打如意算盤。

小雞   雞肉

0345
☐☐☐

chief
[tʃif]

形（作限定詞）首要的，主要的
名 首領，領袖

例句 The chief aim of life is not to get money.
／人生的主要目的不是賺錢。
片語 in chief ①主要地，尤其 ②在首席地位

0346
☐☐☐

child
[tʃaɪld]

名 (pl.children) 小孩，兒童

例句 I am the second child of my family.
／我在家裡排行老二。

0347 ☐☐☐ **childhood**
[ˋtʃaɪldˌhʊd]

图 童年，幼年（時代）

巧記 -hood 加在名詞後構成名詞，表示「時期」：babyhood(嬰兒時期);
childhood(童年時代)；girlhood(少女時代); boyhood(少年時代)。

例句 She was lovely in her childhood.
／她小時候很可愛。

0348 ☐☐☐ **childish**
[ˋtʃaɪldɪʃ]

图 孩子的，稚嫩的；幼稚的

例句 Don't be so childish! ／別這麼孩子氣了！

0349 ☐☐☐ **childlike**
[ˋtʃaɪldˌlaɪk]

图 孩子般的，單純的，天真無邪的

例句 The sight filled her with childlike
excitement.
／這情景讓她像孩子般地興奮起來。

天真無邪的　　孩子氣的

辨析 childish, childlike
以 -ish 結尾者常含貶義，以 -like(-ly) 結尾者常含褒義。所以 childish 多
含有不好的、輕蔑的意味，childlike 多指孩子們好的一面。

0350 ☐☐☐ **chin**
[tʃɪn]

图 下巴，頦（嘴下面的部位）

例句 I hit him on the chin.
／我朝他下巴打了一拳。

0351 ☐☐☐ **China**
[ˋtʃaɪnə]

图 中國

例句 He is the first-class actor of China.
／他是中國的一流演員。

0352 ☐☐☐ **Chinese**
[ˋtʃaɪˋniz]

图 中國的，中國人的
图〔單同複〕中國人；華語

例句 Each day, about 220 million packets of cigarettes are
smoked by Chinese. ／中國人每天要抽掉約 2.2 億包煙。

0353 ☐☐☐ **chocolate**
[ˋtʃɑkəlɪt]

图 巧克力

巧記 諧音：〔英〕chocolate 一音譯→〔漢〕巧克力

例句 Sweet foods such as chocolate can make you fat.
／像巧克力之類的甜食能使人發胖。

0354 □□□ **choice**
['tʃɔɪs']

名 選擇;選擇權

片語 have no choice but to do sth. 除了做某事別無選擇 ‖ make one's choice 作選擇

例句 The tourists had no choice but to wait for the next bus.
／除了等下一輛公車,遊客們別無選擇。

0355 □□□ **choose**
['tʃuz']

動 (chose, chosen) 選擇,挑選;決定

例句 Choose an English name for yourself.
／給自己選個英文名字。

0356 □□□ **chopstick**
['tʃɑpˌstɪk']

名 (常 pl.) 筷子

例句 Chinese people always use chopsticks instead of a knife and fork.
／中國人常使用筷子而不用刀叉。

0357 □□□ **Christmas**
['krɪsməs']

名 耶誕節 (=Xmas)

例句 Merry Christmas to you!
／祝你耶誕節快樂!

片語 at Christmas 聖誕期間 ‖ on Christmas Day 在聖誕日

0358 □□□ **chubby**
['tʃʌbɪ']

形 胖嘟嘟的,豐滿的

例句 Do you think I'm too chubby?
／你會不會覺得我太胖了?

0359 □□□ **church**
['tʃɝtʃ']

名 教堂;教會

例句 Follow this road until you get to the church, then turn left.
／順著這條路一直走到教堂,然後左轉彎。

0360 □□□ **circle**
['sɝkl']

名 圈,圓,環狀物
動 [及物] 盤旋

例句 We danced in a circle.
／我們圍成圓圈跳舞。

0361 □□□
citizen
[`sɪtəzn̩]
名 市民;公民,國民

例句 We need our school to teach students to be good citizens.
／我們需要學校把學生教育成良好的公民。

Group 4

0362 □□□
20
city
[`sɪtɪ]
名 城市,市

例句 I prefer country life to city life.
／我喜歡鄉村生活勝於城市生活。

0363 □□□
claim
[klem]
動 [及物] 聲稱,斷言;對…提出要求,索取

例句 The girls claimed to have seen the fairies.
／這些女孩聲稱見到了仙女。

0364 □□□
clap
[klæp]
動 [及物] 拍,輕拍;振(翼),拍(翅膀)
動 [不及物] 拍手

例句 The audience clapped after his speech.
／他演講完之後,觀眾鼓掌喝彩。

0365 □□□
class
[klæs]
名 (學校裡的)班級;課;等級

例句 What time does the next class begin?
／下一堂課什麼時候開始?

片語 after class 課後 ‖ have class 上課 ‖ in class 在課堂上

0366 □□□
classic
[`klæsɪk]
形 最優秀的,(可作)典範的;古典的,古典主義的

巧記 〔熟〕class 等級 → 〔生〕classic(=of the first or highest class)
例句 This is a classic textbook on English grammar.
／這是一本最優秀的英語語法課本。

0367 □□□
classical
[`klæsɪkl̩]
形 古典的,古典藝術的;第一流的,經典的

例句 I like classical music better than popular music.
／比起流行音樂來,我更喜歡古典音樂。

辨析 classic, classical
(1) classic 主要意思是「最優秀的」、「最上等的」。
(2) classical 指古希臘和古羅馬的文學、藝術,意為「古典(文學或藝術)的」。
在文學藝術上,它分別與 romantic(浪漫主義的) 或 popular(流行的) 相對。

0368 ☐☐☐

classmate
[`klæs,met]

名 同班同學

巧記 class(班級)+mate(同伴)

例句 He took a gift from his classmate.
／他從他的同學那裡拿了一份禮物。

0369 ☐☐☐

clean
[klin]

動 [及物] 打掃，掃除
形 清潔的，乾淨的

例句 Would you mind cleaning the yard?
／你可以打掃一下庭院嗎？

片語 clean away/off 清除，擦去 ‖ clean out 打掃乾淨，收拾乾淨 ‖ clean up
①打掃，整理 ②清除

反義 dirty 形 骯髒的

0370 ☐☐☐

clear
[klɪr]

形 清楚的；晴朗的；清澈的
動 [及物] 收拾，清除

例句 I am not clear about that.
／我對那件事不太清楚。

片語 clear away 把…清除，把…收拾乾淨 ‖ clear out 掃除，清除 ‖ clear up
整理，收拾 ‖ make clear 講清楚，表明

0371 ☐☐☐

clerk
[klɝk]

名 職員，辦事員；店員，售貨員；(旅館) 接待
員

例句 He is a clerk in a software company.
／他是一家軟體公司的職員。

0372 ☐☐☐

clever
[`klɛvə-]

形 聰明的，靈巧的

例句 The clever fox escaped the hunter.
／機靈的狐狸逃脫了獵人的追蹤。

同義 bright adj. 聰明的

0373 ☐☐☐

climate
[`klaɪmɪt]

名 氣候

例句 Los Angeles has a warm and dry climate.
／洛杉磯氣候溫暖乾燥。

0374 ☐☐☐

climb
[klaɪm]

名 動 爬，攀登

例句 Do you like climbing mountains?
／你喜歡爬山嗎？

0375 □□□ **clock**
[klɑk]

名 時鐘

例句 The alarm clock didn't ring.
／鬧鐘沒響。

0376 □□□ **close**
[kloz]

動 關，關閉；結束
名 (sing.) 結束，終止

例句 Close the windows at night.
／晚上要關上窗戶。

片語 close down 關閉，歇業 ‖ come to a close 漸近結束

注意 close 作不及物動詞時，可以用主動形式表示被動意義：
The door won't close. 這門關不上。

0377 □□□ **close**
[klos]

形 近的，接近的；親密的

片語 close by 在近旁，在旁邊 ‖ close to ①將近 ②在…附近 ‖ get close (to)
靠近
The close friend close to the door closed the door. 靠近門的那位好朋友
關上了門。

例句 His house is close to the school.
／他的房子靠近學校。

0378 □□□ **closet**
[`klɑzɪt]

名 櫥櫃，碗櫥，衣櫥

例句 Hang your overcoat in the closet.
／把你的大衣掛在衣櫥裡。

0379 □□□ **clothes**
[kloz]

名 (pl.) 衣服；服裝

例句 I'm packing my suitcase with my clothes.
／我正往我的小提箱裡裝衣服。

用法 clothes 用作複數，可與 many，few 等詞連用，但不能與數詞連用。指
一套衣服時用 a suit of clothes。

0380 □□□ **cloudy**
[`klaʊdɪ]

形 多雲的，陰天的

例句 It was a cloudy day.
／那是一個陰天。

反義 sunny 形 陽光充足的

MEMO

GEPT
Elementary

Week 2

第二週

C

Lesson 1

0381 ☐☐☐
club
[klʌb]
🔊 **21**

名 社團，俱樂部

巧記 諧音：〔英〕club 一音譯→〔漢〕俱樂部
例句 She is among the most active members in our club.
／她是我們俱樂部中最活躍的成員之一。

0382 ☐☐☐
coach
[kotʃ]

名 教練

例句 The coach gave me some advice. ／教練給我一些建議。

0383 ☐☐☐
coast
[kost]

名 海岸，海濱

片語 off the coast 在海面上　on the coast 在岸上，沿岸
例句 The city is on the coast. ／這城市鄰近海岸。

0384 ☐☐☐
coat
[kot]

名 外套，大衣

例句 I need a new winter coat. ／我需要一件新的冬季大衣。

0385 ☐☐☐
cockroach
[ˈkɑkˌrotʃ]

名 蟑螂 (=roach)

例句 Look! There's a big cockroach on your desk light.
／看啊！你的檯燈上有隻大蟑螂。
例句 Cockroaches hide themselves during the day.
／蟑螂白天都躲起來。

0386 ☐☐☐
coffee
[ˈkɔfɪ]

名 咖啡（熱飲料）；咖啡色

例句 I wanted some more coffee, but there was none left.
／我想再要些咖啡，可是一點兒都沒剩下。
用法 coffee 作不可數名詞意為「咖啡」；作可數名詞意為「一杯咖啡」。類似
的詞還有 tea, beer 等。

0387 ☐☐☐
coin
[kɔɪn]

名 硬幣，錢幣

例句 The magician lost the coin. ／魔術師丟失了那枚硬幣。
片語 the other side of the coin 事情的另一面

0388 ☐☐☐
coke
[kok]

名 焦，焦炭；可樂

例句 Coke is used as fuel.
／焦炭被用來當作燃料。

第二週

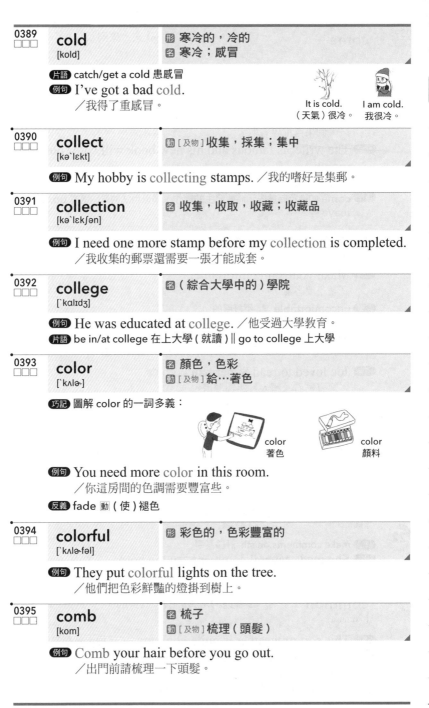

0389 cold
[kold]
形 寒冷的，冷的
名 寒冷；感冒

片語 catch/get a cold 患感冒
例句 I've got a bad cold.
／我得了重感冒。

It is cold.
（天氣）很冷。

I am cold.
我很冷。

0390 collect
[kəˋlɛkt]
動 [及物] 收集，採集；集中

例句 My hobby is collecting stamps. ／我的嗜好是集郵。

0391 collection
[kəˋlɛkʃən]
名 收集，收取，收藏；收藏品

例句 I need one more stamp before my collection is completed.
／我收集的郵票還需要一張才能成套。

0392 college
[ˋkɑlɪdʒ]
名（綜合大學中的）學院

例句 He was educated at college. ／他受過大學教育。
片語 be in/at college 在上大學（就讀）‖ go to college 上大學

0393 color
[ˋkʌlɚ]
名 顏色，色彩
動 [及物] 給…著色

巧記 圖解 color 的一詞多義：

color
著色

color
顏料

例句 You need more color in this room.
／你這房間的色調需要豐富些。

反義 fade 動（使）褪色

0394 colorful
[ˋkʌlɚfəl]
形 彩色的，色彩豐富的

例句 They put colorful lights on the tree.
／他們把色彩鮮豔的燈掛到樹上。

0395 comb
[kom]
名 梳子
動 [及物] 梳理（頭髮）

例句 Comb your hair before you go out.
／出門前請梳理一下頭髮。

0396 ☐☐☐
come
[kʌm]

動 [不及物] (came, come) 來，來到

片語 come across 偶然遇到 ‖ come back 回來 ‖ come from 出生於，來自 ‖ come in 進來 ‖ come on ①趕快，快點兒 ②加油 ‖ come out ①出來 ②出版，發行 ‖ come over 順便來訪 ‖ come true (希望等) 實現，達到

例句 People came from all the corners of the world.
／人們來自世界各地。

例句 The writer is famous and his new book will come out next month.
／這個作家很有名，他的新書下個月即將出版。

用法 come 的進行時態表示將要發生的動作，類似用法的單詞還有 go, arrive, leave 等。

0397 ☐☐☐
comfortable
[ˋkʌmfəˏtəbl]

形 舒服的

例句 Make yourself comfortable.
／請不要客氣。

反義 uncomfortable 形 不舒服的

0398 ☐☐☐
comic
[ˋkamɪk]

形 滑稽的，可笑的
名 (報紙上所刊載的) 連環漫畫

例句 Joe loved to read Superman comics.
／喬喜歡看《超人》連環漫畫。

0399 ☐☐☐
command
[kəˋmænd]

動 命令；指揮
名 命令

例句 He commanded his men to fire. ／他命令手下開火。

Ⓖroup 2

0400 ☐☐☐
🄽22
comment
[ˋkamɛnt]

名 評論，評注；意見
動 評論

片語 make comments on sth. 評論某事
例句 She made several comments on the book.
／對於這本書她做了一些評論。

0401 ☐☐☐
common
[ˋkamən]

形 普通的；共同的；公共的

例句 This sort of weather is quite common. ／這種天氣很常見。
例句 We use English as a common language.
／我們使用英語為通用語言。

片語 have...in common 擁有共同的… ‖ in common 共同，共用

0402 □□□ **company** [ˋkʌmpənɪ]
名 公司;夥伴;客人

例句 I didn't know you had company. ／我不知道你有同伴。

例句 The company produces motorcycle. ／那家公司生產摩托車。

片語 in company with 和…一起 ‖ keep company with sb. 與某人結交

0403 □□□ **compare** [kəmˋpɛr]
動 [及物] 比較,對照;將…比作
動 [不及物] 與…類似

例句 He compared her to a rose. ／他把她比作玫瑰。

用法 作「與…比較」講時,既可以用 with,也可以用 to,但作「把…比作」解時,只能用 to。

0404 □□□ **complain** [kəmˋplen]
動 抱怨,訴說(病痛等);投訴,控告

片語 complain that... 抱怨… ‖ complain to sb. of/about sth. 向某人抱怨某事 ‖ complain of doing sth. 抱怨做某事

例句 He complained to the police about the noise.
／他向員警投訴那個噪音。

0405 □□□ **complete** [kəmˋplit]
動 [及物] 完成,結束
形 完整的,全部的;完全的

例句 This set of tools is not complete.
／這套工具不齊全。

例句 I had completely forgotten it.
／我完全把它忘了。

反義 begin 動 [及物] 開始

0406 □□□ **computer** [kəmˋpjutɚ]
名 電腦

例句 I use a computer to do my homework.
／我用電腦來做作業。

例句 My computer can cope with huge amounts of data.
／我的電腦能夠處理大量資料。

0407 □□□ **concern** [kənˋsɝn]
名 憂慮,關心
動 [及物] 有關;使關心,使擔心

片語 as/so far as...be concerned 就…而言 ‖ show concern for sb. 關心某人

例句 She was more concerned for her son's safety than her own.
／比起自己,她更關心她孩子的安危。

例句 As far as I'm concerned, I agree with you.
／就我而言,我同意你的意見。

0408 confident
[`kɑnfədənt]

形 有信心的，自信的

例句 I'm confident that I will succeed. ／我相信我一定會成功。

片語 名詞 confidence 後接 in，但形容詞 confident 後卻要接 of。
(a) We have confidence in our future.
(b) We are confident of our future.

0409 confirm
[kən`fɝm]

動 [及物] 使（信仰等）堅定；證實，確認

巧記 〔熟〕firm 形 堅定的；結實的 → 〔生〕confirm 動 [及物] 證實，確認

例句 I'd like to confirm a reservation. ／我想確認一項預約。

例句 The new facts will confirm his opinion.
／這些新的事實將使他的想法更加堅定。

0410 conflict
[`kɑnflɪkt]

名 爭論，爭執；抵觸，衝突，矛盾，不一致；戰鬥，戰爭

例句 There was a conflict between the accounts of the witnesses. ／證人們的證詞相互矛盾。

片語 come into conflict with ①與…衝突 ②與…戰鬥
‖ in conflict with 與…相衝突

conflict

0411 Confucius
[kən`fjuʃəs]

名 孔子（西元前 551 年～西元前 479 年，春秋末期思想家、教育家、理論政治家）

例句 Confucius's many words are wisdom.
／孔子的許多語錄都是至理名言。

0412 confuse
[kən`fjuz]

動 [及物] 使困惑，把…弄糊塗；混淆，把…混同

例句 The new rules confused the drivers. ／新規定把駕駛員搞糊塗了。

例句 Never confuse pity with love. ／不要把同情跟愛情相混淆。

0413 congratulation
[kən,grætʃə`leʃən]

名 祝賀，恭喜；(pl.) 賀詞

例句 I offered him my congratulations on his success.
／我祝賀他成功。

0414 consider
[kən`sɪdɚ]

動 [及物] 考慮，思考；認為

片語 consider...(as)... 把…看作… ‖ consider doing sth. 考慮做某事 ‖ consider sb.(to be)... 認為某人…

例句 I consider him (as) a very clever boy.
／我認為他是一個很聰明的男孩。

0415 □□□ **contact** [`kɑntækt]
名 接觸；聯繫
動 [及物] 與…取得聯繫，與…接觸

例句 They contact each other by mail.
／他們透過郵件互相聯繫。

0416 □□□ **contain** [kən`ten]
動 [及物] 包含，含有；容納

例句 What percentage of alcohol does this Kinmen Kaoliang Liquor contain?
／這瓶金門高樑酒含有百分之幾的酒精？

例句 The speech contained some interesting ideas.
／這個演講包含一些有趣的想法。

0417 □□□ **continue** [kən`tɪnjʊ]
動 繼續

例句 He continued working after an operation.
／手術後他仍然繼續工作。

辨析 continue, go on
continue 後可直接跟名詞作受詞，而 go on 後需借助介系詞再接名詞作受詞。continue 後接動詞不定式或 -ing 均可，表示「不停地做某事」；而 go on doing sth. 意為「不停地做某事」(不中斷)或「繼續某事」(中斷後繼續)，go on to do sth. 意為「(做完某事後)繼續做另外的事」。

0418 □□□ **contract** [kɑntrækt]
名 合同，契約
動 [不及物] 訂合同，訂契約　動 [及物] 訂(約)

例句 He was engaged on the contract of five years.
／他以 5 年合同的條件接受聘雇。

Ⓖroup 3

0419 □□□ **control** [kən`trol]
名 動 [及物] 控制，支配

⟨23⟩

例句 He couldn't control his anger.
／他無法控制自己的憤怒。

片語 in control 控制著　out of control 失去控制 ‖ under the control of 受…的控制

0420 □□□ **convenient** [kən`vinjənt]
形 方便的，便利的；近便的，就近的

例句 It is not convenient for me to ring him up now.
／我現在不方便給他打電話。

0421 ☐☐☐
conversation
[ˌkɑnvɚˋseʃən]

名 交談；談話

例句 Conversation is one of the pleasures of life.
／聊天是人生的樂趣之一。

片語 have/hold a conversation with 與…交談

0422 ☐☐☐
cook
[kʊk]

動 烹調；煮
名 廚師

例句 I know how to cook some simple dishes.
／我會做一些簡單的菜。

0423 ☐☐☐
cookie
[ˋkʊkɪ]

名 小甜餅，餅乾

例句 I want a container for these cookies.
／我需要一個容器來裝這些餅乾。

0424 ☐☐☐
cool
[kul]

形 涼爽的；冷靜的
動 (使) 變涼；(使) 冷靜下來

片語 cool down 冷靜下來 ‖ keep cool 保持鎮靜
例句 She kept cool during the argument. ／她在辯論中始終保持冷靜。

0425 ☐☐☐
copy
[ˋkɑpɪ]

名 抄本，副本
動 [及物] 抄寫，複製

例句 Copy this passage into your notebook.
／把這一段抄在你的筆記本上。

0426 ☐☐☐
corn
[kɔrn]

名 穀物，穀粒；玉米

例句 All our chickens are fed on corn.
／我們的雞都是餵玉米。

corn 玉米　　rice 大米　　wheat 小麥

0427 ☐☐☐
corner
[ˋkɔrnɚ]

名 (街道) 街角，角落；牆角

片語 around/round the corner ① 在轉角處 ②
即將來臨 ‖ at/on the corner of 在…拐角
處／上 ‖ in the corner of 在…角落裡
例句 He lives just around the corner.
／他就住在轉角處。
辨析 in the corner 在轉角的裡面；on the
corner 在角上，如床角；at the corner
在轉角的外面。

in the corner
在轉角的裡面
A ●

at the corner
在轉角的外面
● B

第二週

※ In the corner of the office stands a desk, and on the corner of it lies a book. 在辦公室的角落有一張桌子，在桌角上放著一本書。

0428 ☐☐☐
correct
[kə`rɛkt]

形 正確的
動 [及物] 改正

例句 You should correct your bad habits.
／你應該改掉自己的壞習慣。

0429 ☐☐☐
cost
[kɔst]

名 成本
動 [及物] (cost, cost) 價值為；花費

例句 How much does the ticket cost from Shulin to Taoyuan?
／從樹林到桃園的車票多少錢一張？

片語 at all costs 不惜任何代價，無論如何 ‖ at the cost of 以…為代價

用法 cost 的主詞是物或某種活動，不以人作主詞，常用句型為「事／物+cost+ 人 + 金錢 +to do sth.」。

0430 ☐☐☐
cotton
[`kɑtn̩]

名 棉花；棉布

例句 They are picking cotton in the field.
／他們正在田地裡摘棉花。

0431 ☐☐☐
couch
[kaʊtʃ]

名 長沙發，睡椅

例句 He sat on a couch watching TV.
／他坐在長沙發上看電視。

0432 ☐☐☐
cough
[kɔf]

動 [不及物] 名 咳嗽

例句 The girl has a bad cough.
／這女孩咳嗽得很厲害。

0433 ☐☐☐
could
[kəd／(重讀)kʊd]

動 助 (can 的過去式) 能；可以，可能

例句 The teacher said we could all go home.
／老師說我們都可以回家了。

用法 could 可以是 can 的過去式，表示過去的能力；也可表示委婉語氣。

0434 ☐☐☐
count
[kaʊnt]

動 [及物] 計數，點數目 動 [不及物] 數數；有價值
名 計算，總數

例句 My little sister can count from one to ten.
／我的小妹妹能從 1 數到 10。

片語 count down 倒數 ‖ count out ①不把…算入 ②逐一數出

0435 □□□ **country** [ˋkʌntrɪ]
名 國家；(the ～) 鄉下

例句 We went into the country for the vacation.
／我們到鄉下去度假。

0436 □□□ **countryside** [ˋkʌntrɪˏsaɪd]
名 農村，鄉村

例句 The beautiful countryside was polluted.
／這個美麗的鄉村被污染了。

辨析 country, countryside
(1) country 強調區別於城鎮的「鄉村」。
(2) countryside 泛指一切鄉村地區，特別強調擁有山、河、樹林等自然景觀的地方。

0437 □□□ **county** [ˋkaʊntɪ]
名 郡，縣

例句 They did not stay long in that county.
／他們在那個縣沒停留太長的時間。

Group 4

0438 □□□ **couple** [ˋkʌpl̩]
名 夫婦；一對

Track 24

例句 The couple had no children. ／這對夫妻沒有孩子。
片語 a couple of ①兩個 ②一些，幾個 ‖ in couples 成雙成對的

0439 □□□ **courage** [ˏkɝɪdʒ]
名 勇氣，膽量

例句 He had the courage to speak up.
／他有勇氣說出自己的意見。
片語 lose courage 失去勇氣 ‖ with courage 勇敢地

0440 □□□ **course** [kors]
名 過程；經過；課程

例句 During the course of the holiday, we visited a lot of places.
／在假期中，我們參觀了很多地方。
片語 in the course of 在…的過程中，在…期間 ‖ of course 當然

0441 □□□ **court** [kort]
名 法庭，法院；院子

例句 The court case lasted six weeks. ／這場訴訟持續了六周。
片語 take sb. to court 起訴某人

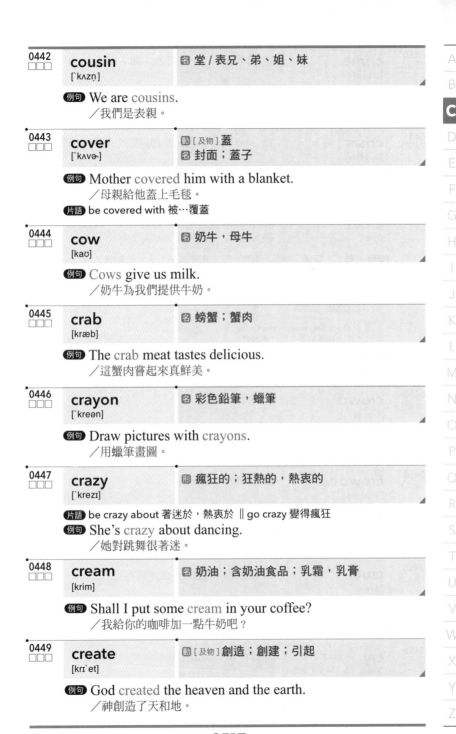

0442 cousin
[`kʌzn̩]
名 堂/表兄、弟、姐、妹

例句 We are cousins.
／我們是表親。

0443 cover
[`kʌvɚ]
動 [及物] 蓋
名 封面；蓋子

例句 Mother covered him with a blanket.
／母親給他蓋上毛毯。
片語 be covered with 被…覆蓋

0444 cow
[kaʊ]
名 奶牛，母牛

例句 Cows give us milk.
／奶牛為我們提供牛奶。

0445 crab
[kræb]
名 螃蟹；蟹肉

例句 The crab meat tastes delicious.
／這蟹肉嘗起來真鮮美。

0446 crayon
[`kreən]
名 彩色鉛筆，蠟筆

例句 Draw pictures with crayons.
／用蠟筆畫圖。

0447 crazy
[`krezɪ]
形 瘋狂的；狂熱的，熱衷的

片語 be crazy about 著迷於，熱衷於 ‖ go crazy 變得瘋狂
例句 She's crazy about dancing.
／她對跳舞很著迷。

0448 cream
[krim]
名 奶油；含奶油食品；乳霜，乳膏

例句 Shall I put some cream in your coffee?
／我給你的咖啡加一點牛奶吧？

0449 create
[krɪ`et]
動 [及物] 創造；創建；引起

例句 God created the heaven and the earth.
／神創造了天和地。

0450 crime [kraɪm]
名 犯罪活動，不法行為；罪，罪行

例句 We moved here because the crime rate was low.
／我們搬到這裡來是因為這裡的犯罪率低。

0451 crisis [ˋkraɪsɪs]
名 (pl.crises) 危機，危急關頭；決定性時刻

例句 We are now in a food crisis.
／我們現在正面臨糧食危機。

0452 cross [krɔs]
動 [及物] 通過，穿過，越過；交，疊放
名 十字架，十字形

巧記 多義：「穿過」街道的蹤跡，不正與街道成「十」字形嗎？

cross the street 穿過街道　　the Cross 十字架

例句 Look right and left before you cross the street.
／過馬路之前，要先向左右兩邊看一下。

0453 crowd [kraʊd]
名 人群，群眾

例句 There was a large crowd of people in the hall.
／大廳裡有一大群人。

0454 crowded [ˋkraʊdɪd]
形 擁擠的，擠滿的

片語 be crowded with 擠滿了…
例句 The car is crowded with people.
／這輛車擠滿了人。

0455 cruel [ˋkruəl]
形 殘忍的，殘酷的；悲慘的

例句 Don't be cruel to animals. ／不要殘忍對待動物。
反義 kind 形 仁慈的

0456 cry [kraɪ]
名 動 [不及物] 哭泣；呼喊

例句 He cried with pain when his father beat him.
／父親打他時，他痛得哭了起來。

0457 □□□ **25**	**culture** [ˈkʌltʃɚ]	名 文化

例句 I love meeting people from different cultures.
／我喜歡認識來自不同文化的人。

0458 □□□	**cup** [kʌp]	名 杯子，酒杯，茶杯；一杯的容量

例句 She drank a whole cup of milk.
／她喝了滿滿的一杯牛奶。

0459 □□□	**cure** [kjʊr]	名 治癒；療法 動 [及物] 治癒，治好

例句 The pills will cure your headache.
／這藥丸能治好你的頭痛。

0460 □□□	**curious** [ˈkjʊrɪəs]	形 好奇的，渴望知道的；奇特的

片語 be curious about sth. 對某事感到好奇 ‖ be curious to do sth. 很想做某事
例句 I'm curious to know what she said.
／我真想知道她說了什麼。

0461 □□□	**current** [ˈkɝənt]	形 流行的；目前的，現行的 名 (空氣、水等的) 流

例句 It was a current belief then that the earth was flat.
／當時人們普遍認為地球是扁平的。

0462 □□□	**curtain** [ˈkɝtn̩]	名 簾，窗簾，門簾

例句 Susan drew the curtains and switched the light on.
／蘇珊拉上了窗簾，打開了燈。

0463 □□□	**curve** [kɝv]	名 曲線，弧線；彎曲處 動 (使) 彎曲

例句 The road curved around the bay.
／那條路沿著海灣蜿蜒伸展。

0464
□□□

custom
[ˋkʌstəm]

名 習慣，習俗，慣例

例句 Most countries in the world have different customs.
／世界上大多數國家有著不同的風俗習慣。

0465
□□□

customer
[ˋkʌstəmə]

名 顧客

例句 The supermarket has thousands of customers.
／這家超市有數千名顧客。

0466
□□□

cut
[kʌt]

動 [及物] (cut, cut)) 割；砍；剪
名 削減；理髮，修剪

例句 She cut the cake with a knife.
／她用刀切開了蛋糕。

片語 cut down ①砍倒 ②減少，降低 ‖ cut in 插嘴 ‖ cut off 割(砍，切)掉，
切斷 ‖ cut up 切碎

0467
□□□

cute
[kjut]

形〔口〕聰明的，伶俐的，可愛的

例句 The baby's so cute. ／這嬰兒真可愛。

0468
□□□

dad
[dæd]

名〔口〕爸爸，爹爹 (=daddy=papa=pa=pop)

例句 He lives with his mom and dad.
／他和爸爸媽媽一起住。

0469
□□□

daily
[ˋdelɪ]

形 每日的；日常的
副 每日

例句 His daily work is sweeping the floor.
／他每天的工作就是掃地。

0470
□□□

damage
[ˋdæmɪdʒ]

名 動 [及物] 損害，毀壞

例句 Smoking can damage your health.
／抽煙會損害你的健康。

片語 do damage to 對…造成損害

0471
□□□

dance
[dæns]

動 [不及物] 跳舞
名 舞蹈，舞步

例句 Lucy dances well.
／露西舞跳得很好。

0472 □□□ **danger**
[`dendʒɚ]

名 危險

片語 in danger 在危險中　out of danger 脫離危險

例句 Many kinds of wild animals are in danger. We must do something to save them.
／許多種野生動物處於危險之中。我們必須一起來拯救它們。

0473 □□□ **dangerous**
[`dendʒərəs]

形 危險的

例句 My work is interesting but kind of dangerous.
／我的工作雖然有趣，但是有些危險。

He is in danger.
他處於險境。

He is a dangerous man.
他是個危險人物。

0474 □□□ **dark**
[dɑrk]

形 黑暗的
名 黃昏；黑暗

例句 It was a dark night. ／那是一個漆黑的夜晚。

0475 □□□ **data**
[`detə]

名 資料〔▲ datum 的複數〕

例句 Feed the data into the computer and have them analyzed.
／將資料輸入電腦並且加以分析。

Ⓖroup 2

0476 □□□ **date**
[det]

26

名 日期
動 [不及物] 追溯（到），屬於過去…年代；約會

片語 out of date 過時的，陳舊的←→ up to date 時新的，現代的 ‖ date from 追溯到…年代

例句 This coat is out of date. ／這件衣服過時了。

0477 □□□ **daughter**
[`dɔtɚ]

名 女兒

例句 She has two daughters.
／她有兩個女兒。

0478 □□□ **dawn**
[dɔn]

名 黎明，拂曉；(sing.) 開端，起始

例句 Dawn is breaking. ／天漸漸亮了。
片語 at dawn 在黎明時刻 ‖ from dawn till dark 從早到晚
反義 dusk 名 黃昏，傍晚

0479 ☐☐☐ **day**
[de]

名 天；白天；一日

例句 Most people work during the day. ／多數人在白天工作。

片語 day after day 日復一日地 ‖ day and night 日日夜夜 ‖ day by day 一天天地，逐日 ‖ the day after tomorrow 後天 ‖ the day before yesterday 前天 ‖ the other day 在不久前的某天

辨析 date, day
(1) date 指用年月日來表示的具體日期。
(2) day 指一個時間單位，是星期、月或年被分隔成 24 小時的期間之一。

0480 ☐☐☐ **dead**
[dɛd]

形 死的

例句 The flowers are dead. ／這些花死了。

用法 the dead 指「死去的人」，用作複數。

反義 alive 形 活（著）的

He died 4 years ago.
他 4 年前去逝了。

now

He has been dead for 4 years.
他去逝 4 年了。

0481 ☐☐☐ **deaf**
[dɛf]

形 聾的；不想聽的

例句 He was deaf to my warning. ／他不聽我的警告。

片語 turn a deaf ear to... 對…充耳不聞

0482 ☐☐☐ **deal**
[dil]

動 [不及物] (dealt, dealt) 處理，應付
名 交易

片語 a good/great deal of (=a lot of) 〔修飾不可數名詞〕大量的，非常多的 ‖ deal with 對付，處理

例句 Many students don't know how to deal with stress and become worried.
／很多學生因為不知道怎麼應付壓力而變得憂慮。

0483 ☐☐☐ **dear**
[dɪr]

形 親愛的 嘆 天啊（表示焦急、驚奇、傷心等）
名 親愛的人

巧記 圖解 dear 的一詞多義：

Oh, dear! 天啊
We don't want it, my dear. 親愛的

例句 Dear me, I'm forgetting my wallet!
／天啊，我差一點兒就忘了我的錢包！

0484 □□□ **death** [dɛθ]

名〔die 的名詞〕死，死亡

例句 Death belongs to life as birth does.
／死亡宛如誕生，都是隸屬於生命的。

片語 put sb. to death 置某人於死地 ‖ to death 極度

0485 □□□ **debate** [dɪˋbet]

動 辯論，爭論
名 辯論（會），爭論（會）

巧記〔熟〕battle 戰鬥 →〔根〕bate 戰 →〔生〕debate〔de-(加強意義) + bate；「唇槍舌劍」→〕辯論，爭論

例句 Parliament will debate the question tomorrow.
／議會明天將辯論這個問題。

0486 □□□ **debt** [dɛt]

名 債務，欠債，負債；(常 sing.) 恩情，情義

例句 I must pay a debt of ＄200 to him.
／我必須還他 200 美元的借款。

片語 get/run into debt 負債 ‖ in debt to sb. (=in sb.'s debt) ①欠某人的債 ②受某人的恩惠 ‖ out of debt 不欠債

0487 □□□ **December** [dɪˋsɛmbɚ]

名 十二月 (=Dec.)

例句 We got married in December. ／我們是在 12 月份結婚的。

0488 □□□ **decide** [dɪˋsaɪd]

動 決定；判決
動 [及物] 使下決心

片語 decide against (doing) sth. 決心不幹某事 ‖ decide (not) to do sth. 決定 (不) 幹某事

例句 They decided to end their relationship. ／他們下定決心斷絕關係。

0489 □□□ **decision** [dɪˋsɪʒən]

名 決定，決心

片語 make a decision 作決定

例句 It was very hard for me to make a decision, but I decided to leave my job.
／對我來說作出決定是非常困難的，但是我決定辭職了。

0490 □□□ **decorate** [ˋdɛkəˏret]

動 [及物] 裝飾，裝潢

例句 We decorated the Christmas tree with glass balls.
／我們用玻璃球裝飾聖誕樹。

用法 decorate 不接雙受詞，而採用 decorate...with sth. 的結構。

| 0491 | **decrease** [dɪ`kris] | 動（使）變小，（使）減少 名 減少，減少的量 |

例句 Student numbers have decreased by 500.
／學生人數減少了 500 名。

| 0492 | **deep** [dip] | 形 深的 副 深深地 |

例句 The sea there is very deep. ／那裡的海很深。
片語 deep in thought 沉思

| 0493 | **deer** [dɪr] | 名〔單同複〕鹿 |

例句 The purse was made of deer skin.
／那個錢包是用鹿皮做的。

| 0494 | **degree** [dɪ`gri] | 名 度（數）；學位 |

例句 The thermometer showed five degrees below zero.
／溫度計顯示零下五度。

Ⓖroup 3

| 0495 | **delay** [dɪ`le] | 動［及物］耽擱；推遲，使延期 動［不及物］拖延 名 遲延，延期 |
| 27 | | |

例句 We decided to delay our holiday. ／我們決定把放假延期。
片語 without delay 毫不遲延地

| 0496 | **delicious** [dɪ`lɪʃəs] | 形 美味的 |

例句 What a delicious apple! ／多好吃的蘋果啊！

| 0497 | **deliver** [dɪ`lɪvɚ] | 動［及物］投遞，郵送；解救；釋放 |

〔根義〕釋放 →〔多義〕

及物動詞
(1) 釋放（人）① 釋放，救出
② 接生
(2) 釋放（物）① 發表，表達
② 遞送，交付

片語 deliver sth. (over) to sb. 把某物交給某人
例句 We can deliver goods to your door.
／我們可以到府送貨。

0498 ☐☐☐ **democracy** [dɪ`mɑkrəsɪ] 图 民主，民主主義；民主國家

例句 The new democracies are facing tough challenges.
／這些新興的民主國家面臨著嚴峻的挑戰。

0499 ☐☐☐ **democratic** [ˌdɛmə`krætɪk] 形 民主的

例句 The Liberal Democratic Party swept the nation last year.
／自由民主黨在去年全國的選舉中大獲全勝。

0500 ☐☐☐ **dentist** [`dɛntɪst] 图 牙醫

例句 I'm going to the dentist this afternoon.
／今天下午我要看牙醫。

0501 ☐☐☐ **deny** [dɪ`naɪ] 動 [及物] 否認，不承認；拒絕…的要求

例句 The boss denied our request for higher wages.
／老闆拒絕了我們加薪的要求。
片語 deny doing... 否認做過… ‖ deny sb.sth. 拒絕給予某人某物

0502 ☐☐☐ **department** [dɪ`partmənt] 图（企業、機構等的）部門；（學術機構的）…學部，系

例句 The company united the two departments.
／該公司合併了那兩個部門。

0503 ☐☐☐ **depend** [dɪ`pɛnd] 動 [不及物] 依靠；信賴

片語 depend on/upon 依靠 ‖ It all depends. (=That depends.) 視情況而定。
例句 Whether I'll go to New York depends on the result of the examination. ／我能否去紐約取決於我的考試成績。

0504 ☐☐☐ **describe** [dɪ`skraɪb] 動 [及物] 描述，形容

例句 Can you describe the man you saw?
／你能不能描述一下你看到的那個男子？

0505 ☐☐☐ **desert** [dɪ`zɝt] 動 [及物] 遺棄，拋棄；擅離，離開

例句 The man deserted his family.
／這個人拋棄了他的家庭。

0506 desert
[`dɛzə-t]
名 沙漠

巧記 圖解 desert 的不同詞義：

掰掰～

n. 沙漠　　　　　　　　vt. 拋棄

例句 These plants live in deserts.
／這些植物生長在沙漠中。

0507 design
[dɪ`zaɪn]
名 設計；圖案，圖樣
動 [及物] 設計，構思

例句 The design is formed with several triangles.
／這設計由若干三角形組成。

片語 of the latest design 最新式的，最新設計的

0508 desire
[dɪ`zaɪr]
名 願望，想要
動 [及物]（不用在進行時）願望，期望；要求

例句 I've no desire for wealth.
／我沒有發財的慾望。

片語 desire sb. to do sth. 想讓某人做某事 ‖ desire to do sth. 想要做某事
用法 desire 及其派生詞 (desirable, desirous) 所接的從句用虛擬語氣。

0509 desk
[dɛsk]
名 書桌，辦公桌

例句 Mary is sitting at her desk.
／瑪麗正坐在書桌前。

0510 dessert
[dɪ`zɝt]
名（餐後的）甜食，甜點

例句 What are we having for dessert?
／我們吃什麼甜點呢？

0511 determine
[dɪ`tɝmɪn]
動 決定，決心

片語 determine on (doing) sth. 決定（做）某事 ‖ determine to do...（動作）決定做…
例句 We have determined to get the work done before Friday.
／我們已決定在週五前完成工作。

0512 ☐☐☐
develop
[dɪ`vɛləp]

🔴（使）發展；開發

例句 Shenzhen has developed into a commercial center.
／深圳已發展成為一個商業中心。

片語 developed countries 發達國家 ‖ developing countries 發展中國家

0513 ☐☐☐
dial
[`daɪəl]

🔴[不及物] 撥打，撥（電話號碼）

例句 I dialed my friend's number but the line was busy.
／我給朋友打電話，可是他的電話占線。

辨析 dial, telephone/call/ring
(1) dial sb.=telephone/call/ring sb.
(2) dial 可接電話號碼，而 telephone/call/ring 則不能。

Group 4

0514 ☐☐☐
diamond
[`daɪəmənd]

🔴 鑽石；（撲克牌的）方塊

28

例句 I've only the six of diamonds. ／我只有方塊 6。
片語 diamond cut diamond 硬碰硬，棋逢對手，勢均力敵

0515 ☐☐☐
diary
[`daɪərɪ]

🔴 日記

例句 It's a good habit to keep a diary. ／寫日記是個好習慣。

0516 ☐☐☐
dictionary
[`dɪkʃən‚ɛrɪ]

🔴 字典，辭典，詞典

例句 Are these your dictionaries? ／這些詞典是你的嗎？

0517 ☐☐☐
die
[daɪ]

🔴[不及物] 死；枯萎

例句 Her husband died yesterday.
／她丈夫昨天去世了。

片語 die away 逐漸停止，逐漸消失 ‖ die
from 死於…（外因）‖ die of 死於…
（內因）‖ die out 逐漸消失

die from an
accident
死于車禍

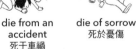
die of sorrow
死於憂傷

辨析 die, dead, death
(1) die 是瞬態性動詞，動作不延續，與時間點連用，常用於一般過去時。
(2) dead 是形容詞，與系動詞構成系表結構，可與時間段連用，用於現在時。
(3) death 是 die 的名詞形式。

0518 diet [`daɪət]
名 節食

片語 go/be on a diet 節食
例句 She is on a low-fat diet. ╱她正在接受低脂節食治療。

0519 difference [`dɪfərəns]
名 差異，不同，區別

例句 There are many differences in their points of view.
╱他們的觀點有很多不同。
片語 make a difference (to) (對…) 有差別，有關係 ‖ make no difference 沒有差別

0520 different [`dɪfərənt]
形 不同的

片語 be different from 與…不同
例句 Life in the countryside is quite different from that in modern cities. ╱農村生活與現代城市生活相當不同。
反義 same 形 相同的

0521 difficult [`dɪfə͵kʌlt]
形 困難的

例句 English is a difficult language for me to master.
╱對我來說，英語是門很難掌握的語言。
反義 easy 形 容易的

0522 difficulty [`dɪfə͵kʌltɪ]
名 困難，費力

片語 have difficulty in (doing) sth. 幹某事有困難 ‖ without difficulty 容易地，毫不費力地
例句 They had great difficulty in finding a good doctor.
╱他們費了很大勁才找到一個好醫生。

0523 dig [dɪg]
動 (dug, dug) 挖

例句 He is digging in his garden. ╱他正在花園裡挖土。

0524 diligent [`dɪlədʒənt]
形 勤奮的，勤勉的

例句 He is diligent in his studies. ╱他學習勤奮。
反義 lazy 形 懶惰的

0525 □□□
dinner
[`dɪnɚ]
名 正餐；晚宴

例句 It's time for dinner.
／吃飯時間到了。
片語 be at dinner 在吃飯 ‖ have a big dinner 大吃一頓
用法 dinner 前一般不用冠詞或限定詞，除非指某一頓正餐，或其前有形容詞修飾。

0526 □□□
dinosaur
[`daɪnə,sɔr]
名 恐龍

例句 Have you ever seen a dinosaur?
／你見過恐龍沒有？

0527 □□□
diplomat
[`dɪpləmæt]
名 外交官，外交家

例句 We need a diplomat to deal with these problems.
／我們需要一個外交家來處理這些問題。

0528 □□□
direct
[də`rɛkt]
形 直接的
動 [及物] 指示方向；指導；導演

例句 She directed him to the station.
／她告訴他去車站的路怎麼走。

0529 □□□
direction
[də`rɛkʃən]
名 方向；指導

片語 in all directions (=in every direction) (向) 四面八方
例句 The bees flew in all directions.
／蜜蜂向四面八方飛去。

0530 □□□
director
[də`rɛktɚ]
名 導演；指揮者

例句 Who is the director of the film?
／這部電影的導演是誰？

0531 □□□
dirty
[`dɝtɪ]
形 髒的，弄髒的
動 [及物] 弄髒 動 [不及物] 變髒

例句 My hands are dirty. ／我的手很髒。

0532 □□□
disappear
[dɪsə`pɪr]
動 [不及物] 消失

例句 The plane disappeared among clouds. ／飛機消失在雲層裡。

0533
□□□
discover
[dɪ`skʌvə-]
動 [及物] 發現

29

巧記 dis-(否定首碼，表相反動作)+cover(蓋，掩蓋)；取掉蓋 → 發現

例句 Do you ever discover who did it?
／你發現那是誰做的了嗎？

dis- (= apart) +cover
乃取掉 cover 之意

discover 發現

0534
□□□
discuss
[dɪ`skʌs]
動 [及物] 討論，議論

例句 We discussed when to go.
／我們商量了什麼時候去。

片語 discuss sth. with sb. 和某人討論某事

0535
□□□
discussion
[dɪ`skʌʃən]
名 討論

例句 The discussion went on for hours.
／那場討論持續了好幾個小時。

片語 under discussion 在討論中

0536
□□□
dish
[dɪʃ]
名 盤，碟；一道菜

例句 He picked up a dish from the table.
／他從桌上拿起一個盤子。

0537
□□□
dishonest
[dɪs`ɑnɪst]
形 不誠實的

巧記 dis-(不)+honest(誠實的)

例句 It is dishonest to lie about one's age.
／虛報年齡是不誠實的。

0538
□□□
distance
[`dɪstəns]
名 距離

例句 What is the distance from Los Angeles to San Francisco?
／洛杉磯到三藩市的距離有多遠？

片語 at a distance 離一段距離，從遠處
‖ in the distance 在遠處，在遠方

at a distance
離一段距離

in the distance
在遠處

0539 ☐☐☐

divide
[dəˋvaɪd]

動 [及物] 分成；劃分

例句 Let's divide ourselves into two groups.
／我們分成兩個小組吧。

0540 ☐☐☐

division
[dəˋvɪʒən]

名 分，分開；(sing.) 分配；除 (法)

巧記 已知：〔動〕decide → 〔名〕decision
易記：〔動〕divide → 〔名〕division

例句 Are you good at division?
／ 你的除法好嗎？

0541 ☐☐☐

dizzy
[ˋdɪzɪ]

形 頭暈目眩的，極高的

例句 The boy climbed to a dizzy height.
／那個男孩爬到了令人頭暈目眩的高度。

0542 ☐☐☐

do
[du]

動 [及物] (did, done) 做
動〔構成疑問句及否定句，無實際詞義〕

例句 What are the boys doing over there?
／那邊的那些男孩們在幹什麼？

片語 do well in 在 … 方面做得好 ‖ do with 處理 ‖ have something to do
with... 與…有關　have nothing to do with... 與…無關

辨析 do with, deal with
(1) do with 在問句中多和 what 連用，常譯為「處理」。
(2) deal with 在問句中多和 how 連用，其基本意思為「應付，處理」。

例句 They didn't go to Paris.
／他們沒去巴黎。

0543 ☐☐☐

doctor
[ˋdɑktɚ]

名 醫生，醫師；博士

巧記 doctor 是「醫生」，為什麼又是「博士」？因為 doctor 過去作「學者，先生」講。

例句 He received a doctor's degree in physics.
／他獲得了物理學博士學位。

片語 see a doctor 看醫生，就診 ‖ send for a doctor 請醫生

0544 ☐☐☐

document
[ˋdɑkjəmənt]

名 檔案，文獻；(電腦中的) 文件，檔案

例句 The policeman wanted to see all our documents.
／員警想查看我們所有的檔。

0545 □□□
dog
[dɔg]
名 狗

例句 I keep a dog.
／我養了一隻狗。

0546 □□□
doll
[dɑl]
名 玩偶，玩具娃娃

例句 She has a pretty doll.
／她有個漂亮的洋娃娃。

0547 □□□
dollar
[`dɑlɚ]
名 元，美元（符號為 $）

巧記 詞源：美元符號是一個大 S 加上一條分隔號。關於這個符號的來歷，一個說法是認為在這個符號中將一個窄寫的 U 放在一個寬寫的 S 上，它代表了美國 (United States)。

例句 He earned ten million dollars last year.
／去年他賺了 1,000 萬美元。

0548 □□□
dolphin
[`dɑlfɪn]
名 海豚

例句 A dolphin is an intelligent animal.
／海豚是一種聰明的動物。

0549 □□□
donkey
[`dɑŋkɪ]
名 驢

例句 The little donkey rolled on the ground.
／小驢在地上打滾。

0550 □□□
door
[dor]
名 門；通道

例句 Remember to lock the door.
／記住要鎖門。

片語 from door to door 挨家挨戶

Group 2

0551 □□□
30
dot
[dɑt]
名 點，小圓點；小數點；句號

片語 on the dot 準時
例句 I'll be there on the dot.
／我會準時到達那裡。

0552 ☐☐☐

double
[ˋdʌbl̩]

形 兩倍的;雙的
動 (使) 加倍　名 兩倍數

例句 Ten is double five. ／ 10 是 5 的兩倍。
辨析 double, two
(1) double 表示「雙」,後面的名詞不用複數。
(2) two 表示「兩個」,後面的名詞用複數。

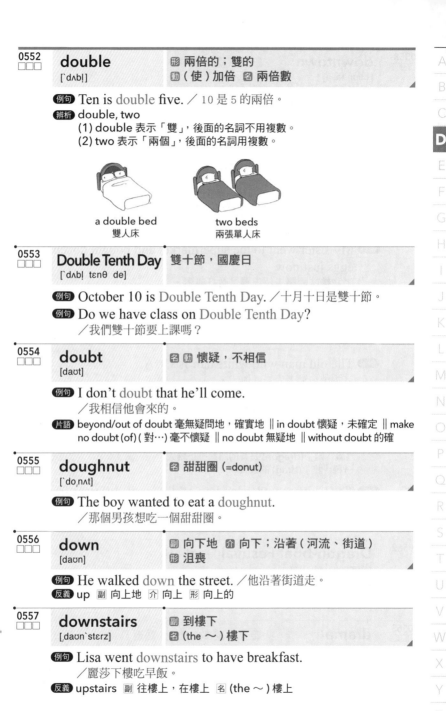

a double bed
雙人床

two beds
兩張單人床

0553 ☐☐☐

Double Tenth Day
[ˋdʌbl̩ tɛnθ de]

雙十節,國慶日

例句 October 10 is Double Tenth Day. ／十月十日是雙十節。
例句 Do we have class on Double Tenth Day?
／我們雙十節要上課嗎?

0554 ☐☐☐

doubt
[daʊt]

名 動 懷疑,不相信

例句 I don't doubt that he'll come.
／我相信他會來的。
片語 beyond/out of doubt 毫無疑問地,確實地 ‖ in doubt 懷疑,未確定 ‖ make no doubt (of) (對…) 毫不懷疑 ‖ no doubt 無疑地 ‖ without doubt 的確

0555 ☐☐☐

doughnut
[ˋdo͵nʌt]

名 甜甜圈 (=donut)

例句 The boy wanted to eat a doughnut.
／那個男孩想吃一個甜甜圈。

0556 ☐☐☐

down
[daʊn]

副 向下地　介 向下;沿著 (河流、街道)
形 沮喪

例句 He walked down the street. ／他沿著街道走。
反義 up 副 向上地　介 向上　形 向上的

0557 ☐☐☐

downstairs
[͵daʊnˋstɛrz]

副 到樓下
名 (the ～) 樓下

例句 Lisa went downstairs to have breakfast.
／麗莎下樓吃早飯。
反義 upstairs 副 往樓上,在樓上　名 (the ～) 樓上

0558 □□□ downtown
[ˈdaʊnˈtaʊn]

名 商業區，市中心

例句 Shall we go downtown this evening?
／今晚我們去市中心好嗎？

用法 英語中的 downtown 是指商店、銀行、戲院等集中所在的都市中心地帶，如 downtown Los Angeles 是指洛杉磯的商業區。

0559 □□□ dozen
[ˈdʌzn̩]

名 (一)打，12 個；(pl.) 幾十，許多

巧記 諧音：〔英〕dozen 一音譯→〔漢〕打
片語 dozens of 許多，數打 ‖ for dozens of years 數十年以來 ‖ in dozens 一打一打地，成打地

例句 My sister went to the supermarket and bought dozens of eggs just now.
／我妹妹剛剛去超市買了數打雞蛋。

用法 無論 dozen 是否是複數，後面的名詞必須是複數。

0560 □□□ Dr./Dr
[ˈdɑktɚ]

醫生；博士

例句 The old man with white hair is Dr. A.
／那位白髮老人是 A 博士。

0561 □□□ dragon
[ˈdræɡən]

名 龍

巧記 〔熟〕drag 拖，拉→〔生〕dragon
▲「龍」(dragon) 長長的體態不正給人一種「拖」(drag) 的感覺嗎？

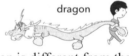
dragon

例句 The Chinese understanding of dragon is different from that of Westerners.
／中國人對龍的理解跟西方人不一樣。

0562 □□□ Dragon-boat Festival
[ˈdræɡən bot ˈfɛstəvl̩]

端午節

例句 Wish Dragon-boat Festival happiness!
／祝端午節快樂！

0563 □□□ drama
[ˈdrɑmə]

名 戲，劇本；戲劇 (藝術)

例句 Ben played a major part in the drama.
／本在這部戲中扮演主要的角色。

0564 ☐☐☐ **draw** [drɔ] 　動 (drew, drawn) 畫；拉；取出

例句 I'm going to draw a picture. ／我打算畫一幅畫。

0565 ☐☐☐ **drawer** [`drɔɚ] 　名 抽屜

例句 She took a file from her desk drawer.
／她從書桌的抽屜裡拿出一個資料夾。

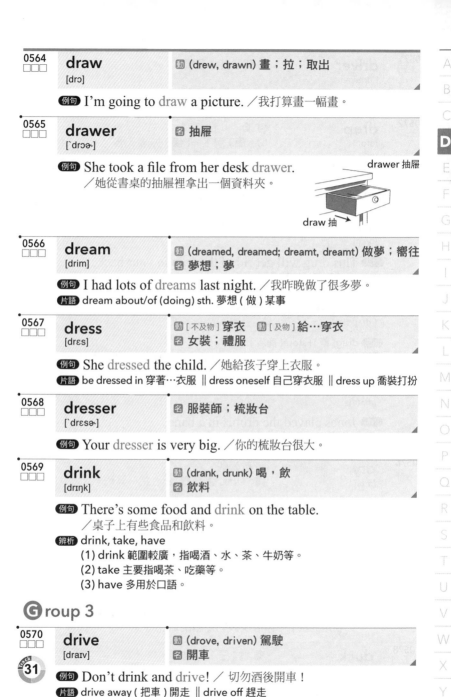

drawer 抽屜

draw 抽➡

0566 ☐☐☐ **dream** [drim] 　動 (dreamed, dreamed; dreamt, dreamt) 做夢；嚮往
名 夢想；夢

例句 I had lots of dreams last night. ／我昨晚做了很多夢。
片語 dream about/of (doing) sth. 夢想 (做) 某事

0567 ☐☐☐ **dress** [drɛs] 　動 [不及物] 穿衣　動 [及物] 給⋯穿衣
名 女裝；禮服

例句 She dressed the child. ／她給孩子穿上衣服。
片語 be dressed in 穿著⋯衣服 ‖ dress oneself 自己穿衣服 ‖ dress up 喬裝打扮

0568 ☐☐☐ **dresser** [`drɛsɚ] 　名 服裝師；梳妝台

例句 Your dresser is very big. ／你的梳妝台很大。

0569 ☐☐☐ **drink** [drɪŋk] 　動 (drank, drunk) 喝，飲
名 飲料

例句 There's some food and drink on the table.
／桌子上有些食品和飲料。
辨析 drink, take, have
(1) drink 範圍較廣，指喝酒、水、茶、牛奶等。
(2) take 主要指喝茶、吃藥等。
(3) have 多用於口語。

Ⓖroup 3

0570 ☐☐☐ ③①(Track) **drive** [draɪv] 　動 (drove, driven) 駕駛
名 開車

例句 Don't drink and drive! ／ 切勿酒後開車！
片語 drive away (把車) 開走 ‖ drive off 趕走

0571 □□□ **driver**
[ˋdraɪvɚ]

名 駕駛員，司機

例句 Lewis is a driver.／路易斯是一名司機。

0572 □□□ **drop**
[drɑp]

名 滴
動（使）滴下，（使）掉落；扔

例句 I think I dropped my mobile phone during the concert.
／我想我的手機是在音樂會時掉的。
片語 drop in 偶然來訪，順便走訪 ‖ drop out ①退出 ②退學

0573 □□□ **drug**
[drʌg]

名 藥，藥物；麻醉劑，毒品

例句 This drug will get rid of the pain in your back.
／這藥可以消除你的背痛。

0574 □□□ **drugstore**
[ˋdrʌg͵stor]

名 藥店，藥房

巧記 drug(藥)+store(商店)
例句 There is a drugstore around the corner.／轉角處有一家藥店。

0575 □□□ **drum**
[drʌm]

名 鼓

例句 Jones played the drums in a band.
／鐘斯在一個樂隊裡打鼓。

0576 □□□ **dry**
[draɪ]

形 乾燥的
動 [不及物] 變乾 動 [及物] 把…弄乾

例句 I dried my clothes by the heater.／我用暖爐烘乾衣服。
片語 dry up ①（使）乾涸，（使）幹透 ②（使）枯竭 ‖ keep dry 保持乾燥，請勿受潮
反義 wet 形 潮濕的

0577 □□□ **dryer**
[ˋdraɪɚ]

名 烘乾機，吹風機

例句 My hair is wet. Can you get me the hair dryer?
／我頭髮濕了，你可以拿吹風機給我嗎？

0578 □□□ **duck**
[dʌk]

名 鴨（子）；鴨肉

例句 The main course of this restaurant is roast duck.
／這家飯店的主菜是烤鴨。

0579 □□□ **dumb** [dʌm]
形 啞的；(因驚恐等)說不出話的

例句 She was dumb with fear. ／她怕得說不出話來。

0580 □□□ **dumpling** [`dʌmplɪŋ]
名 湯圓；餃子

例句 We have dumplings for lunch. ／我們中午吃了餃子。

0581 □□□ **during** [`djʊrɪŋ]
介 在…期間

例句 The road is usually very busy, especially during the rush hours. ／這條路通常很塞，尤其是在上下班尖峰時段。

0582 □□□ **duty** [`djutɪ]
名 職責，職務；責任

例句 It is your duty to share in the housework. ／分擔家事是你的責任。

片語 do one's duty 盡義務，盡本分 ‖ fail in one's duty 失職 ‖ off duty 下班，不值勤　on duty 上班，值勤

0583 □□□ **each** [itʃ]
代 每個，各個　形 每個的，各自的
副 各個地

例句 Each of us has a room. ／我們每人有一個房間。

片語 each other 互相，彼此

0584 □□□ **eagle** [`ig!]
名 鷹

例句 An eagle is flying up into the sky. ／一隻雄鷹飛向天空。

0585 □□□ **ear** [ɪr]
名 耳朵

例句 The news eventually reached the ears of the king. ／消息最終傳到了國王的耳裡。

ear 耳朵　　ear 穗　　ear 耳狀物

0586 □□□ **early** [`ɝlɪ]
形 副 早的(地)

例句 It is good for health to keep early hours. ／早睡早起身體好。

反義 late 形 副 晚的(地)

0587 ☐☐☐
earn
[ɝn]

動 [及物] 賺得；獲得，獲利
動 [不及物] 掙錢

例句 He earns £ 20 a week.
／他一周賺 20 英鎊。
片語 earn one's living/bread 謀生

0588 ☐☐☐
earth
[ɝθ]

名 地球；大地；泥土

片語 on earth ①在地球上 ②〔常用在疑問詞後加強語氣〕究竟，到底
例句 What on earth has happened to him?
／他到底怎麼了？

Group 4

0589 ☐☐☐
east
[ist]
㉜

名 東，東方
形 副 東方的（地）

片語 in the east (of) 在 (…的) 東部 ‖ on the east (of) 在 (…的) 東面
例句 The sun rises in the east. ／太陽從東邊升起。
反義 west 名 西，西方 形 副 西方的（地）

0590 ☐☐☐
Easter
[ˋistɚ]

名 復活節；復活節期間

例句 We'll probably go away at Easter.
／復活節期間我們可能會外出度假。

0591 ☐☐☐
eastern
[ˋistɚn]

形 朝東的；東方的，東部的

例句 They are farmers in eastern England.
／他們是英格蘭東部的農民。
反義 western 形 西方的；來自西方的

0592 ☐☐☐
easy
[ˋizɪ]

形 容易的

例句 Easy come, easy go. ／〔諺〕來得容易，去得快。
片語 take it easy 別著急，慢慢來
反義 difficult 形 難的，困難的；hard 形 困難的，不易的

0593 ☐☐☐
eat
[it]

動 (ate, eaten) 吃

片語 eat up 吃光，消滅
例句 The children ate up the cakes as soon as they appeared.
／蛋糕一上來，孩子們就把它吃光了。

0594 edge [ɛdʒ]
名 邊，邊緣；刀口，鋒刃

片語 on the edge of 在…邊緣上
例句 Jill sat on the edge of the bed. ／吉爾坐在床沿上。

0595 education [ˌɛdʒʊˋkeʃən]
名 教育

例句 We need a good education environment.
／我們需要一個良好的教育環境。

0596 effect [ɪˋfɛkt]
名 結果；效果
動 [及物] 實現，使生效，引起

例句 Study the cause and effect of the matter.
／研究該問題的因果關係。
片語 bring/carry/put... into effect 實行，使生效 ‖ come/go into effect 開始生效，開始實行 ‖ effect on/upon 對…的作用／影響 ‖ have an/no effect on 對…有／沒有影響／效果 ‖ in effect ①事實上 ②在實施中，有效 ‖ take effect 生效，起作用

0597 effective [ɪˋfɛktɪv]
形 有效的，起作用的

例句 The law is no longer effective. ／該法令已失效。

0598 effort [ˋɛfɚt]
名 努力，盡力

例句 Getting a high grade in every subject requires great effort.
／想要每門課都得高分需要非常努力。
片語 make an effort 努力 ‖ without effort 毫不費力

0599 egg [ɛg]
名 蛋，雞蛋；卵

例句 The fish lay thousands of eggs at a time.
／這種魚一次產數千枚卵。

0600 eight [et]
名 形 八（個）（的）

例句 They woke at eight. ／他們是八點鐘醒的。

0601 eighteen [eˋtɪn]
名 形 十八（個）（的）

例句 He is eighteen years old this year. ／他今年 18 歲。

0602
□□□

eighty
[ˈetɪ]

名 形 八十（個）（的）

例句 He fought against cancer and lived to be eighty.
／他和癌症抗爭，活到了 80 歲。

0603
□□□

either
[ˈiðɚ]

副（用在否定句或否定片語後加強語氣）也

例句 I haven't seen the movie and my brother hasn't either.
／我沒看過這部電影，我弟弟也沒有。

辨析 also, either, too/as well
(1) also 置於實義動詞之前，助動詞、be 動詞之後，間或用於句末。
(2) either 常用於否定句。 (3) too/as well 常用於口語中，多置於句末。

0604
□□□

either
[ˈiðɚ]

代 形 兩者之一（的）

片語 either...or... 或者…或者…

例句 Either you or your brother can join us. We want one of you.
／你或者你兄弟可以加入我們。我們只要你們其中一個。

用法 either...or 連接並列成分作主詞時，述語動詞要與後面所接的名 / 代詞在
數方面保持一致，遵循「就近原則」。

辨析 any, either
(1) any 指三者或三者以上的任何一個。 (2) either 指兩者中的任何一個。

0605
□□□

elder
[ˈɛldɚ]

形 較年長的
名 年長者；長輩

例句 My elder brother is seven years older than my younger sister.
／我哥哥比我妹妹大七歲。

辨析 elder, older
(1) elder 通常作限定詞，不作主詞補語，不與 than 連用；常加在
   brother, sister 等詞前，指「哥哥」、「姐姐」。
(2) older 可作限定詞和主詞補語，通常指「歲數比…大些」，是比較級形式。

0606
□□□

elect
[ɪˈlɛkt]

動 [及物] 選舉，推舉

例句 He was elected mayor last year. ／他去年被選為市長。

用法 在「elect sb.+ 職務」句式中，像總統、市長等獨一無二的職位前不用任
何冠詞：We elected him Chairman. 我們選他當主席。

0607
□□□

election
[ɪˈlɛkʃən]

名 選舉，競選；當選

例句 He will be fighting local elections next May.
／他將在明年 5 月參加當地的競選。

0608 ☐☐☐
electric
[ɪˋlɛktrɪk]
⑮ 電的；導電的；電動的

33

例句 My electric shaver works on these batteries.
／我的電動剃鬍刀就是用這種電池。

0609 ☐☐☐
element
[ˋɛləmənt]
名 要素；元素

例句 Is money an element of happiness?
／金錢是幸福的一個要素嗎？

0610 ☐☐☐
elephant
[ˋɛləfənt]
名 象

例句 African elephants have trunks.
／非洲象長著長鼻子。

0611 ☐☐☐
eleven
[ɪˋlɛvn]
代 名 形 十一（個）（的）

例句 The college gate closes at eleven at night.
／學院大門夜晚 11 點關閉。

0612 ☐☐☐
else
[ɛls]
副 另外，其他

例句 Who else can I ask to help me?
／我還能讓誰來幫我呢？
片語 or else 否則，要不然

0613 ☐☐☐
e-mail
[ˋiˋmel]
名 電子郵件
動 [及物] 給…發電子郵件

例句 Will you e-mail me about it?
／關於這件事，你能給我傳一封電子郵件嗎？

0614 ☐☐☐
embarrass
[ɪmˋbærəs]
動 [及物] 使尷尬，使人為難

巧記 em-(= im- , in) + bar(障礙) + -ass；陷於障礙中 → 進退維谷 → 使人為難

例句 I was embarrassed because I had no money.
／我因為沒錢而不知如何是好。

0615 emotion
[ɪ`moʃən]
名 情感，情緒

例句 I was overcome by emotion. ／我激動得無法自已。

0616 emphasize
[`ɛmfə,saɪz]
動 [及物] 強調，著重

例句 He emphasized the need for practical English.
／他強調了實用英語的必要性。

用法 emphasize 後面直接跟受詞。

0617 employ
[ɪm`plɔɪ]
動 [及物] 雇用

例句 He employed fifty men in his factory.
／他雇用了 50 個人在他的工廠工作。

片語 be employed to do sth. 受雇做某事 ‖ employ oneself/be employed in (doing) sth. 從事某事

0618 empty
[`ɛmptɪ]
形 空的
動 [不及物] (一場所) 變空，人全走光

例句 The classroom emptied at 4:30. ／四點半教室裡空無一人。

反義 full 形 滿的

0619 encourage
[ɪn`kɝɪdʒ]
動 [及物] 鼓勵，激勵

巧記 en-(使)+courage(勇氣)；使充滿勇氣 → 鼓勵

片語 encourage sb. to do sth. 鼓勵某人做某事

例句 This kind of contest encourages people to speak English.
／這類比賽鼓勵人們講英語。

0620 end
[ɛnd]
名 結束；結尾；終點
動 [不及物] 結束，終止

片語 at the end of 在…的盡頭 ‖ by the end of 到…時為止 ‖ end in... 以…結束 ‖ end up 最終成為，最終處於 ‖ in the end 最後，終於

例句 The man tried several times to start the car, and he succeeded in the end.
／這位男士嘗試了好幾次發動這輛車，最終成功了。

0621 enemy
[`ɛnəmɪ]
名 敵人

例句 He has many enemies.
／他樹敵很多。

0622 ☐☐☐

energy
[ˋɛnɚˎdʒɪ]

名 精力，活力；能源

例句 Young people usually have more energy than the old.
／年輕人通常比老年人更有活力。

0623 ☐☐☐

engine
[ˋɛndʒən]

名 發動機，引擎

巧記 諧音：〔英〕engine 一音譯→〔漢〕引擎

例句 The engine won't start. ／該引擎無法發動。

0624 ☐☐☐

engineer
[ˎɛndʒəˋnɪr]

名 工程師

例句 I want to be an engineer. ／我想成為一名工程師。

0625 ☐☐☐

England
[ˋɪŋglənd]

名 英格蘭；英國

例句 England is his second home. ／英格蘭是他的第二故鄉。

0626 ☐☐☐

English
[ˋɪŋglɪʃ]

形 英國的，英格蘭的
名 英語

例句 How long have you learned English? ／你學英語學多久了？

Ⓖroup 2

0627 ☐☐☐
34

Englishman
[ˋɪŋglɪʃmən]

名 (pl.Englishmen) 英國人，英格蘭人

例句 She has married an Englishman.
／她嫁給了一個英國人。

0628 ☐☐☐

enjoy
[ɪnˋdʒɔɪ]

動 [及物] 喜歡，享受…的樂趣

片語 enjoy doing sth. 喜愛做某事 ‖ enjoy oneself 玩得高興

例句 More and more foreigners enjoy listening to Peking Opera.
／喜歡聽京劇的外國人越來越多。

辨析 appreciate, enjoy
(1) price(價) → appreciate〔根義〕評價，估價 → 因而它作「欣賞」講時指對事物有深入的瞭解並能鑒賞。
(2) joy(樂) → enjoy〔根義〕使快樂 → 因而它作「欣賞」講時不像 appreciate 那樣需要較高的修養，僅指從中得到快樂。
※ The foreigner enjoys Peking opera very much although he doesn't appreciate it. 這個老外很愛聽京劇，雖然他聽不出個子丑寅卯。

0629 □□□
enough
[ə`nʌf]
形 副 足夠的（地），充分的（地）

例句 The problem is easy enough for me to solve.
／這個問題很簡單，我可以解決。
用法 enough 放在所修飾的名詞前或後均可，但只能用在形容詞或副詞之後。

0630 □□□
enter
[`ɛntə]
動 [及物] 進入

例句 There was no one there, so she entered the room.
／屋子裡沒人，於是她走了進去。

0631 □□□
entire
[ɪn`taɪr]
形 整個的，全部的

例句 The entire village was destroyed. ／整個村子都被毀了。

0632 □□□
entrance
[`ɛntrəns]
名 入口，門口；入學

例句 He passed the college entrance examination.
／他通過了大學入學考試。
反義 exit 名 出口

ENTRANCE WAY IN

EXIT WAY OUT

0633 □□□
envelope
[`ɛnvəˌlop]
名 信封

例句 She sealed the envelope. ／她把信封封上。

0634 □□□
environment
[ɪn`vaɪrənmənt]
名 （自然）環境

例句 An unhappy home environment may affect a child's
behavior. ／不幸的家庭環境可能對孩子的行為造成影響。

0635 □□□
envy
[`ɛnvɪ]
名 動 [及物] 羨慕，妒忌

例句 Andy looked with envy at his neighbor's new car.
／安迪以羨慕的目光看著鄰居的新車。
片語 feel envy at 對…感到妒忌／羨慕 ‖ out of envy 出於妒忌
辨析 envy, admire
(1) envy「羨慕，妒忌」，是希望自己擁有他人的好運、財物或長處。
(2) admire「欽佩」，因認定他人或某物具有卓越的價值而對其懷有愛慕、尊敬之情。

0636 □□□

equal
[`ikwəl]

形 平等的
動 [及物] 等於

例句 All men are created equal.
／人人生而平等。

片語 be equal to doing sth. 勝任… ‖ be equal to sth. 與…相等 ‖ equal sb. in sth. 在…方面與某人匹敵 ‖ equal sth. 與…相等

反義 unequal 形 不平等的

0637 □□□

eraser
[ɪ`resə-]

名 橡皮擦

例句 Can I use your eraser?
／我可以用你的橡皮擦嗎？

0638 □□□

error
[`ɛrə-]

名 錯誤，過失，差錯

例句 The accident was caused by human error.
／這次的事故是人為的過失所引起的。

片語 in error (=by mistake) 錯誤地

0639 □□□

especially
[ə`spɛʃəlɪ]

副 特別；尤其

例句 I think winter is a beautiful season, especially when it snows.
／我覺得冬天是一個美麗的季節，尤其是下雪的時候。

0640 □□□

Europe
[`jʊrəp]

名 歐洲

例句 Ann travelled around Europe for a few months.
／安在歐洲各地旅遊了幾個月。

0641 □□□

European
[jʊrə`piən]

形 歐洲的，歐洲人的
名 歐洲人

例句 We are keeping a good relationship with our European partners.
／我們與我們的歐盟夥伴保持著良好的關係。

0642 □□□

eve
[iv]

名 (常 sing.) 前夜；(the ～)(大事件的) 前夕

例句 We're arriving on Christmas Eve.
／我們將在耶誕節前夕到達。

片語 on the eve of... 在…的前夕

0643 ☐☐☐

even
[ˋivən]

副 甚至，更

片語 even if/though 即使，雖然

例句 My father has spent much money on books, even though he's not rich. ／我爸爸花了很多錢買書，雖然他並不富有。

0644 ☐☐☐

evening
[ˋivnɪŋ]

名 黃昏，傍晚，晚上；晚會

例句 I'll call you up this evening. ／我今晚給你打電話。

片語 in the evening 在晚上 ‖ on the evening of... 在…的晚上

0645 ☐☐☐

event
[ɪˋvɛnt]

名 事件，大事；(運動)項目，比賽

例句 My sister's wedding was a big event for our family.
／我姐姐的婚禮是我們家的大事。

片語 in the event of... 倘若…，萬一在…的時候 ‖ in the event that 倘若，萬一

Ⓖroup 3

0646 ☐☐☐

35

ever
[ˋɛvɚ]

副 曾，曾經

例句 Have you ever seen the Queen? ／你曾經見過女王嗎？

片語 ever since 自…以來

0647 ☐☐☐

every
[ˋɛvrɪ]

形 每個，每一

例句 Every dog has his day. ／〔諺〕誰都有得意的時候。

用法 every 後接單數名詞作主詞時，述語動詞用單數形式；every+ 基數詞 + 名詞 (複數)，意為「每隔」；由 every 所修飾的名詞，其前不能用介系詞修飾，如不能說 on every week, in every year 等。

辨析 each, all, every
each 和 every 都可指三個或三個以上的人或物中的「每個」。
(1) each 指「各個」，以個別為主。
(2) all 指「所有」，概括全體。
(3) every 相當於 each and all，不僅逐指每個，而且概括全體。each 後可跟 of 短語，而 every 不可以。

each   all   every

※ Every one of them went to the meeting and each made a speech. 他們每人都到會了，並且人人都發了言。

0648 □□□ **everybody**
[ˈɛvrɪˌbɑdɪ]

代 每個人，人人

例句 He doesn't know that rule which everybody knows.
／他不知道每個人都知道的那條規則。

0649 □□□ **everyone**
[ˈɛvrɪˌwʌn]

代 每個人，人人

例句 If everyone is ready, I'll begin.
／如果大家都準備好了，我就開始了。

辨析 everybody/everyone, every one
(1) everybody/everyone 只指人，不指事物，後不接 of...。
(2) every one 既可指人，也可指事物，後可接 of...。

0650 □□□ **everything**
[ˈɛvrɪˌθɪŋ]

代 每件事物；一切

例句 I decided to tell her everything.
／我決定把一切都告訴她。

0651 □□□ **everywhere**
[ˈɛvrɪˌhwɛr]

副 到處，處處，各地

例句 This flower is found everywhere. ／這種花到處可見。

0652 □□□ **evil**
[ˈivl]

名 邪惡
形 邪惡的，壞的

例句 Love of money is the root of all evil.
／〔諺〕貪財是萬惡之源。

0653 □□□ **exact**
[ɪgˈzækt]

形 確切的，精確的

例句 Tell me the exact time, please.
／請告訴我確切的時間。

片語 to be exact〔作插入語〕說得確切些
※ To be exact, she is a very exact person. 確切地說，她是個一絲不苟的人。

0654 □□□ **exam**
[ɪgˈzæm]

名 考試；檢查 (=examination)

例句 He passed the English exam.
／他通過了英語考試。

片語 do/pass well in an exam 通過考試 / 考得好　do/fail badly in an exam 考試不及格 / 考得差 ‖ take/do an exam 參加考試

0655 ☐☐☐
examine
[ɪg`zæmɪn]

動 [及物] 檢查，審查；測驗

例句 The doctor examined her but could find nothing wrong.
／醫生給她作了檢查，但沒發現什麼問題。

0656 ☐☐☐
example
[ɪg`zæmpl̩]

名 例子；榜樣

例句 I'll give you an example.
／我會給你舉一個例子。

片語 for example 例如… ‖ set an example (to sb.)(給某人) 樹立榜樣
‖ take...for example 以…舉例說明

0657 ☐☐☐
excellent
[`ɛksl̩ənt]

形 極好的；優秀的

例句 Singapore is an excellent place to try new food.
／新加坡是一個品嘗新食品的好地方。

片語 be excellent in 在…方面極好

0658 ☐☐☐
except
[ɪk`sɛpt]

連 介 除…之外

例句 Everybody except John was able to answer it.
／除了約翰以外大家都能回答它。

辨析 1 except, except for
(1) except 表示除去的和非除去的是同類事物。
(2) except for 表示除去的和非除去的不是同類事物。

辨析 2 besides, except
(1) besides 指「除…外 (還有)」，著重於「另外還有」。
(2) except 的含義是「從整體裡減去一部分」，因為所說的道理或事實不
能適用於減去的那部分，著重於「排除在外」。

0659 ☐☐☐
excite
[ɪk`saɪt]

動 [及物] 使激動，使興奮

例句 The news excited me.
／這個消息使我感到興奮。

0660 ☐☐☐
excited
[ɪk`saɪtɪd]

形 興奮的，激動的

例句 We were excited at the thought of going on vacation.
／一想到要去度假我們就感到很興奮。

第二週

0661
☐☐☐

exciting
[ɪk`saɪtɪŋ]

形 使人興奮的，令人激動的

例句 He was so excited when he heard the exciting news that he got the first prize in the contest.
／當他得知自己在比賽中得了一等獎的那個令人振奮的消息時，他是那麼的興奮。

辨析 excited, exciting
(1) excited 形容人「感到興奮的，激動的」。
(2) exciting 形容事物「令人激動的，刺激的」。

0662
☐☐☐

excuse
動 [ɪk`skjuz] 名 [ɪk`skjus]

動 [及物] 原諒
名 藉口

巧記 圖解 excuse 的一詞多義：

You made an excuse.
你編了一個藉口。

Excuse me...
請原諒…

例句 There is no excuse for your conduct.
／你的行為沒有辯解的餘地。

片語 Excuse me. 勞駕 / 對不起 / 請原諒。 ‖ make an excuse 找藉口 ‖ without excuse 沒有理由

0663
☐☐☐

exercise
[`ɛksɚ‚saɪz]

名 練習；運動
動 [及物] 訓練 動 [不及物] 鍛煉，運動

例句 You need to exercise a bit more.
／你需要多做些運動。

片語 do morning exercises 做早操 ‖ take exercise 做運動

辨析 exercise 作「運動」講時，為不可數名詞；作「體操；練習；習題」講時，為可數名詞，且作「體操」講時常用複數形式。

0664
☐☐☐

exist
[ɪg`zɪst]

動 [不及物] 存在，實際上有；生存，生活

例句 We cannot exist without food or water.
／沒有食物和水我們無法生存。

片語 exist on 靠…活下去，靠…生存

E

Lesson 4

0665
□□□

exit
[`ɛksɪt`]

名 出口

(track 36)

例句 They all hurried toward the exit.
／他們都急忙湧向出口。

※ Every exit is an entry somewhere. 每一個出口又是某處的入口。

反義 entrance 名 入口；enter 動 進入

0666
□□□

expect
[ɪk`spɛkt`]

動 [及物] 期望，期待

例句 I am expecting a letter from him.
／我正期待著他的來信。

片語 expect sb. to do sth. 期望某人去做某事

0667
□□□

expensive
[ɪk`spɛnsɪv`]

形 昂貴的

例句 This is an expensive camera.
／這是一台昂貴的照相機。

辨析 expensive, dear
(1) expensive「貴的」，常用來形容價格高而品質、外觀都較好的物品。
(2) dear「貴的」，常指由於特殊原因而價格上漲的一般物品。

反義 cheap 形 便宜的

0668
□□□

experience
[ɪk`spɪrɪəns`]

名 經驗；經歷
動 [及物] 經歷

例句 Mr. Kroll is an officer with experience, who has many odd experiences.
／克羅爾先生是個實戰經驗豐富的軍官，他有著很多奇特的經歷。

用法 experience 作「經驗」講時，是不可數名詞；作「經歷」講時，是可數名詞。

0669
□□□

expert
[`ɛkspɚt`]

名 專家，能手

例句 He is an expert in economics.
／他是經濟學領域的專家。

反義 layman 名 外行人，門外漢

0670
□□□

explain
[ɪk`splen`]

動 解釋，說明

片語 explain sth. to sb. 向某人解釋某事

例句 I explained the situation to my boss.
／我向我的老闆說明了情況。

用法 explain 通常接名詞或從句作受詞；explain 不能帶雙受詞。

第二週

0671 □□□

export
動 [ɪksˋport] 名 [ˋɛksport]

動 出口，輸出
名 出口；(常 pl.) 出口商品

例句 Wheat is one of the country's chief exports.
／小麥是該國的主要出口商品之一。

0672 □□□

express
[ɪkˋsprɛs]

動 [及物] 表達
名 特快列車 形 迅速的

例句 Nancy freely expressed her ideas.
／南茜坦率地表達了自己的想法。

片語 express oneself 表達自己的思想或感情

0673 □□□

extra
[ˋɛkstrə]

形 額外的，臨時的

例句 The bus company provided extra buses because there were so many people.
／因為人太多，公共汽車公司派出了加班車。

0674 □□□

eye
[aɪ]

名 眼睛；眼光；(sing.) 眼力，觀察力

例句 She looked at me with hate in her eyes.
／她用憎恨的眼光看著我。

片語 an eye for an eye 以牙還牙 ‖ give an eye to 照顧 ‖ in the eyes of 在…看來 ‖ see with one's own eyes 親眼所見

0675 □□□

face
[fes]

名 臉
動 [及物] 面對

例句 The house faces the sea.
／這座房子面向大海。

片語 face to face 面對面 ‖ lose one's face 失面子 ‖ make a face/faces 做鬼臉 ‖ save one's face 挽回面子

0676 □□□

fact
[fækt]

名 事實；實際情況

片語 as a matter of fact 事實上 ‖ in fact 實際上
例句 In fact, she always comes top in the school exams.
／事實上，她在學校考試中一直名列前茅。

0677 □□□

factory
[ˋfæktərɪ]

名 工廠，製造廠

例句 He has been working in the factory for 16 years.
／他已經在這家工廠工作了 16 年。

0678 fail
☐☐☐
[fel]

🔲 動 失敗；不及格

片語 fail (in) the exam 考試不及格 ‖ fail to do sth. 未能做成某事
例句 The student failed in the examination.
／這個學生考試不及格。
反義 succeed 動〔不及物〕成功；pass 動 考試及格

0679 failure
☐☐☐
[ˋfeljə]

🔲 名〔fail 的名詞〕失敗；失敗的人（或事）

例句 Failure is the mother of success.
／〔諺〕失敗是成功之母。
反義 success 名 成功；成功的人（或事）

0680 fair
☐☐☐
[fɛr]

🔲 形 公平的；（膚色）白皙的，（頭髮）金色的

例句 It's not fair for you to treat the fair man with fair hair like that.
／你那樣對待那位金髮白皙男子是不公平的。
片語 fair and square 光明正大地
反義 unfair 形 不公平的，不公正的

0681 fair
☐☐☐
[fɛr]

🔲 名（定期）集市；商品展覽會

例句 She bought a large doll at the fair.
／她在集市上買了一個大娃娃。

0682 fall
☐☐☐
[fɔl]

🔲 名 秋季

例句 The war broke out in the fall of 1962.
／戰事在 1962 年的秋天爆發了。
同義 autumn 名〔英〕秋天

0683 fall
☐☐☐
[fɔl]

🔲 動〔不及物〕名（fell, fallen）落下；跌倒

例句 Be careful on the ice, or you will fall.
／在冰上要小心，否則你會跌倒。
片語 fall asleep 入睡 ‖ fall down 倒下，落下 ‖ fall in love with... 愛上…

0684 □□□ 🔊**37**

false
[fɔls]

形 錯的，不真實的；偽造的

例句 She gave a false name to the police.
／她向警方供出的是假名字。

反義 true 形 真的，真實的

0685 □□□

family
[ˈfæməlɪ]

名 家庭；家族；孩子，子女

例句 She has a large family on her hand.
／她有許多子女要照顧。

用法 family 是集體名詞。指整體時，用作單數，述語動詞用單數形式；指成員時，用作複數，述語動詞用複數形式。

0686 □□□

famous
[ˈfeməs]

形 著名的，出名的

片語 be famous as 作為…而著名 ‖ be famous for 因…而著名
例句 Dai-Kang Yang is famous for playing baseball.
／陽岱鋼因打棒球而出名。

0687 □□□

fan
[fæn]

名 扇子；迷；狂熱愛好者

巧記 諧音：〔英〕fans 一音譯→〔漢〕粉絲
例句 He switched on the electric fan.
／他打開了電扇。

0688 □□□

fancy
[ˈfænsɪ]

形 奇特的，花式的；昂貴的

例句 I just want a basic sports coat—nothing fancy.
／我只要一件簡單的輕便外套——別太花俏的。

0689 □□□

fantastic
[fænˈtæstɪk]

形 異想天開的，不切實際的；奇異的；極好的

例句 She told me a fantastic story about a frog becoming a prince. ／她給我講了一個關於一隻青蛙成為王子的奇異故事。

0690 □□□

far
[fɑr]

形 副 (farther, farthest；further, furthest) 遠的（地）；遙遠的（地）

例句 The stranger seems to have come from a far country.
／這個陌生人似乎來自遙遠的國度。

片語 as far as ①遠到，直到 ②就…，盡… ‖ so far〔與現在完成式連用〕到現在為止

0691 ☐☐☐
farm
[farm]

名 農場；農莊

例句 His father runs a farm.
／他的父親經營一家農場。

片語 on the farm 在農場裡

0692 ☐☐☐
farmer
[ˋfɑrmɚ]

名 農夫；農場主，牧場主

例句 The farmer employs many farmhands.
／那個農場主人雇用了許多農場工人。

0693 ☐☐☐
fashionable
[ˋfæʃənəbḷ]

形 流行的，時髦的

例句 It was fashionable to have short hair those days.
／那時流行短髮。

0694 ☐☐☐
fast
[fæst]

形 副 快的（地），迅速的（地）

例句 He is very fast in reading.
／他的閱讀速度很快。

辨析 fast, quickly
(1) fast「迅速地」，指運動的物體和運行的速度。
(2) quickly「快」，強調立刻行動，毫不遲緩，毫不耽擱。

0695 ☐☐☐
fat
[fæt]

形 (fatter, fattest) 肥胖的，多脂肪的
名 脂肪，肥肉

例句 If you eat less, you won't get so fat.
／你如果少吃點兒，就不會長得這麼胖。

反義 thin 形 瘦的

fat   thin

0696 ☐☐☐
father
[ˋfɑðɚ]

名 父親

例句 My father enjoys the peace and quiet of the country.
／我父親喜愛鄉下的安祥與寧靜。

0697 ☐☐☐
faucet
[ˋfɔsɪt]

名 水龍頭

例句 She turned off the faucet and dried her hands.
／她關掉水龍頭，把手擦乾。

0698 □□□

fault
[fɔlt]

名 缺點，毛病；過失，責任

例句 Nobody lives without faults. ／〔諺〕人無完人。

片語 at fault 有責任，出毛病 ‖ find fault in... 看出…的缺點，找出…的毛病 ‖ find fault with... 對…不滿，挑剔…

辨析 fault, mistake
(1) fault 多指性格上的弱點，行為上的過失，強調過失所導致的應負的責任。
(2) mistake 指「錯誤，誤會，誤解」，多指因缺乏正確理解而造成行動上或認識上的錯誤。
※ It's your fault to make such a mistake. 是你的過失導致了這樣的錯誤。

反義 merit 名 長處，優點

0699 □□□

favor
[`fevɚ]

動 [及物] 對…表示好感，支持；有利於；偏愛
名 偏袒；幫助；贊同

片語 ask a favor of 請求…幫忙 ‖ do sb. a favor 幫某人的忙，給某人做好事 ‖ in favor of 支持，贊同 ‖ in favor with... 得…寵愛，受…鼓勵

例句 You did me a great favor.
／你幫了我一個大忙。

0700 □□□

favorite
[`fevərɪt]

形 〔無比較等級，作限定詞〕特別喜愛的
名 特別喜歡的人（或物）

例句 This is my favorite among his novels.
／在他的小說中我最喜愛這一本。

0701 □□□

fear
[fɪr]

名 動 害怕，擔憂

例句 I have a fear that it will rain.
／我擔心天就要下雨了。

片語 for fear 唯恐，生怕 ‖ in fear of 擔憂，恐怕，為…而擔心

0702 □□□

February
[`fɛbrʊ͵ɛrɪ]

名 二月 (=Feb.)

例句 February is the second month of the year.
／二月是一年中的第二個月。

Group 2

0703 □□□

38

fee
[fi]

名 費用，學費，會費

例句 Park entrance fees have gone up to $15.
／公園的門票漲到了 15 美元。

0704 feed
[fid]

動 [及物] (fed, fed) 餵養，飼養

例句 Have you fed the cat yet?
／你餵貓了沒有？

片語 be fed up (with) (對…) 感到厭煩 ‖ feed on(=live on) 以…為食 ‖ feed sth. to sb. (=feed sb. on/with sth.) 用某物餵某人

0705 feel
[fil]

動 [不及物] (felt, felt) 感覺
動 [及物] 摸；感知

例句 I feel that he has done his best.
／我覺得他已經盡了最大的努力了。

片語 feel cold/hungry/happy 感到冷 / 餓 / 高興 ‖ feel like (doing) sth. 想要 (做)…

0706 feeling
[`filɪŋ]

名 (a ～) 感覺，感觸；(pl.) 心情；看法，意見

例句 My personal feeling is that we should buy the cheaper one.
／我個人的意見是我們應該買較便宜的那個。

片語 have a feeling that... 有…的感覺 ‖ hurt one's feelings 傷害某人的感情

0707 fellow
[`fɛlo]

名 夥伴，同事，傢伙

例句 Her fellows share her interest in computers.
／她的同伴們跟她一樣對電腦都很感興趣。

0708 female
[`fimel]

形 女 (性) 的；雌的
名 女子

例句 Over half of the staff is female.
／半數以上的職員是女性。

反義 male 形 男 (性) 的；雄的 名 男性；雄性動物

0709 fence
[fɛns]

名 籬笆，柵欄

巧記 「籬笆，圍欄」(fence) 原意是「護」(defence) 家的東西。

例句 The garden was surrounded by a wooden fence.
／花園被木柵欄圍了起來。

0710 festival
[`fɛstəvl]

名 (音樂、芭蕾舞、戲劇等) 節日

例句 Christmas is an important Christian festival.
／耶誕節是基督教的重要節日。

0711 □□□ **fever**
[ˈfivɚ]

名 發燒，發熱

例句 My fever has gone, but I still have a cough.
／我的燒已經退了，但還是會咳嗽。

0712 □□□ **few**
[fju]

形 少數的，幾乎沒有的
代〔表示否定〕幾乎沒有

例句 He has few friends.
／他沒有多少朋友。

片語 a few 少數 ‖ only a few 只有幾個 ‖ quite a few 好幾個

0713 □□□ **field**
[fild]

名 田地；領域

例句 He works in the fields on Sunday.
／他周日在田裡工作。

片語 in the field of 在…方面，在…領域

0714 □□□ **fifteen**
[ˈfɪfˈtin]

代 名 形 十五（個）（的）

例句 Three multiplied by five is fifteen.
／3 乘以 5 等於 15。

0715 □□□ **fifty**
[ˈfɪftɪ]

代 名 形 五十（個）（的）

例句 He must be well past fifty.
／他肯定早就年過半百了。

0716 □□□ **fight**
[faɪt]

動 (fought, fought)（與…）戰鬥；（與…）打架

例句 They fought their enemies bravely.
／他們英勇地與敵人戰鬥。

片語 fight against... 與…戰鬥 ‖ fight for... 為…而戰 ‖ fight with... 與…並肩戰鬥

0717 □□□ **figure**
[ˈfɪgjɚ]

名 外形，體形
動 [及物] 計算　動 [不及物] 計算

片語 figure out ①算出，解決 ②領會到，理解 ‖ figure up 合計，計算
例句 I can't figure out the total cost.
／我算不出全部的費用。

0718 □□□
fill
[fɪl]

動（使）充滿
動 [及物] 擠滿，占滿；

例句 A big audience filled the hall. ／觀眾濟濟一堂。
片語 be filled with (=be full of) 充滿，裝滿 ‖ fill...with 把⋯裝滿

0719 □□□
film
[fɪlm]

名 電影，影片；膠片，膠捲

巧記 圖解 film 的一詞多義：

電影　　　膠卷

例句 I saw a good film at the theater yesterday.
／昨天我在電影院看了一部好電影。
片語 go to (see) a film 去看電影

0720 □□□
final
[ˋfaɪnḷ]

形 最終的；決定性的
名（常 pl.）期終考試

例句 When do you take your finals? ／ 你什麼時候參加期終考試？

0721 □□□
finally
[ˋfaɪnḷɪ]

副 最終，最後

例句 The performance finally started half an hour later.
／延遲了半小時後終於開始上演了。

ⓖroup 3

0722 □□□
39
find
[faɪnd]

動 [及物]（found, found）尋找，查找；找到

例句 I found the book he was looking for. ／我找到了他正在找的書。
片語 find out 查明，發現，瞭解
辨析 look for, find
(1) look for 強調「尋找」的動作。
(2) find 強調「找到」的結果。

0723 □□□
fine
[faɪn]

形 美好的；晴朗的；健康的

巧記 圖解 fine 的一詞多義：

晴朗的

健康的

精美的

例句 It's a fine day today, isn't it? ／今天天氣很好，不是嗎？

0724 ☐☐☐

fine
[faɪn]

動 [及物] 對…處以罰款
名 罰金，罰款

例句 The court fined him $500.
／法院罰了他 500 美元。

用法 注意 fine 是可數名詞：pay a fine of 100 dollars 交 100 元的罰金。

0725 ☐☐☐

finger
[`fɪŋgɚ]

名 手指

例句 We ate with our fingers.
／我們用手抓著吃。

0726 ☐☐☐

finish
[`fɪnɪʃ]

動 完成；結束
名 結束，末尾

片語 finish (doing) sth. 做完某事
例句 May I have a rest? I have already finished writing the
report.
／我可以休息一下嗎？我已經寫完報告了。

0727 ☐☐☐

fire
[faɪr]

名 火；火災
動 開（槍或炮）動 [及物]（口）解雇

例句 He was fired for not coming to work on time.
／他因為遲到而被解雇。

片語 be on fire 著火 ‖ catch fire 燃著，著火 ‖ play with fire ①玩火 ②幹冒險
的事 ‖ set fire to 放火燒，點燃

0728 ☐☐☐

firm
[fɝm]

名 商店，公司，企業

例句 She works for an electronics firm.
／她在一家電子公司工作。

0729 ☐☐☐

firm
[fɝm]

形 堅固的，結實的；堅決的

例句 The shelf isn't very firm, so don't put too many books on it.
／架子不太結實，上面別放太多書。

片語 as firm as a rock 堅如磐石 ‖ be on firm ground 腳踏實地 ‖ hold firm (to)
固守，抓緊 ‖ stand firm 站穩立場

0730 first
[fɝst]

形 副 第一的（地）；最初的（地）

例句 Let's read the first lesson.
／讓我們來讀第一課的課文。

片語 at first 起先，最初 ‖ first aid 急救 ‖ first and last 始終，一貫 ‖ first of all 首先，第一

0731 fish
[fɪʃ]

名〔單同複〕魚；魚肉
動〔不及物〕捕魚，釣魚

例句 Dad really loves to fish.
／爸爸很喜歡釣魚。

衍生 fishes 指不同種類的魚

0732 fisherman
['fɪʃɚ-mən]

名 (pl.fishermen) 漁民，漁夫

例句 The fisherman caught a fish at his first cast.
／那漁夫第一次拋釣線就釣到一條魚。

0733 fit
[fɪt]

動 (fit, fit；fitted, fitted) 適合；適應

例句 This coat doesn't fit me.
／這件大衣我穿起來不合身。

0734 five
[faɪv]

代 名 形 五（個）（的）

例句 Sales have doubled in five years.
／銷售額在 5 年內翻了一倍。

0735 fix
[fɪks]

動〔及物〕修理；安裝；確定

片語 fix on/upon 確定，決定，選定 ‖ fix one's attention on 專心於，把注意力集中在 ‖ fix up ①修理，修補 ②安排

例句 Have you fixed on a date for the wedding?
／你們定好婚期了嗎？

0736 flag
[flæg]

名 旗；信號旗

例句 The flag went down, and the race began.
／信號旗落下，比賽開始了。

0737 ☐☐☐
flashlight
[ˈflæʃˌlaɪt]
名〔美〕手電筒

例句 Please shine your flashlight over here.
／請把手電筒往這兒照。

同義 torch 名〔英〕手電筒

0738 ☐☐☐
flat
[flæt]
名〔英〕（樓房的）一層；一套房間

例句 They have a flat in Chicago.
／他們在芝加哥有一套公寓。

同義 apartment 名〔美〕一套住房

0739 ☐☐☐
flat
[flæt]
形 平坦的，平的；扁平的，淺的

例句 The countryside near there is very flat.
／那兒附近的鄉間地勢非常平坦。

0740 ☐☐☐
flight
[flaɪt]
名〔fly 的名詞〕飛翔，飛行

例句 The success of the test flight depends on the weather.
／試飛是否成功取決於天氣。

片語 in flight 在飛行中

Ⓖroup 4

0741 ☐☐☐
40
floor
[flor]
名（室內的）地面，地板；樓層（=fl.）

例句 Her office is on the top floor.
／她的辦公室在頂樓。

用法 (1) 英式英語和美式英語對樓層稱呼不同，在英式英語中「一樓」是 the ground floor，「二樓」是 the first floor；而在美式英語中「一樓」是 the first floor，「二樓」是 the second floor。其他依此類推。

(2) 建築物的層數用 story 不用 floor：a three-story building 一棟三層的樓房。

	美	英
the 3rd floor	三層	the 2nd floor
the 2nd floor	二層	the 1st floor
the 1st floor	一層	the ground floor

0742 ☐☐☐ **flour**
[flaʊr]

名 麵粉，（任何穀類磨成的）粉

例句 Flour can be used for making bread, cake, etc.
／麵粉可用來做麵包、蛋糕等。

| wheat 麥子 | flour mill 磨坊 | flour 麵粉 | dough 麵團 | bread, cake, biscuit 麵包、蛋糕、餅乾 |

0743 ☐☐☐ **flow**
[flo]

動 [不及物]（河水等）流動，流；湧出
名（常 sing.）流（動），流量

例句 The river flows from north to south.
／那條河由北向南流。

0744 ☐☐☐ **flower**
[`flaʊɚ]

名 花，花草，花卉

例句 The plant has a red flower.
／那株植物開著一朵紅花。

0745 ☐☐☐ **flu**
[flu]

名 流行性感冒（＝influenza）

例句 I couldn't go because I had flu.
／我得了流感，去不了了。

0746 ☐☐☐ **flute**
[flut]

名 長笛

例句 I like to play the flute.
／我喜歡吹長笛。

0747 ☐☐☐ **fly**
[flaɪ]

動 [不及物]（flew, flown）飛；（乘飛機）飛行

例句 I flew from London to Paris last Sunday.
／我上星期天從倫敦搭飛機去巴黎。

0748 ☐☐☐ **fly**
[flaɪ]

名 蒼蠅

例句 There were flies buzzing all around us.
／蒼蠅嗡嗡地在我們周圍飛來飛去。

0749 ☐☐☐

focus
[`fokəs]

名 焦點，聚焦
動 (使)聚焦，(使)集中

片語 focus on... 集中於… ‖ in focus 焦距對準，清晰　out of focus 焦距沒對準，模糊

例句 The children's attention was focused on the stage.
／孩子們的注意力集中在舞臺上。

0750 ☐☐☐

fog
[fag]

名 霧；迷茫，困惑

例句 We get heavy fogs on this coast in winter.
／這裡的海邊冬季有濃霧。

0751 ☐☐☐

follow
[`falo]

動 [及物] 跟隨；(表示時間、順序等)接著；理解

例句 You speak so fast that I can't quite follow you.
／你講得太快了，我有點兒聽不懂。

片語 follow one's advice 聽從某人的建議

0752 ☐☐☐

following
[`faləwɪn]

形 接著的；下述的
介 在…之後，跟著

例句 Following the meeting, coffee will be served.
／會後將有咖啡供應。

反義 previous 形 以前的

0753 ☐☐☐

food
[fud]

名 食物，食品

例句 We went on a hike but forgot to bring food.
／我們去遠足，但是忘了帶食物。

0754 ☐☐☐

fool
[ful]

名 傻瓜　形 愚蠢的，傻的
動 [及物] 愚弄，欺騙

例句 They know he can't be fooled.
／他們知道他是不會被欺騙的。

片語 April/All Fools' Day 愚人節 (4 月 1 日) ‖ fool sb. into doing sth. 哄騙某人做某事 ‖ make a fool of 愚弄，欺騙

0755 ☐☐☐

foolish
[`fulɪʃ]

形 笨的，愚蠢的，傻的；可笑的

例句 It was foolish of you to leave school. /You were foolish to leave school.
／你中途退學，真是傻瓜。

反義 bright 形 聰明的；clever 形 聰明的

0756 □□□
foot
[fʊt]

名 (pl.feet) 腳 , 足；英尺

例句 The giant's feet are big, measuring three feet.
／巨人的腳很大，有三英尺長。

片語 at the foot of... 在…的腳下 ‖ foot by foot 一步一步地，逐漸地 ‖ on foot 步行

0757 □□□
football
[`fʊt͵bɔl]

名 足球，橄欖球

例句 I saw them playing football on the meadow.
／我看見他們在草坪上踢球。

0758 □□□
for
[fɔr]

介 為了
連 因為，由於

例句 I don't want to go, for it is raining.
／因為下雨，所以我不想去。

辨析 as, because, for
(1) as 表原因時 語氣和從屬關係不如 because 那樣強烈、直接 常譯為「既然，由於」。
(2) because 回答 why 提問的問句，表示直接的原因，可用於強調句。
(3) for 語氣更弱，關係更間接，用來補充說明理由或提供一種解釋。

0759 □□□
force
[fors]

名 力量；暴力 動 [及物] 強制，強迫

例句 I had to force myself to get up this morning.
／今天早晨我不得不強迫自己起床。

片語 by force 用暴力，強迫 ‖ come into force 生效，實施

GEPT
Elementary

Week 3

第三週

F

Lesson 1

0760
☐☐☐

41

foreign
[`fɔrɪn]

形 外國的;涉外的

例句 He lives in a foreign country.
／他住在國外。

0761
☐☐☐

foreigner
[`fɔrɪnə]

名 外國人

例句 How many foreigners are there in your company?
／你公司有多少外國人?

0762
☐☐☐

forest
[`fɔrɪst]

名 森林,森林地帶

例句 Thousands of old trees were lost in the forest fire.
／成千上萬棵的古樹在森林大火中被燒毀了。

0763
☐☐☐

forget
[fə`gɛt]

動 (forgot, forgotten) 忘記

片語 forget doing sth. 忘記已經做過某事 ‖ forget to do sth. 忘記去做某事
例句 Don't forget to bring your history and politics books
tomorrow morning.
／明天早上別忘了帶著你的歷史書和政治書。

0764
☐☐☐

forgive
[fə`gɪv]

動 [及物] (forgave, forgiven) 原諒,饒恕,寬恕

片語 forgive sb. for doing sth. 饒恕／原諒某人做某事
例句 I forgave him for stealing the money.
／我原諒他偷了這筆錢。

0765
☐☐☐

fork
[fɔrk]

名 叉,餐叉;(路、河等)分岔,岔口

例句 They eat with a knife and fork.
／他們使用刀叉吃東西。

0766
☐☐☐

form
[fɔrm]

名 形式;形狀;表格;種類
動 (使)形成

例句 An idea formed in my mind.
／我心中產生了某種想法。
片語 in form 形式上 ‖ in the form of 以…的形式

第三週

0767 □□□ **formal**
[`form!`]

形 形式上的，表面的；正式的，合乎禮儀的

例句 She is wearing a formal dress for dinner.
／她穿著正裝赴宴。

0768 □□□ **former**
[`formɚ`]

形 以前的，(兩者之中) 前者的
名 (the ～) 前者

片語 the former...the latter... 前者…後者…
例句 They keep horses and cattle, the former for riding, the latter for food.
／他們養馬和牛，前者供乘騎，後者供食用。

0769 □□□ **forty**
[`fɔrtɪ`]

代 名 形 四十 (個)(的)

例句 Jim's father is forty years old.
／吉姆的父親 40 歲。

0770 □□□ **forward**
[`fɔrwɚd`]

形 副 往前方的 (地)；向前的 (地)；進步的 (地)

片語 look forward to 期待，盼望
例句 Each of us is looking forward to getting a good result. Let's do it more carefully.
／我們每個人都期盼一個好結果。讓我們做得更仔細點吧。
辨析 look forward to, expect
(1) look forward to 具有主觀上以愉快的心情盼望的意思，注意 to 為介系詞，後接名詞、代詞或動詞 -ing 形式。
(2) expect 是指據客觀情況做出的估計，不涉及主觀上是否願意 (用在好事、壞事都可以)。

0771 □□□ **four**
[for]

代 名 形 四 (個)(的)

例句 There are four books in the bag.
／包包裡有 4 本書。

0772 □□□ **fourteen**
[`for`tin`]

代 名 形 十四 (個)(的)

例句 There were fourteen people on the bus.
／公共汽車上有 14 個人。

0773 fox
[fɑks]
图 (pl.foxes) 狐狸

例句 The clever fox escaped the hunter.
／聰明的狐狸逃脫了獵人的追蹤。

0774 France
[fræns]
图 法國

例句 He went to France to perfect his French.
／為了精通法語，他去了法國。

0775 frank
[fræŋk]
形 坦白的，直率的

例句 I like his frank manner.
／我喜歡他那率直的態度。

片語 to be frank (with you)〔作插入語〕坦率地說

0776 free
[fri]
形 空閒的；免費的
動 [及物] 釋放，解放

例句 "Are you free this evening? " "I am free after six. "
／「你今晚有空嗎？」「我六點以後有空。」

0777 freedom
[ˋfridəm]
图 自由

例句 Kids have too much freedom these days.
／現在的孩子太自由了。

0778 freezer
[ˋfrizɚ]
图 冰箱

例句 We keep frozen food in a freezer.
／我們在冰箱裡保存了冷凍食品。

Group 2

0779 French
[frɛntʃ]
形 法國的，法國人的；法語的
图 法語

例句 She is at the top of her class in French.
／她的法語是班上的第一名。

0780 fresh
[frɛʃ]

形 新鮮的；清新的

例句 Eat plenty of fresh fruit and vegetables.
／多吃新鮮水果和蔬菜。

0781 Friday
[ˋfraɪ,de]

名 星期五 (=Fri.)

例句 We are going to have our sports meeting next Friday.
／我們將於下週五舉行運動會。

0782 friend
[frɛnd]

名 朋友

例句 We are old friends.
／我們是老朋友。

片語 be friends with 跟⋯做朋友 ‖ make friends with sb. 和某人交朋友

0783 friendly
[ˋfrɛndlɪ]

形 友好的

例句 That's not very friendly of you.
／你那樣不太友善了。

注意 friendly 是形容詞，而不是副詞。類似的詞還有 lovely。

0784 friendship
[ˋfrɛndʃɪp]

名 友誼

例句 Real friends do not talk about friendship in words.
(Belinskiy)
／真正的朋友不把友誼掛在嘴邊。(別林斯基)

0785 frighten
[ˋfraɪtn]

動 [及物] 使驚恐，嚇唬
動 [不及物] 驚嚇，害怕

例句 She was frightened by the anger in his eyes.
／她被他眼中的怒火給嚇住了。

片語 frighten sb. into/out of doing sth. 恐嚇某人使其做 / 不做某事

0786 Frisbee
[ˋfrɪzbi]

名 (塑膠玩具) 飛盤

例句 We always go to the park on weekends and play Frisbee.
／週末我們經常到公園玩飛盤。

0787 □□□ **frog**
[frɑg]

名 蛙，青蛙

例句 Frogs generally feed at night.
／青蛙一般在夜間進食。

0788 □□□ **from**
[frɑm]

介 從…起，從

片語 from now/then on 從現在 / 那時起 ∥ from...to... 從…到…
例句 From now on, I'll only be working in the mornings.
／從現在起，我只上上午班。

0789 □□□ **front**
[frʌnt]

名 前面；前線
形 前面的

例句 I was sitting right in the front of the cinema but someone sat in front of me, so I couldn't see anything.
／我就坐在電影院的前部，但有人坐在我的前面，所以我什麼也看不見。
辨析 in the front of, in front of
(1) in the front of 指內部的「前部」。
(2) in front of 指位置「在…的前面」。

0790 □□□ **fruit**
[frut]

名〔總稱〕水果；(pl.) 成果，收穫

例句 Is a tomato a fruit or a vegetable?
／番茄是水果還是蔬菜？
用法 fruit 指同種類時不加 -s，指不同種類時要加 -s。

fruit   fruits

0791 □□□ **fry**
[fraɪ]

動 油煎，油炸
名（常 pl.）油炸食品

例句 She is frying fish.
／她在炸魚。

0792 □□□ **full**
[fʊl]

形 滿的，充滿的；吃飽的

片語 be full of 充滿
例句 The bag is full of books.
／書包裡滿滿都是書。

0793 □□□ **fun**
[fʌn]

名 愉快，開心
形 有趣的；令人愉快的

片語 for fun 開玩笑地 ‖ have fun 玩得高興 ‖ make fun of... 取笑…
例句 We had great fun at the festival.
／聯歡節上我們玩得高興極了。

0794 □□□ **function**
[ˈfʌŋkʃən]

名 功能，作用
動 [不及物] 工作，起作用

例句 The machine does not function properly.
／這台機器運轉不正常。

0795 □□□ **funny**
[ˈfʌnɪ]

形 有趣的，滑稽的

例句 What a funny story it is!
／那是一個多麼好笑的故事呀！

0796 □□□ **furniture**
[ˈfɝ·nɪtʃə·]

名〔總稱〕傢俱

例句 They have bought much furniture.
／他們已經買了不少傢俱。

用法 furniture 是不可數名詞，要表達「一件／套傢俱」時，應說 a piece/set of furniture。

0797 □□□ **further**
[ˈfɝ·ðə·]

副 更遠地；進一步
形（距離、時間上）較遠的；更進一步的

例句 The hospital is further down the road.
／醫院在這條路上，再往前走就到了。

Group 3

0798 □□□ **future**
43 [ˈfjutʃə·]

名 未來，將來
形 將來的

例句 No one knows what will happen in the future.
／沒有人知道將來會發生什麼事。

辨析 in the future, in future
(1) in the future 特指將來的某一時刻。
(2) in future 指從今往後的全部將來。

| 0799 | **gain** [gen] | 動 [及物] 獲得；贏得；(體重) 增加 動 [不及物] 受益；增加 |

例句 The man gained much money in the business.
／那個人做這生意賺了很多錢。

| 0800 | **game** [gem] | 名 遊戲；比賽 |

例句 They've won their last three games.
／他們打贏了最近三場比賽。

| 0801 | **garage** [gə`rɑʒ] | 名 車庫；汽車修理廠 |

例句 I'll just go and put the car in the garage.
／我這就把車子停到車庫去。

| 0802 | **garbage** [`gɑrbɪdʒ] | 名 垃圾，廢物 |

例句 Don't talk such a load of garbage.
／不要說這麼多廢話。

| 0803 | **garden** [`gɑrdṇ] | 名 (花、菜、果) 園，庭園；(常 pl.) 公園，園 |

例句 We have only a small garden.
／我們只有一個小花園。

| 0804 | **gas** [gæs] | 名 煤氣；氣體，氣態 |

例句 Do you cook by electricity or gas?
／你做飯是用電還是用煤氣？

※ Water is liquid, but it becomes solid when it freezes and becomes gas when it is boiled. 水是液體，但它遇冷凝結就成了固體，煮沸則變成氣體。

soild 固體　　　liquid 液體　　　gas 氣體

0805 ☐☐☐

gasoline
[ˋgæsəˌlin]

名〔美〕汽油

例句 What happens when food and gasoline supplies run low?
／如果食物和汽油的供應量減少，會產生什麼情況呢？
同義 petrol 名〔英〕汽油

gate 大門

gateway 走道

0806 ☐☐☐

gate
[get]

名 大門，城門，牆門

例句 The gate is closed.
／大門關起來了。
辨析 gate, door
(1) gate 指上面與屋頂不相連的門，通常有兩扇，如籬笆、院牆、花園、院子等的「大門」。
(2) door 指上面連著屋頂的「門」，可指大樓房間的或傢俱、車輛上的「門」。

0807 ☐☐☐

gather
[ˋgæðɚ]

動 收集（資料等），收（莊稼等）；聚集，集合

例句 The novelist gathered materials for his work.
／小說家收集了寫作的資料。
辨析 collect, gather
(1) collect 指精心地、有目的地、有選擇地「收集」。
(2) gather 是把分散的東西「聚集」到一起。

0808 ☐☐☐

general
[ˋdʒɛnərəl]

形 一般的，普通的；整體的；全面的，普遍的

例句 The general condition of our company is not good.
／我們公司的整體狀況不太好。
片語 in general 一般，總的說來

0809 ☐☐☐

general
[ˋdʒɛnərəl]

名 將軍，上將

例句 A captain is below a general. ／上尉的軍階比將軍低。

0810 ☐☐☐

generation
[ˌdʒɛnəˋreʃən]

名 一代一代，世代

片語 for generations 一連好幾代，數代相傳 ‖ from generation to generation/generation after generation
例句 The story has been handed down from generation to generation.
／這個故事一代接著一代傳了下來。

0811
□□□

generous
[`dʒɛnərəs]

形 慷慨的，大方的；寬宏大量的

例句 She is very generous—she often buys me presents.
／她為人很大方——常常買禮物給我。

0812
□□□

genius
[`dʒinjəs]

名 天才，天賦；精靈

巧記 〔漢〕基因 —音譯→〔英〕gene 基因，遺傳因數 →〔生〕genius 天才，天賦

例句 Leonardo da Vinci was a genius in many fields.
／李奧納多 · 達文西在許多領域中都是天才。

0813
□□□

gentle
[`dʒɛntl]

形 溫柔的，文雅的；輕輕的

例句 He is a very gentle person.
／他是一位很溫和的人。

0814
□□□

gentleman
[`dʒɛntlmən]

名 紳士；先生

例句 The gentleman whom I met yesterday was a teacher.
／昨天跟我碰面的紳士是老師。

用法 像 gentleman 這類的複合詞，變複數時只變化後面的 -man。

0815
□□□

geography
[`dʒɪ`agrəfɪ]

名 地理，地理學；(sing.) 地形，地勢

例句 Geography was my weak subject.
／地理是我需要加強的科目。

0816
□□□

German
[`dʒɝ·mən]

形 德國的，德國人的，德語的
名 德國人；德語

例句 He can't speak English, let alone German.
／他連英語都不會說，更別提德語了。

0817
☐☐☐

Germany
[ˋdʒɝˏmənɪ]

🔊44

名 德國

例句 He spent his youth in Germany.
／他的青少年時代是在德國度過的。

0818
☐☐☐

gesture
[ˋdʒɛstʃɚ]

名 姿勢，手勢
動 [不及物] 比手勢

例句 Gesture is another way of communication.
／比手畫腳也是一種溝通的方式。

0819
☐☐☐

get
[gɛt]

動 [及物] (got, got; got, gotten) 得到，獲得；拿來；
變得

例句 Each of them gets a new book.
／他們各得一本新書。

片語 get back 回來 ‖ get down 下來，落下 ‖ get in 上車　get off 下 (火車、公共汽車等) ‖ get on ①上 (車、馬等) ②相處，進展 ‖ get over ①克服②恢復 ‖ get together 聚集 ‖ get up 起床

0820
☐☐☐

ghost
[gost]

名 鬼魂，幽靈；幻影

例句 Do you believe in ghosts?
／你相信有鬼嗎？

0821
☐☐☐

giant
[ˋdʒaɪənt]

形 巨大的
名 巨人；偉人，卓越人物

例句 He caught a giant fish.
／他抓到一條特別大的魚。

0822
☐☐☐

gift
[gɪft]

名 贈品；禮物；天賦

片語 have a gift for 有…的天賦
例句 Having a gift for music, he received a piano as a birthday gift.
／因為在音樂方面有天賦，他收到一架鋼琴作為生日禮物。

0823
☐☐☐

girl
[gɝl]

名 女孩，少女

例句 This girl is my classmate.
／這個女生是我的同班同學。

0824 □□□ **give**
[gɪv]

動 [及物] (gave, given) 給；授予

片語 give away 贈送，分發 ‖ give back 歸還 ‖ give in 屈服，讓步，投降 ‖ give up 放棄，不再做某事

例句 You should really give up smoking. It's a terrible habit.
／你真的應該戒煙。它是個可怕的習慣。（本例句用「give up」這個片語，不容易與單字結合。）

0825 □□□ **glad**
[glæd]

形 高興；樂意

例句 I'll be glad to help you wash your car.
／我很樂意幫你洗車。

0826 □□□ **glass**
[glæs]

名 玻璃；玻璃杯；(pl.) 眼鏡

巧記 圖解 glass 的一詞多義：

| glass 玻璃 | two glasses 兩隻玻璃杯 | a glass of orange 一杯柳橙汁 | (a pair of) glasses 一副眼鏡 |

例句 These glasses are all made of glass.
／這些杯子都是用玻璃做的。

辨析 glass 作可數名詞意為「玻璃杯」，作不可數名詞意為「玻璃」。

0827 □□□ **glove**
[glʌv]

名 手套

例句 I need a new pair of gloves.
／我需要一雙新的手套。

用法 像 glove, shoe 等這種成雙出現的名詞，通常用複數。

0828 □□□ **glue**
[glu]

名 膠水
動 [及物] 膠合，黏貼

例句 Glue the two pieces of wood together.
／把這兩塊木頭黏在一起。

0829 □□□ **go**
[go]

動 [不及物] (went, gone) 去；走；變成
名 嘗試

例句 I went to London by train. ／我坐火車去倫敦。

片語 go away 走開，離開 ‖ go back 回去 ‖ go home 回家 ‖ go on 進展，繼續 ‖ go up 上漲，上升

第三週

0830 ☐☐☐ **goal** [gol] | 名 目的，目標；終點；（足球）球門

例句 My goal is to play in the World Cup.
／我的目標是打進世界杯。

片語 get/kick a goal 踢進一顆球 ‖ keep goal 守球門

0831 ☐☐☐ **goat** [got] | 名 山羊

例句 The young goat was just beginning to grow horns.
／這隻小山羊才剛開始長角。

0832 ☐☐☐ **God** [gɑd] | 名（基督教）上帝，（天主教）天主

例句 Thank God, I've found my iPhone 6.
／謝天謝地，我找到了我的 iPhone 6。

0833 ☐☐☐ **gold** [gold] | 名 黃金；金幣

例句 Her ring was made of gold.
／她的戒指是黃金做的。

0834 ☐☐☐ **golden** [ˋgoldn] | 形 金（黃）色的；金（質）的；極好的

例句 Speech is silver, silence is golden.
／〔諺〕雄辯是銀，沉默是金。

辨析 golden 雖也有「金質的」意義，但原則上 gold(形) 作「金質的」講，golden 卻常為「金色的」。

0835 ☐☐☐ **golf** [gɑlf] | 名 高爾夫球

巧記 諧音：〔英〕golf 一音譯→〔漢〕高爾夫
例句 My father always plays golf on Sundays.
／我爸爸星期天都會去打高爾夫球。

G

Lesson 2

0836 ☐☐☐

good
[gʊd]

形 好的；令人滿意的
名 善良；利益

45

例句 I'm telling you this for your own good.
／我是為了你好才告訴你這件事。

片語 as good as 和…一樣好 ‖ be good at 善於，擅長… ‖ be good/bad for 對…有益／害

0837 ☐☐☐

good-bye
[gʊd`baɪ]

名 再見，再會 (=goodbye, bye)

例句 They said good-bye and left.
／他們道別後就離開了。

片語 say goodbye (to sb.) (向某人) 告別

0838 ☐☐☐

goose
[gus]

名 (pl.geese) 鵝；鵝肉

例句 All his geese are swans. ／〔諺〕敝帚自珍／自誇自讚。

0839 ☐☐☐

government
[`gʌvə-nmənt]

名 政府

例句 The program is organized by the local government.
／這個計劃是由地方政府所組織的。

0840 ☐☐☐

grade
[gred]

名 年級，學年；分數，成績

例句 She got a grade of 80 in English.
／她的英語得了 80 分。

0841 ☐☐☐

gram
[græm]

名 (重量、品質) 公克 (=g=gm)

例句 A football weighs about 400 grams.
／一顆足球的重量約 400 公克。

0842 ☐☐☐

grand
[grænd]

形 雄偉的，豪華的；絕佳的，重要的

例句 He lives in a grand house.
／他住在一間豪華的房子裡。

0843 ☐☐☐

granddaughter
[`græn,dɔtə-]

名 (外) 孫女

例句 Her granddaughter lives abroad.
／她的孫女住在國外。

第三週

0844 grandfather
[`grænd,faðɚ]
图 祖父，爺爺，外公 (=grandpa)

例句 My grandfather is in very poor health.
／我祖父的健康狀況很糟。

0845 grandmother
[`grænd,mʌðɚ]
图 祖母，奶奶，外婆 (=grandma)

例句 My grandmother told me stories about when she was a child.
／我奶奶跟我說她小時候的故事。

0846 grandson
[`grænd,sʌn]
图 孫子，外孫

例句 My grandson is very clever but naughty.
／我的孫子既聰明又調皮。

0847 grape
[grep]
图 葡萄（樹）

例句 Wine is made from grapes.
／葡萄酒是由葡萄釀成的。

0848 grass
[græs]
图 草；草地，牧場

例句 Keep off the grass.
／請勿踐踏草地。

0849 gray
[gre]
形 灰色的；（頭髮）灰白的
图 灰色

例句 She has gray eyes.
／她的眼睛是灰色的。

0850 great
[gret]
形 偉大的；重大的；大量的；大的

例句 He is a great artist.
／他是一位偉大的藝術家。

0851 greedy
[`gridɪ]
形 貪吃的；貪婪的，貪心的

例句 The company had become more and more greedy for profit.
／這家公司變得對獲利越來越貪婪。

0852 ☐☐☐ **green** [grin]

形 綠（色）的，青（色）的；未熟的
名 綠色；綠地

例句 The grass in the yard is green.
／院子裡的草地綠油油的。

0853 ☐☐☐ **greet** [grit]

動 [及物] 歡迎，問候，招呼

例句 The girl greeted us with a smile when we arrived.
／當我們抵達時，那女孩笑著歡迎我們。

0854 ☐☐☐ **ground** [graʊnd]

名 (the～) 地面；場地；（供特殊目的用的）運動場

例句 There are many leaves on the ground.
／地上有許多樹葉。

Ｇroup 2

0855 ☐☐☐ **group** [grup]

名 群，（小）組；團體，派

片語 a group of 一群，一組，一批 ‖ group by group 分批地 ‖ in a group/in groups 成群地

例句 A group of boys are coming this way.
／一群男孩朝這邊走來。

0856 ☐☐☐ **grow** [gro]

動 [不及物] (grew, grown) 生長；變成
動 [及物] 種植

例句 Tomatoes grow best in direct sunlight.
／番茄在陽光照射下長得最好。

片語 grow into 長成，變成 ‖ grow out 長出 ‖ grow up 長大成人

0857 ☐☐☐ **growth** [groθ]

名 增加；生長，成長；發展，增長

例句 Can we measure the growth of a tree during the year?
／我們能測量樹木在一年內生長多少嗎？

0858 ☐☐☐ **guard** [gard]

名 警衛；哨兵
動 [及物] 保衛，守衛；看守，監視

例句 The dog guarded the child day and night.
／那條狗整天都在看守那個孩子。

片語 keep guard 放哨，守望 ‖ off guard 沒有提防，疏忽 ‖ on guard 值班，警戒

0859 ☐☐☐ **guava** [ˈgwɑvə]　名 芭樂（一種熱帶水果）

例句 Where can we buy guava?
／我們可以在哪裡買到芭樂？

0860 ☐☐☐ **guess** [gɛs]　動 猜測；想，認為
名 猜測，猜想

例句 Guess what I did yesterday.
／猜猜我昨天做了什麼事。

片語 make a guess at 猜一猜

0861 ☐☐☐ **guest** [gɛst]　名 客人

例句 There were 200 guests at the wedding.
／那場婚禮有 200 位賓客。

0862 ☐☐☐ **guide** [gaɪd]　名 嚮導，導遊
動 指引，指導；帶領

例句 A guide will show you around the castle.
／導遊將帶你們參觀城堡。

0863 ☐☐☐ **guitar** [gɪˈtɑr]　名 吉他，六弦琴

巧記 諧音：〔英〕guitar —音譯→〔漢〕吉他
例句 He likes playing the guitar.
／他喜歡彈吉他。

0864 ☐☐☐ **gun** [gʌn]　名 槍，砲

例句 He aimed the gun at a bird.
／他用槍瞄準一隻鳥。

0865 ☐☐☐ **guy** [gaɪ]　名 傢伙；朋友 (pl.) 大家，各位

例句 He's a great guy. ／他是個了不起的小伙子。

0866 ☐☐☐ **gym** [dʒɪm]　名 體育館，健身房 (=gymnasium)

例句 I go to the gym as often as I can.
／我一有空就去健身房健身。

0867 ☐☐☐ **habit**
[`hæbɪt]

名 習慣

例句 You need to change your eating habits. ／你得改變你的飲食習慣。

片語 be in the habit of/have the habit of 有…的習慣 ‖ get into/form/ develop the habit of 養成…的習慣

辨析 custom, habit
(1) custom 一般指整個社會在長時期內形成的習俗。
(2) habit 一般指個人的習慣行為。

0868 ☐☐☐ **hair**
[hɛr]

名 毛髮，頭髮；獸毛

例句 Her hair is the same color as her mother's.
／她的頭髮顏色跟她母親的一樣。

片語 do up one's hair 梳理頭髮，把頭髮盤起來

用法 hair 作「頭髮，毛髮」講時為不可數名詞，作「幾根頭髮」講時則為可數名詞。
※ She found a few grey hairs while doing up her hair. 她梳頭髮時
發現了幾根白髮。

0869 ☐☐☐ **haircut**
[`hɛr͵kʌt]

名 理髮；剪髮

例句 He is going to have a haircut. ／他準備去剪頭髮。

0870 ☐☐☐ **half**
[hæf]

代 名 一半
形 副 一半的（地）

例句 He banks half his salary every month.
／他將每月薪水的一半存入銀行。

片語 an hour and a half (=one and a half hours) 一個半小時 ‖ half an hour
(=a half hour) 半個小時 ‖ in half (=into halves) 分為兩半

0871 ☐☐☐ **hall**
[hɔl]

名 會堂，大廳；（大學的）餐廳

例句 Leave your coat in the hall.
／把你的大衣放在大廳裡。

0872 ☐☐☐ **Halloween**
[͵hæloˋin]

名 萬聖節前夕，萬聖夜

例句 Halloween is an autumn holiday that Americans celebrate
every year. ／萬聖節前夕是美國人每年秋天都會慶祝的一個節日。

0873 ☐☐☐ **ham**
[hæm]

名 火腿

例句 I have ham and eggs for breakfast. ／我早餐吃火腿和雞蛋。

0874 ☐☐☐

hamburger
[`hæmbɝɡɚ]

名 漢堡 (=burger)

(Track 47)

巧記 hamburger 是因 Hamburg(德國漢堡)而得名,原為德國一般家庭的常見食品。

例句 You can buy hamburgers in McDonald's.
／你可以在麥當勞買到漢堡。

0875 ☐☐☐

hammer
[`hæmɚ]

名 榔頭,鐵錘

例句 Damn! I hit my thumb with the hammer.
／該死,我搥到大拇指了。

0876 ☐☐☐

hand
[hænd]

名 手

例句 Clean your hands before a meal. ／飯前要將手洗乾淨。

片語 by hand 手工製作 ‖ give/lend sb. a hand 幫某人忙 ‖ hand in hand 手拉手 ‖ hands up 舉手

0877 ☐☐☐

hand
[hænd]

動 [及物] 傳遞,交給

例句 Monica handed the book to me. ／莫妮卡把書交給我。

片語 hand in 交出,繳交 ‖ hand out 分發,發送

0878 ☐☐☐

handkerchief
[`hæŋkɚˌtʃɪf]

名〔d 不發音〕(pl.-s 或 handkerchieves) 手帕,手絹

例句 He put his handkerchief over his face. ／他將手帕蓋在臉上。

0879 ☐☐☐

handle
[`hændl̩]

動 [及物] 操作;處理,應付;經營

例句 He is very hard to handle. ／他很難應付。

0880 ☐☐☐

handle
[`hændl̩]

名 柄,把手;把柄

例句 He turned the handle and went in.
／他轉了一下把手就走了進去。

handle

0881 ☐☐☐

handsome
[`hænsəm]

形 英俊的;大方的

例句 He's the most handsome man I've ever met.
／他是我見過的最英俊的男人。

0882 □□□
hang
[hæŋ]

働 (hung, hung) 吊，懸掛；徘徊
働 [及物] (hanged, hanged) 絞死

例句 Hang your coat up on the hook.
／把你的外套掛在掛鉤上。

片語 hang on 稍等，(電話) 別掛斷 ‖ hang out
閒逛 ‖ hang up ①掛斷電話 ②懸掛，掛起

hang up

0883 □□□
hanger
[`hæŋɚ]

名 衣架

例句 She took off her jacket and hung it on a hanger.
／她把夾克脫下來掛在衣架上。

0884 □□□
happen
[`hæpən]

働 [不及物] (偶然) 發生；碰巧做

例句 How did the accident happen? ／這個意外是怎麼發生的？

片語 happen to (sb.) (某人) 發生 (不幸的事) ‖ happen to do sth. 碰巧做某事
‖ It happened that... 碰巧…

0885 □□□
happy
[`hæpɪ]

形 愉快的，高興的，幸福的

例句 All happy families are like one another; each unhappy
family is unhappy in its own way. (Leo Tolstoy)
／所有幸福的家庭都十分相似，而每個不幸的家庭則各有各的不幸。
（列夫・托爾斯泰）

反義 unhappy 形 不高興的

0886 □□□
hard
[hard]

形 困難的；堅硬的
副 努力地；猛烈地

巧記 圖解 hard 的一詞多義：

堅硬的

困難的

努力的

猛烈的

例句 It is hard to hold the attention of children for a long time.
／要長時間吸引孩子們的注意，是一件困難的事。

辨析 hard, difficult
(1) hard 最普遍用詞，是 easy 的反義詞。
(2) difficult「困難的」，指克服某種障礙需要特別的技能、才智、知識或
勇氣，常用于表示難以應付、對付。

反義 soft 形 柔軟的

0887 □□□

hardly
[`hɑrdlɪ]

副 幾乎不；幾乎沒有

例句 I'm so tired that I can hardly stay awake.
／我太累了，以至於幾乎睜不開眼了。

用法 hardly 放在句首時，句子要倒裝；如果一個句子含有 no, hardly, never, little, few 等否定意義的詞，其反意疑問句要用肯定的疑問形式。

0888 □□□

hat
[hæt]

名（指有邊的）帽子，禮帽

例句 Mary is wearing a beautiful new hat.
／瑪麗戴著一頂漂亮的新帽子。

辨析 cap, hat
(1) cap「便帽」，常指無邊的帽子，如校帽、運動帽、軍帽等。
(2) hat「帽子」，常指有邊的帽子，婦女的帽子通稱 hat，又指帽子的總稱。

cap　　sports cap

hat　　top hat

0889 □□□

hate
[het]

動[及物] 名 憎恨；討厭

例句 My sister hates cats.
／我妹妹討厭貓。

片語 hate doing 不喜歡做…，不願做…〔表示經常性動作〕‖ hate to do 不喜歡做…，不願做…〔表示一次性動作〕

0890 □□□

have
[hæv]

動[及物] (had, had) 擁有；做；得到；吃，喝；生育
助〔與過去分詞一起構成完成式〕有

例句 Let me have a try.
／讓我試一下。

片語 have to do sth. 不得不做某事

例句 You have to wear sports shoes when you climb a mountain.
／爬山的時候你必須穿運動鞋。

例句 I have waited for half an hour. ／我等了半個小時。

辨析 have been to, have gone to
(1) have been to 表示「曾經去過某地」，現在已經回來，可以和 once, twice, never, ever 等連用。
(2) have gone to 表示「已經去了某地」，指現在不在說話人所在地（可能在去某地的途中或已經到達目的地），此句型主要用於第三人稱。

0891 □□□

he
[hi]

代〔主格〕他

例句 He is our English teacher.
／他是我們的英語老師。

0892
□□□

head
[hɛd]

名 頭;首腦
動 [不及物] 前進

🔊**48**

例句 The horse has a white mark on its head.
／這匹馬的頭上有個白色的斑紋。

片語 keep one's head 保持鎮靜 ‖ lose sb.'s head 慌亂,倉皇失措 ‖ use your head 動動腦筋

0893
□□□

headache
[`hɛd͵ek]

名 頭痛

例句 I had a really bad headache, and couldn't go to work.
／我頭很痛,沒辦法去上班。

0894
□□□

health
[hɛlθ]

名 健康;衛生

片語 in bad/poor health 身體不健康 ←→ in good health 身體健康
例句 She is in a poor state of health.
／她的健康狀況不佳。

0895
□□□

healthy
[`hɛlθɪ]

形 健康的

例句 Although 80 years old, my grandmother is still healthy.
／我祖母雖然 80 歲了,但是還很健康。

反義 unhealthy 形 不健康的

0896
□□□

hear
[hɪr]

動 (heard, heard) 聽;聽見;聽說

片語 hear from (=get/receive a letter from) 得到⋯消息,收到⋯的來信 ‖ hear of/about 聽說
例句 I thought she was famous, but none of my friends have ever heard of her.
／我以為她很有名,但是我朋友沒人聽說過她。

辨析 hear sb. do sth., hear sb. doing sth.
(1) hear sb. do sth. 表示聽到動作的全過程或經常聽到動作發生。
(2) hear sb. doing sth. 則表示聽到動作正在進行。

0897
□□□

heart
[hɑrt]

名 心(臟)

例句 Can you hear my heart beating?
／他交代廚師燒一些開水。

片語 by heart 記住,背誦 ‖ lose heart 失去勇氣

0898 ☐☐☐ **heat**
[hit]

名 熱；熱度
動 [及物] 把…加熱

例句 He ordered the cook to heat some water.
／他吩咐廚師燒些水。

0899 ☐☐☐ **heater**
[`hitɚ]

名 加熱器，暖氣機，暖爐

例句 Did you turn the heater off?
／你關掉暖氣機了嗎？

0900 ☐☐☐ **heavy**
[`hɛvɪ]

形 沉重的，多的

例句 The bag is too heavy for me to carry.
／這個袋子太重，我提不動。

heavy 重的　　light 輕的

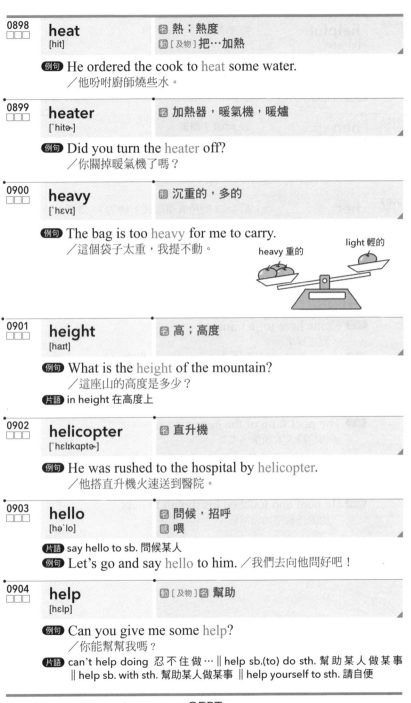

0901 ☐☐☐ **height**
[haɪt]

名 高；高度

例句 What is the height of the mountain?
／這座山的高度是多少？
片語 in height 在高度上

0902 ☐☐☐ **helicopter**
[`hɛlɪkɑptɚ]

名 直升機

例句 He was rushed to the hospital by helicopter.
／他搭直升機火速送到醫院。

0903 ☐☐☐ **hello**
[hə`lo]

名 問候，招呼
感 喂

片語 say hello to sb. 問候某人
例句 Let's go and say hello to him. ／我們去向他問好吧！

0904 ☐☐☐ **help**
[hɛlp]

動 [及物] 名 幫助

例句 Can you give me some help?
／你能幫幫我嗎？
片語 can't help doing 忍不住做… ‖ help sb.(to) do sth. 幫助某人做某事
‖ help sb. with sth. 幫助某人做某事 ‖ help yourself to sth. 請自便

0905 □□□
helpful
[`hɛlpfəl]

形 有幫助的，有益的

例句 Thank you for your advice; it's been very helpful.
／謝謝你的建議，它非常有用。

片語 helpful advice/information/suggestions 有用的勸告 / 資訊 / 建議

0906 □□□
hen
[hɛn]

名 母雞；雌禽

例句 The hens don't lay during such cold weather.
／母雞不會在這麼冷的天氣下蛋。

0907 □□□
her
[hɝ]

代〔she 的所有格形式〕她的；〔受格〕她

例句 I learned of her illness from him.
／我從他那裡得知她生病了。

0908 □□□
here
[hɪr]

副 這裡，在這裡，向這裡

例句 Come here for a minute.
／到這裡來一下。

片語 here and now 此時此地 ‖ here and there 到處

0909 □□□
hero
[`hɪro]

名 (pl.heroes) 英雄，勇士

例句 The poet sang of the hero.
／那位詩人歌頌那名英雄。

0910 □□□
hers
[hɝz]

代〔名詞性物主代詞〕她的

例句 He bent and touched his mouth to hers.
／他俯身親吻她的嘴唇。

0911	**herself** [hə·ˋsɛlf]	代〔反身代名詞〕她自己；〔加強語氣〕她親自

49

例句 She cut herself on some broken glass.
／她用碎玻璃割傷自己。

0912	**hey** [he]	感 嘿

例句 Hey! Where are you going?
／嘿！你要去哪裡？

0913	**hi** [haɪ]	感〔表示打招呼、問候或引起注意〕你好

例句 Hi! How are you?
／嗨！你好嗎？

0914	**hide** [haɪd]	動 (hid, hidden) 藏

例句 He hid the letter in a drawer.
／他把信藏在抽屜裡。

0915	**high** [haɪ]	形 高的 副 在高處

例句 The mountain is 2,000 meters high.
／那座山有 2,000 公尺高。

反義 low 形 低的

0916	**highway** [ˋhaɪ͵we]	名 公路

例句 The village people will benefit from the new highway.
／新的公路讓村民得到好處。

0917	**hike** [haɪk]	動 名 遠足，徒步旅行

例句 He wants to hike in the woods.
／他想在樹林間徒步旅行。

0918	**hill** [hɪl]	名 小山，丘陵

例句 The house is on the side of a hill.
／這間房子在山坡上。

0919 ☐☐☐
him
[hɪm]

代〔受格〕他

例句 His son cared for him when he was ill.
／他生病時，他的兒子照顧他。

0920 ☐☐☐
himself
[hɪm`sɛlf]

代〔反身代名詞〕他自己；〔用於加強語氣〕他本人，親自

例句 He went to night school to improve himself.
／他上夜校來改善自己。

0921 ☐☐☐
hip
[hɪp]

名 髖部，臀部

例句 He stood with his hands on his hips.
／他兩手叉腰站著。

0922 ☐☐☐
hippopotamus
[ˌhɪpə`pɑtəməs]

名 河馬 (=hippo)

例句 The children enjoyed watching the hippopotamus wallowing in the mud.
／孩子們喜歡看河馬在泥中打滾。

0923 ☐☐☐
hire
[haɪr]

名 動〔及物〕租用，雇用

例句 Can I hire a car for three days?
／我能租車租三天嗎？
片語 hire out 出租
辨析 employ, hire
(1) employ 是長時間「雇用」。
(2) hire 是臨時或一次性「雇用」。

0924 ☐☐☐
his
[hɪz]

代〔he 的所有格〕他的

例句 Tom took off his coat and sat down.
／湯姆脫掉外套坐了下來。

0925 ☐☐☐
history
[`hɪstərɪ]

名 歷史（學）

例句 History repeats itself.
／〔諺〕歷史會重演。
片語 make history ①創造歷史 ②做名垂青史的大事

0926 □□□ **hit**
[hɪt]

動 [及物] (hit, hit) 打；擊中；撞；猜對
名 擊中；碰撞

例句 The bullet hit the mark.
／子彈擊中了目標。

用法 hit sb.+in the+ 較軟的身體部位 (如 face, eye, mouth)；hit sb.+on the+ 較硬的身體部位 (如 head, nose, back)。

辨析 beat, hit
(1) beat 指連續地「敲打」。
(2) hit 側重指「擊中」，有時也指「打一下」。

0927 □□□ **hobby**
[`hɑbɪ]

名 業餘愛好，嗜好

例句 My hobby is growing flowers.
／我的嗜好是種花。

0928 □□□ **hold**
[hold]

動 [及物] (held, held) 握住，抓住；舉行；持有
名 抓住，握

例句 The girl was holding her father's hand.
／那個女孩抓住她爸爸的手。

片語 hold back 阻止，抑制 (眼淚等) ‖ hold on ①繼續 ② (打電話) 不掛斷 ‖ hold out 伸出

0929 □□□ **hole**
[hol]

名 坑洞；洞穴

例句 There is a huge hole in the road.
／路上有一個大坑洞。

Group 2

0930 □□□ **holiday**
[`hɑlə,de]

50

片語 have/take a holiday 放假，度假 ‖ on holiday 在度假 ‖ summer holiday 暑假

例句 He's on holiday.
／他正在度假。

0931 □□□ **home**
[hom]

名 家；家鄉
副 回家；在本國，回本國

例句 I saw him on my way home.
／我在回家的路上看到他。

片語 at home 在家 ‖ make sb. feel at home 使某人感到賓至如歸 ‖ make yourself at home 別拘束

0932 homesick
[`hom,sɪk]
形 想家的，思鄉的

例句 Alone in the big city, I began to get homesick.
／一個人獨自在大都市，我開始想家了。

0933 homework
[`hom,wɝk]
名 家庭作業

片語 do one's homework 做家庭作業
例句 Have you done your homework? ／你做完家庭作業了嗎？

0934 honest
[`anɪst]
形 誠實的，正直的

例句 An honest person has a lot of friends.
／誠實的人朋友多。
片語 to be honest〔作插入語〕老實說，說實在的
反義 dishonest 形 不誠實的

0935 honesty
[`anɪstɪ]
名 誠實，老實，正直

例句 I have a firm belief in his honesty. ／我堅信他的誠實。
反義 dishonesty 名 不誠實

0936 honey
[`hʌnɪ]
名 蜂蜜；寶貝，親愛的

例句 I love you, honey. ／親愛的，我愛你。

0937 Hong Kong
[`haŋ `kaŋ]
名 香港

例句 Have you ever been to Hong Kong? ／你去過香港嗎？

0938 hop
[hap]
動 [不及物]（人）單腳跳，（蛙、鳥等）跳

例句 He had hurt his left foot and had to hop along.
／他左腳受傷了，只好單腳跳行。

0939 hope
[hop]
動 名 希望；盼望，期待

片語 hope for 希望發生某種情況 ‖ hope to do sth. 希望做某事 ‖ in (the) hope of... 懷著…的希望
例句 We hope to see you tomorrow.
／我們希望明天能見到你。

0940 □□□

horrible
[ˈhɔrəbḷ]

形 令人恐懼的，恐怖的，可怕的

例句 The sight of the traffic accident was horrible.
／車禍現場令人毛骨悚然。

0941 □□□

horse
[hɔrs]

名 馬；(the -s) 賽馬

例句 His horse jumped across the stream.
／他的馬跳過小溪。

片語 get off a horse 下馬 ‖ ride a horse 騎馬

0942 □□□

hospital
[ˈhɑspɪtḷ]

名 醫院

例句 The hospital was founded in 1920.
／這家醫院創立於 1920 年。

片語 be in hospital 住在醫院〔指病人〕‖ be in the hospital 在醫院〔不一定是病人〕‖ go to hospital 到醫院看病

0943 □□□

host
[host]

名 主人；節目主持人；電腦主機
動 [及物] 招待

例句 The host cut the turkey for the guests.
／這位主人在客人面前切開火雞。

0944 □□□

hot
[hɑt]

形 熱的；辣的

例句 I like hot soup.
／我喜歡熱湯。

0945 □□□

hotel
[hoˈtɛl]

名 旅館，賓館

例句 She is watching TV in her hotel room.
／她正在旅館的房間裡看電視。

0946 □□□

hour
[aʊr]

名 小時；(pl.)(工作或學習等的) 固定時間

例句 She'll be home in half an hour.
／她半小時後到家。

片語 business hours 營業時間 ‖ by the hour 按鐘點 ‖ hour after hour 連續地 ‖ on the hour 準點

辨析 hour 指時間段，如 3 hours 3 個小時；o'clock 指時間點，如 3 o'clock 3 點鐘。

0947 □□□ **house** [haʊs]
名 (pl.houses) 房屋，住宅

例句 He lives in a large house.
／他住在一間大房子裡。

0948 □□□ **how** [haʊ]
副 連〔指程度、數量〕多麼；多少；怎樣；怎麼

片語 how about (doing)...〔表示徵求同意〕(做什麼)怎麼樣 ‖ how do you like...〔常用於詢問對方感受、印象、看法〕你覺得 / 認為…如何 ‖ how far〔指距離〕到…多遠 ‖ how long 多長，多久 ‖ how many〔跟可數名詞複數〕多少 ‖ how much ①〔跟不可數名詞〕多少 ②多少錢 ‖ how often 多久一次 ‖ how soon 多久 ‖ how old 幾歲

例句 How about taking a walk?
／去散步怎麼樣？

辨析 how often, how long, how soon
(1) how often「隔多久一次」，指動作的頻率。
(2) how long「(延續)多久(時間)」，回答一般用 for... 或 since 引導的時間副詞。
(3) how soon「還要多久(時間)才…」，回答一般都用表將來時的時間副詞 in...。

Group 3

0949 □□□ **however** [haʊ`ɛvɚ]
Track 51
連 不管怎樣
副 無論如何；然而

例句 I tried to do the right thing; however, I failed.
／我努力做該做的，然而我卻失敗了。

辨析 however, but
(1) however 是副詞，在句中作副詞並起連接作用，可位於句首、句中或句末，用逗號與句子分開。
(2) but 是連詞，連接兩個並列分句。

0950 □□□ **Hualien** [`hua`lɪɛn]
名 花蓮

例句 We took our holidays in Hualien and had a good time.
／我們到花蓮度假，玩得很愉快。

0951 □□□ **huge** [hjudʒ]
形 巨大的，龐大的

例句 The elephant is a huge animal.
／大象是種龐大的動物。

0952 human
[`hjumən]
形 人類的
名 人

例句 Men, women and children are all human.
／男人、女人和小孩都是人類。

片語 human nature 人性 ‖ human right 人權

0953 humble
[`hʌmbḷ]
形 謙虛的，謙遜的

例句 The doctor was humble about his work, although he cured many people.
／儘管這位醫生治癒了很多人，但他對自己的工作很謙虛。

0954 humid
[`hjumɪd]
形 潮濕的，濕潤的

例句 Tokyo is very humid in mid-autumn.
／東京到了秋天非常潮濕。

0955 humor
[`hjumɚ]
名 幽默（感），詼諧

巧記 諧音：〔英〕humor 一音譯→〔漢〕幽默

例句 He has a good sense of humor. ／他很有幽默感。

0956 humorous
[`hjumərəs]
形 幽默的，詼諧的

例句 Good humor is a promoter of friendship.
／良好的幽默能促進友誼。

0957 hundred
[`hʌndrəd]
名 代 一百

例句 Our school is so famous that hundreds of people come and visit it every term.
／我們學校很有名，每個學期都有上百人前來參觀。

用法 hundred，thousand，million 前有具體數字時，只能用單數，如 two hundred people 兩百人；前面無數字時，用複數，如 hundreds of people 數百人。

0958 hunger
[`hʌŋgɚ]
名 饑餓；渴望

例句 Ted was weak with hunger.
／泰德餓得全身無力。

片語 hunger for 渴望

0959 hungry
☐☐☐
[ˋhʌŋgrɪ]

形 饑餓的，感到餓的；渴望得到的

例句 Are you hungry?
／你餓嗎？

片語 be hungry for 渴望…

0960 hunt
☐☐☐
[hʌnt]

動 [不及物] 打獵　動 [及物] 獵殺；追捕
名 打獵

例句 He hunted animals in the mountains.
／他在山上獵動物。

片語 go hunting 去打獵 ‖ hunt for 尋找，搜尋

0961 hunter
☐☐☐
[ˋhʌntɚ]

名 獵人

例句 He is a brave hunter. ／他是一個勇敢的獵人。

0962 hurry
☐☐☐
[ˋhɝɪ]

名 動 趕快，匆忙

例句 You'd better hurry if you want to catch that bus.
／如果想趕上那輛公車，你最好快一點。

片語 hurry up 快一點 ‖ in a hurry 匆忙，很快地

0963 hurt
☐☐☐
[hɝt]

動 [不及物] (hurt, hurt) 疼痛
動 [及物] 傷害；受傷

例句 I was rather hurt by what he said about me.
／他講有關我的話讓我受到傷害。

0964 husband
☐☐☐
[ˋhʌzbənd]

名 丈夫

例句 He is a very good husband. ／他是一個好丈夫。

0965 I
☐☐☐
[aɪ]

代 〔主格〕我

例句 I am very busy now. ／我現在很忙。

0966 ice
☐☐☐
[aɪs]

名 冰，冰塊；冰層

例句 Ice turns into water.
／冰變成水。

片語 on thin ice 如履薄冰，處境極其危險

0967 ☐☐☐

idea
[aɪˋdɪə]

名 主意，想法

52

例句 What a good idea!
／好主意！

片語 have no idea 不知道

0968 ☐☐☐

if
[ɪf]

連 假如，如果；是否

例句 We will have no water to drink if we don't protect the earth.
／如果我們不保護地球，我們將會無水可喝。

用法 if 當「如果」講時，常引導條件副詞從句，主句是一般將來時，從句用一般現在時表示將來；if 當「是否」講時，引導受詞從句，常放在 ask, remember, know 等動詞的後面，通常可與 whether 互換。

0969 ☐☐☐

ignore
[ɪgˋnor]

動 [及物] 不理，忽視

例句 I said hello to her, but she ignored me!
／我向她打招呼，她卻不理我！

0970 ☐☐☐

ill
[ɪl]

形 生病的，不適的；壞的

例句 She can't go to school because she is ill.
／她不能去上學，因為她生病了。

0971 ☐☐☐

image
[ˋɪmɪdʒ]

名 影像，圖像；形象；印象

例句 The company has to protect its right image.
／公司要保護其正面形象。

0972 ☐☐☐

imagine
[ɪˋmædʒɪn]

動 [及物] 想像，猜想

例句 Can you imagine the life on a lonely island?
／你能想像在孤島上的生活是什麼樣的嗎？

0973 ☐☐☐

impolite
[ˏɪmpəˋlaɪt]

形 無禮的，不禮貌的

例句 It is impolite to turn your back on someone who is
speaking to you.
／背對著對你說話的人是不禮貌的。

反義 polite 形 有禮貌的

0974 ☐☐☐
import
[`ɪmport]
動 [及物] 進口，輸入
名 進口商品

巧記 im-(=in) + port(港口) → import 進口
例句 Britain imports wine from France.
／英國從法國進口葡萄酒。

0975 ☐☐☐
importance
[ɪm`pɔrtn̩s]
名 重要 (性)；重大

例句 Oil is of great importance to industry.
／石油對工業是極為重要的。

0976 ☐☐☐
important
[ɪm`pɔrtn̩t]
形 重要的

例句 Safety is more important than speed.
／安全比速度重要。
反義 unimportant 形 不重要的

0977 ☐☐☐
impossible
[ɪm`pasəbl̩]
形 不可能的

例句 It is impossible for fish to walk.
／魚是不可能走路的。
用法 以人或事作主詞時，必須用 it 作形式主詞，用「It is impossible (for sb./sth.) to do...」來表達。
反義 possible 形 可能的

0978 ☐☐☐
improve
[ɪm`pruv]
動 改善，改進

例句 His spoken English has improved much.
／他的英語口語進步許多。
片語 improve on/upon 改進，做得比…更好，超過

0979 ☐☐☐
in
[ɪn]
介 在…之內；穿著；在…之中

例句 Suddenly she saw a lady all in white standing in front of her.
／她突然看見一個全身白衣的女士站在她的面前。
反義 out 代 在…外面 形 不再時髦的

0980 ☐☐☐
inch
[ɪntʃ]
名 英吋；一點點

例句 The ice is two inches thick. ／冰有兩英吋厚。
片語 inch by inch 慢慢地，一步一步地

第三週

0981 □□□ **include** [ɪnˋklud]　　動 [及物] 包括，包含

巧記 in-(在內)+clude(關)；把…關在裡面 → 包含
例句 The price includes the tax.
／這價錢包括稅金。

0982 □□□ **including** [ɪnˋkludɪŋ]　　介 包括，包含在內 [ɪnˋkludɪŋ]

例句 Thirty people, including six children, went to visit the factory.
／ 30 個去參觀工廠的人之中，包括了 6 個小孩。
反義 excluding prep. 不包括，除去

0983 □□□ **income** [ˋɪnˏkʌm]　　名 收入，收益，所得

例句 On her small income, they lived very simply.
／他們靠她微薄的收入，過著非常簡樸的生活。
用法 expense(費用)，fortune(財產)，income(收入) 等談其多少，不用 much/little，而用 high/large 或 low/small。

0984 □□□ **increase** [ɪnˋkris]　　動 增加；增長

例句 Travel increases one's knowledge of the world.
／旅行增長了人們對世界的瞭解。
用法 increase by+ 倍數或百分數，表示「增加了…倍或百分之…」；increase to+ 具體增長後的數字，表示「增加到…」。

0985 □□□ **independent** [ˏɪndɪˋpɛndənt]　　形 獨立的，自主的

例句 That country became independent of France in the sixties.
／那個國家在 60 年代脫離法國而獨立。
用法 可說 depend/dependence/dependent on，卻只能說 independent of。
※ I used to be dependent on my parents. Now I'm independent of them. 過去我常常依賴父母，現在我獨立了。

0986 □□□ **indicate** [ˋɪndəˏket]　　動 [及物] 指出，指示；顯示；是…的徵兆

例句 The arrow indicates the way to the park.
／箭頭指示前往公園的路。

0987
☐☐☐

individual
[ˌɪndə`vɪdʒʊəl]

图 個體，個人
形 單獨的，個別的；獨特的

巧記 in-(= not) + divid(e) + -ual(= of)；無法再分割的

例句 Each individual boy in the class has his own personality.
／這個班上的每個男孩都有自己的個性。

0988
☐☐☐

industry
[`ɪndəstrɪ]

图 工業；產業；行業

例句 Chicago is famous for its auto industry.
／芝加哥以汽車製造業而聞名於世。

片語 heavy/light industry 重 / 輕工業

0989
☐☐☐

influence
[`ɪnflʊəns]

图 影響；影響力
動 [及物] 影響

例句 The weather in summer influences the rice crops.
／夏天的天氣影響稻穀的收成。

片語 have an influence on sth. 對某物有影響 ‖ under the influence of... 受…的影響

0990
☐☐☐

information
[ˌɪnfə`meʃən]

图 通知；資訊，情報

巧記 information 縮寫為 info，在公共場所常縮寫為「 i 」，指「資訊台」等。

例句 Can you give me any information on this matter?
／ 你能給我任何有關這件事的資訊嗎？

information

用法 information 為不可數名詞，表示一條消息，用 a piece of information。

0991
☐☐☐

injury
[`ɪndʒərɪ]

图 損害，傷害

例句 She was taken to hospital with serious head injuries.
／她因為頭部嚴重受傷被送到醫院。

0992
☐☐☐

ink
[ɪŋk]

图 墨水，油墨

片語 write in ink 用墨水寫〔不用 with〕
例句 Please write in black ink.
／請用黑色墨水書寫。

0993 ☐☐☐ **insect** [ˈɪnsɛkt]　名 昆蟲

例句 Butterflies, bees, flies, and ants are insects.
／蝴蝶、蜜蜂、蒼蠅和螞蟻都是昆蟲。

0994 ☐☐☐ **inside** [ɪnˈsaɪd]
介 在…裡　副 在裡面
名 裡面

例句 Don't let the dog come inside the house.
／不要讓狗進到房子裡來。
片語 inside out ①裡朝外，從裡到外 ②徹底地
反義 outside 介 在…外

0995 ☐☐☐ **insist** [ɪnˈsɪst]
動[不及物] 堅持，堅決要求
動[及物] 堅決主張，堅持認為

例句 I insisted that she was innocent.
／我堅持認為她是清白的。
片語 insist on (one's) doing 堅持 (某人) 做
用法 insist that... 並非總用虛擬語氣。若表示「堅持應該幹…」，從句動詞用
「(should+) 動詞原形」表示虛擬；若表示「堅持某一事實或看法」則用
陳述語氣。
　※ Insisting that Tom had stolen his car, Mr. Smith insisted that
　　Tom (should) be put in prison. 由於堅持認為湯姆偷了他的汽車，
　　史密斯先生堅持把湯姆關進監獄。

0996 ☐☐☐ **inspire** [ɪnˈspaɪr]　動[及物] 鼓舞，激勵

巧記 in-(入)+spire(精神，靈氣)；注入精氣神 → 鼓舞，激勵
例句 The teacher inspired us to make greater efforts.
／老師激勵我們更加努力。

0997 ☐☐☐ **instance** [ˈɪnstəns]　名 例子，實例

例句 Let me give you some instances.
／我舉幾個例子給你看。
片語 for instance 例如，比如

0998 ☐☐☐ **instant** [ˈɪnstənt]
形 立即的；(食品) 即溶的，方便的
名 瞬間

片語 on the instant 立即，馬上 ‖ the instant (that) 一…就…
例句 I had instant noodles as a midnight snack.
／我泡了一碗泡麵當作宵夜。
辨析 in an instant, for an instant

(1) in an instant (=in a while, in a moment, in a minute)，「一會兒，馬上，立刻」，通常用於將來時，常與終止性動詞連用。

(2) for an instant (=for a while, for a moment, for a minute)「暫時，一時」，一般用於完成時態、一般時態或將來時態，常與持續性動詞連用。

0999
☐☐☐
instrument
[ˋɪnstrəmənt]

图〔廣義〕儀器，器具；〔狹義〕樂器

例句 The pilot checked the instruments before the plane took off.
／飛行員在飛機起飛前檢查了儀器。

1000
☐☐☐
intelligent
[ɪnˋtɛlədʒənt]

形 聰明的，有才智的

例句 A monkey is an intelligent animal. ／猴子是聰明的動物。

1001
☐☐☐
interest
[ˋɪntərɪst]

图 興趣，愛好
動〔及物〕使…感興趣

例句 This subject has no interest for me.
／我對這個議題不感興趣。

片語 have/take/show an interest in 對…感興趣　lose interest in 對…失去興趣

1002
☐☐☐
interested
[ˋɪntərɪstɪd]

形 感興趣的，關心的

片語 be interested in (doing) sth. 對 (做)…感興趣 (表狀態) ‖ be interested to do sth. 對 (做)…感興趣 (表一次性動作)

例句 I am interested in comic books.
／我對漫畫書很感興趣。

1003
☐☐☐
international
[͵ɪntəˋnæʃənl]

形 國際的

巧記 inter-(…之間)+nation(國家)+-al(…的)；國與國之間的 → 國際的
例句 English is one of the official languages in international conferences.
／英語是國際會議上的官方語言之一。
片語 International Labour Day 國際勞動節

1004
☐☐☐
Internet
[ˋɪntə͵nɛt]

图 (the ～) 網際網路

巧記 inter-(…之間)+net(網)；網與網之間 → 互聯網
例句 You can find all kinds of information on the Internet.
／你可以在網際網路上找到各式各樣的資訊。

1005 □□□

interrupt
[ˌɪntəˈrʌpt]

動 [及物] 打斷（談話），打擾（某人）；使中斷
動 [不及物] 打斷

巧記 圖解 interrupt 的構詞：

interrupt（中斷） ＝ inter(在…中間) ＋ rupt (break)

例句 It is impolite to interrupt when someone is talking.
／打斷別人講話是不禮貌的。

Group 2

1006 □□□
54

interview
[ˈɪntəˌvju]

名 動 [及物] 接見，會見；面試；採訪

巧記 inter-(相互之間) + view(看，見) → 相見 → 接見，會見
例句 I have an interview for a new job tomorrow.
／我明天有一個新工作的面試。

1007 □□□

into
[ˈɪntu]

介 進，入，到…裡；成為，轉為，變成

例句 The eggs were put into the box. ／雞蛋放進盒子裡了。

be in the room
走進室內

go into the room
走進室內

go out of the room
走進室內

into ⇨ in ⇨ out of

1008 □□□

introduce
[ˌɪntrəˈdjus]

動 [及物] 介紹（給）；引入

例句 May I introduce myself？／我可以自我介紹一下嗎？
片語 introduce...to 把…介紹給〔to 後常跟人〕‖ introduce...into 把…引入
〔into 後常跟地點〕

1009 □□□

invent
[ɪnˈvɛnt]

動 [及物] 發明，創造

例句 Gilbert discovered electricity, and Edison invented the
electric light bulb. ／吉伯特發現了電，愛迪生發明了電燈泡。
辨析 discover, invent
(1) discover 指客觀存在的事物被人「發現」。
(2) invent 指客觀不存在，被人「發明」。

1010
☐☐☐

investigate
[ɪnˋvɛstəˌget]

動 調查，研究

例句 The police are investigating the cause of the accident.
／警方正在調查意外發生的原因。

1011
☐☐☐

invitation
[ˌɪnvəˋteʃən]

名 邀請

例句 Thank you for your kind invitation.
／謝謝你的好意邀請。
片語 send sb. an invitation 向某人發出邀請

1012
☐☐☐

invite
[ɪnˋvaɪt]

動 [及物] 邀請

例句 Peter invited me to go on a trip to Sun-Moon Lake.
／彼得邀我去日月潭旅行。

1013
☐☐☐

iron
[ˋaɪɚn]

名 鐵；熨斗
動 熨，燙

例句 Strike while the iron is hot. ／〔諺〕打鐵趁熱。
用法 iron 作不可數名詞意為「鐵」；作可數名詞意為「熨斗」。
　　※ Nowadays some electric irons are made of plastics instead of iron. 現在一些電熨斗是用塑膠而不是用鐵做的了。

1014
☐☐☐

is
[ɪz]

動 〔be 的第三人稱單數現在式〕是

例句 It is a dog. ／這是一條狗。

1015
☐☐☐

island
[ˋaɪlənd]

名 〔s 不發音〕島，島狀物

例句 No cars are allowed on the island.
／這座島上禁止汽車通行。

1016
☐☐☐

it
[ɪt]

代 〔指剛剛提到的事物〕它；〔指不明確表示性別的嬰兒〕他，她；〔指天氣、時間、距離等〕；〔作形式主詞或形式受詞〕

例句 "Do you like wine?" "No, I don't like it."
／「你喜歡酒嗎?」「不，我不喜歡它。」

1017
☐☐☐

item
[ˋaɪtəm]

名 條款，項目，品項

例句 We have many items to be discussed in our meeting today.
／我們今天的會議有許多項目要討論。

1018 ☐☐☐

its
[ɪts]

代〔it 的所有格〕它的

例句 The hotel has its own pool. ／這家飯店有自己的游泳池。

1019 ☐☐☐

itself
[ɪt`sɛlf]

代 它自己；…本身

例句 The monkey is looking at itself in the mirror.
／猴子正在望著鏡子裡的自己。

片語 by itself 獨自地

1020 ☐☐☐

jacket
[`dʒækɪt]

名 上衣，夾克

巧記 諧音：〔英〕jacket 一音譯→〔漢〕夾克

例句 These trousers are not an exact match for my jacket.
／這條褲子和我的夾克不太搭。

1021 ☐☐☐

jam
[dʒæm]

名 果醬；擁擠，堵塞

例句 I'd like some jam on my bread, please.
／請幫我抹一些果醬在麵包上。

1022 ☐☐☐

January
[`dʒænjʊ͵ɛrɪ]

名 一月 (=Jan.)

例句 I haven't heard from him since last January.
／我從去年一月後就沒他的消息了。

1023 ☐☐☐

Japan
[dʒə`pæn]

名 日本

例句 He came to Japan by way of China. ／他經由中國到了日本。

1024 ☐☐☐

Japanese
[͵dʒæpə`niz]

形 日本的，日本人的，日語的
名〔單同複〕日本人；日語

例句 You have to learn Japanese customs if you want to go there.
／如果你想去日本，你就得學習日本的風俗。

Ⓖroup 3

1025 ☐☐☐

jazz
[dʒæz]

名 爵士樂，爵士舞曲

55

巧記 諧音：〔英〕jazz 一音譯→〔漢〕爵士

例句 He is more familiar with modern jazz than I.
／他比我更懂現代爵士樂。

1026 jealous
☐☐☐ [ˋdʒɛləs]
形 妒忌的，猜忌的

片語 be jealous of... 妒忌，羨慕…

例句 Don't be jealous of other people's success.
／不要嫉妒別人的成功。

辨析 envious, jealous
(1) envious 意為「羨慕的，妒忌的」，不一定帶有不滿的情緒。
(2) jealous 意為「妒忌的」。這是一種強烈且令人不快的感情，還指 (男女間的)「吃醋」。比 envious 更強烈，並帶有不滿。

1027 jeans
☐☐☐ [dʒinz]
名 (pl.) 牛仔褲

例句 She was wearing a pair of tight blue jeans.
／她穿著一條藍色緊身牛仔褲。

1028 jeep
☐☐☐ [dʒip]
名 吉普車

巧記 諧音：〔英〕jeep 一音譯→〔漢〕吉普

例句 The jeep was found lying in a thick bush.
／吉普車被發現翻倒在茂密的叢林裡。

1029 job
☐☐☐ [dʒɑb]
名 工作；任務；職位

例句 The job requires five-years work experience in editing.
／這份工作需要五年的編輯工作經驗。

片語 do a good job 幹得好 ‖ out of a job 失業

1030 jog
☐☐☐ [dʒɑg]
動 [不及物] 慢跑
動 [及物] 輕輕碰撞

例句 He jogs to work every morning. ／他每天早上都慢跑去上班。

1031 join
☐☐☐ [dʒɔɪn]
動 參加；聯合；加入

例句 He joined the tennis club. ／他加入了網球俱樂部。

片語 join in 參加 (某項活動) ‖ join sb. in (doing) sth. 和某人一起做某事 ‖ join the army 加入軍隊

1032 joint
☐☐☐ [dʒɔɪnt]
形 連接的；聯合的
名 接合處；關節

例句 My knee joints have been aching for a week.
／我的膝關節痛了一個星期。

片語 out of joint ①脫臼 ②出了問題，處於混亂狀態

第三週

1033 ☐☐☐

joke
[dʒok]

名 笑話，玩笑；笑柄，笑料
動 [不及物] 開玩笑

例句 I didn't mean that seriously—I was only joking.
／我不是認真的——只是開開玩笑罷了。

片語 have a joke with sb. 跟某人說笑話 ‖ make a joke （about）（拿…）開玩笑 ‖ play a joke on sb. 戲弄某人

1034 ☐☐☐

journalist
[ˈdʒɝnəlɪst]

名 新聞工作者，記者

巧記 journal(日報，期刊 → 新聞) + -ist(…者)

例句 John Smith is a journalist, and he helps to write newspapers.
／約翰史密斯是一名記者，他幫報紙寫文章。

1035 ☐☐☐

joy
[dʒɔɪ]

名 高興，樂趣；使人高興的人或事

例句 Success brought him joy. ／成功帶給他喜悅。

片語 for joy 因為高興 ‖ to one's joy 使 (某人) 高興的是

1036 ☐☐☐

judge
[dʒʌdʒ]

名 法官，裁判；評判員
動 [不及物] 判斷；審判

例句 You can't judge a man by his appearance.
／〔諺〕不能以貌取人。

片語 judging by/from 從…判斷，依據…判斷

1037 ☐☐☐

juice
[dʒus]

名 果汁，菜汁；肉汁

例句 One tomato juice and one soup, please.
／請給我一杯番茄汁和一碗湯。

1038 ☐☐☐

July
[dʒuˋlaɪ]

名 七月 (=Jul.)

例句 It's very hot in July.
／七月裡天氣很熱。

1039 ☐☐☐

jump
[dʒʌmp]

動 跳，跳躍
名 跳，跳躍

例句 Tom can jump much higher than me.
／湯姆比我跳得高得多。

片語 jump rope 跳繩 ‖ jump the queue 插隊 ‖ jump to one's feet 跳起來

A
B
C
D
E
F
G
H
I
J
K
L
M
N
O
P
Q
R
S
T
U
V
W
X
Y
Z

1040

☐☐☐

June
[dʒun]

名 六月 (=Jun.)

例句 His precious roses bloom in June.
／他珍貴的玫瑰六月開花。

1041

☐☐☐

just
[dʒʌst]

副 只不過，只是；正好；剛才

片語 just as 正像 ‖ just now ①剛才 ②此刻，現在 ‖ just so-so 一般般
例句 Where did you go just now? ／你剛才去哪裡了？

1042

☐☐☐

kangaroo
[ˌkæŋgəˈru]

名 (pl.kangaroos) 袋鼠

例句 A kangaroo is an interesting animal. ／袋鼠是一種有趣的動物。

1043

☐☐☐

Kaohsiung
[ˈkɑʊˈʃɪʊŋ]

名 高雄

例句 What is the most famous place in Kaohsiung?
／高雄最著名的景點是哪裡？

Ⓖroup 4

1044

☐☐☐

56

keep
[kip]

動 [及物] (kept, kept) 保留；保持；繼續

片語 keep away from 遠離 ‖ keep from... 使…免於 ‖ keep off 避開，不讓接近
‖ keep on 繼續，保持 ‖ keep out 使在外面 ‖ keep up with 跟上，趕上
例句 Medicine is dangerous for children, so it should be kept
away from them.
／藥物對孩子來說很危險，所以應該讓他們遠離藥物。

1045

☐☐☐

ketchup
[ˈkɛtʃəp]

名 番茄醬 (=catsup)

例句 Don't forget to buy me some ketchup on your way back.
／回來路上別忘了幫我買番茄醬。

1046

☐☐☐

key
[ki]

名 鑰匙；答案；關鍵

例句 This is the key to the front door.
／這是前門的鑰匙。
片語 the key to success 成功的關鍵

1047 key
[ki]
形〔作限定詞〕至關重要的，關鍵的

例句 He makes all the key decisions in our company.
／他決定我們公司所有的重要決定。

1048 kick
[kɪk]
名 動 踢

例句 He kicked the ball into the goal. ／他把球踢進球門裡。

1049 kid
[kɪd]
名 小孩，兒童

例句 He's married with three kids. ／他已婚，有三個小孩。

1050 kill
[kɪl]
動〔及物〕殺死；消磨（時間）
動〔不及物〕致死

片語 kill time 打發時間
例句 We kill time by watching TV during the night.
／我們晚上看電視打發時間。

1051 kilogram
[ˋkɪləˌɡræm]
名 千克，公斤 (=kg)

巧記 kilo-(千)+gram(克)
例句 Ken gained two kilograms during the summer vacation.
／肯在暑假增加了兩公斤。

1052 kilometer
[ˋkɪləˌmitɚ]
名 公里 (=km)

例句 The place is two kilometers away from here.
／這個地方離這裡兩公里遠。

1053 kind
[kaɪnd]
名 種類

片語 a kind of 某種 ‖ all kinds of 各式各樣的 ‖ kind of〔修飾動詞或形容詞〕有一點
例句 Teenagers have all kinds of dreams.
／青少年有各式各樣的夢想。

1054 kind
[kaɪnd]
形 仁慈的；友愛的

片語 be kind to sb. 對某人很好
例句 It will pay to be kind to others. ／善待別人，必有好報。

1055 kindergarten
[ˋkɪndɚˏgɑrtn̩]
名 幼稚園

巧記 〔熟〕garden 花園 → 〔生〕kindergarten 〔kinder (一群兒童)
+garten(=garden)〕幼稚園

例句 She's in kindergarten now. ／她現在在上幼稚園。

1056 king
[kɪŋ]
名 國王，王；⋯大王；王牌，王棋

巧記 圖解 king 的一詞多義：

| king | king (chess piece) | the king of beasts | king of diamonds |
| 國王 | 王棋 | 萬獸之王 | 方框老K |

例句 They made him king. ／他們擁戴他當國王。

1057 kingdom
[ˋkɪŋdəm]
名 王國

例句 The kingdom's power declined. ／這個王國的國力衰退了。

1058 kiss
[kɪs]
動 名 吻；(風、波浪等) 輕拂，輕觸

例句 He gave his daughter a kiss. ／他給了他女兒一吻。
片語 kiss sb. hello/goodbye 以親吻問候某人 / 吻別

1059 kitchen
[ˋkɪtʃɪn]
名 廚房

例句 She is in the kitchen making a meal. ／她正在廚房裡做飯。

1060 kite
[kaɪt]
名 風箏

例句 I can fly a kite. ／我會放風箏。

1061 kitten
[ˋkɪtn̩]
名 小貓 (=kitty)

例句 I have three kittens, they are so pretty.
／我有三隻小貓，牠們都很漂亮。

1062 knee
[ni]
名 膝蓋，(坐姿時) 腿部

片語 fall/go on one's knees 跪下 ‖ on one's knees 跪著
例句 Tim fell on his knees and started to pray. ／提姆跪下來開始禱告。

1063 knife
[naɪf]

名 (pl.knives) 小刀，菜刀，手術刀

57

例句 Is that knife sharp or dull?
／那把刀是鋒利的還是鈍的？

1064 knock
[nɑk]

動 敲，擊，打；碰撞

例句 He knocked his leg against the table.
／他的腿撞到桌子了。

片語 knock at/on 敲擊 (門、窗等) ‖ knock down 擊倒，撞倒 ‖ knock into 撞上

1065 know
[no]

動 (knew, known) 知道；懂得；認識

例句 Do you know the answer to the question?
／你知道這個問題的答案嗎？

片語 be known as 作為…而出名 ‖ be known for 因…而出名 ‖ be known to 為…所熟悉

1066 knowledge
[`nɑlɪdʒ]

名 知識；學問

例句 Knowledge is power.
／〔諺〕知識就是力量。

用法 漢語說「學到…知識」，但英語說 obtain/gain/acquire(NOT learn) a knowledge of...。knowledge 沒有複數形式，但它之前可加不定冠詞 a，表示「某種知識」。

1067 koala
[ko`alə]

名 (澳洲) 無尾熊

例句 The koala is the most popular animal in this zoo.
／無尾熊是這個動物園裡最受歡迎的動物。

1068 Korea
[ko`riə]

名 朝鮮；韓國

例句 She traveled to Korea last Monday.
／她上星期一去韓國旅遊。

1069 Korean
[ko`riən]

形 韓國 (人) 的，韓語的
名 朝鮮人，韓國人

例句 He has translated her latest book into Korean.
／他把她的新書翻譯成韓語。

A
B
C
D
E
F
G
H
I
J
K
L
M
N
O
P
Q
R
S
T
U
V
W
X
Y
Z

1070 ☐☐☐ **KTV**
[ˈkeˈtiˈvi]

🔵名 包廂式卡拉 OK

🔵例句 Do you want to go to the KTV with us?
／你要跟我們去唱 KTV 嗎？

1071 ☐☐☐ **lack**
[læk]

🔵動[及物] 名 (sing.) 缺乏，缺少

🔵例句 She lacked the experience to get the job.
／她缺乏經驗，無法獲得這份工作。

🔵片語 lack of 缺少

1072 ☐☐☐ **lady**
[ˈledɪ]

🔵名 女士；夫人，小姐；淑女

🔵例句 Ladies and gentlemen, now let's begin the meeting.
／各位女士、先生，會議正式開始。

1073 ☐☐☐ **lake**
[lek]

🔵名 湖，湖泊

🔵例句 The lake is near our school.
／那個湖在我們學校附近。

🔵衍生 lakeside 名 湖濱

1074 ☐☐☐ **lamb**
[læm]

🔵名〔b 不發音〕羔羊，小羊；羔羊肉

🔵例句 I like lamb, but my husband doesn't.
／我喜歡羔羊肉，但是我先生不喜歡。

1075 ☐☐☐ **lamp**
[læmp]

🔵名 燈

🔵例句 I turned on the table lamp.
／我打開了檯燈。

1076 ☐☐☐ **land**
[lænd]

🔵名 陸地；土地
🔵動（使）著陸；（使）上岸

🔵巧記 圖解 land（動）的一詞多義：

上岸

著陸

例句 The pilot landed the plane safely in the heavy snow.
／飛行員在大雪中讓飛機安全著陸。

片語 by land 由陸路 ‖ land on (飛機等) 降落於…

辨析 land, ground, earth, soil, floor
(1) 視為財產的「一塊地」，稱為 a piece of land 或 a piece of ground。
(2) 植物所賴以生長的「地」稱為 ground, earth 或 soil。
(3) 供人行走的室外的「地」稱 ground，室內稱 floor。
(4) 與海相對的「陸地」叫 land，但與天空相對的「陸地」叫 earth。

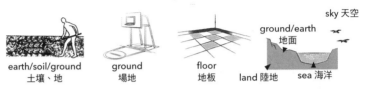

earth/soil/ground　　ground　　floor　　land 陸地
土壤、地　　　　　場地　　　地板　　sea 海洋

sky 天空
ground/earth
地面

1077 □□□

language
[ˋlæŋgwɪdʒ]

名 語言

例句 He is familiar with three languages.
／他熟悉三種語言。

片語 spoken/written language 說 / 寫語言

1078 □□□

Lantern Festival
[ˋlæntɚnˋfɛstəvl]

名 元宵節

例句 People usually eat rice glue balls on Lantern festival.
／元宵節大家通常都吃湯圓。

1079 □□□

large
[lardʒ]

形 寬廣的；大的

例句 The market is very large.
／這個市場非常大。

辨析 large, big, great, huge
(1) large 一般指範圍、面積、體積、數量等的大。
(2) big 常用來修飾有形的東西，應用範圍較廣。
(3) great 指超常的長度、高度等，指人時表示「偉大的」。
(4) huge 指具體的事物或人時，表示體積或數量大得超過一般情況。

反義 small 形 小的

1080 □□□

last
[læst]

形 最後的；(表示時間) 上一個 **名** **代** (the ~) 最後一個

例句 This is the last week of the term.
／這是本學期的最後一周。

片語 at last 終於，最後

反義 first 形 第一的

1081
☐☐☐

late
[let]

形 遲到；末期的；最近的
副 遲，晚

例句 He was ten minutes late this morning.
／今天早上他遲到了十分鐘。

片語 be late for 做…遲到
反義 early 形 早的 副 提前，提早

Ⓖroup 2

1082
☐☐☐
58

later
[`letɚ]

副 較晚的，晚一點；後來

例句 I'll see you later. ／待會兒見。

片語 later on 後來，再過些時候
用法 「一段時間 +later」用於過去時或將來時的將來，表示「…之後」。

1083
☐☐☐

latest
[`letɪst]

形 最近的，最新的

例句 What are the latest developments?
／有什麼最新進展嗎？

1084
☐☐☐

laugh
[læf]

動 [不及物] 笑，大笑
名 笑，笑聲

例句 He who laughs last laughs best.
／〔諺〕最後笑的人，才笑得最得意。（還不知道鹿死誰手呢！）

片語 laugh at sb. 嘲笑某人

1085
☐☐☐

law
[lɔ]

名 法律（體系）；法則

例句 His actions were within the law.
／他的行為在法律允許範圍之內。

片語 by law 依據法律 ‖ obey/break the law 守 / 犯法

1086
☐☐☐

lawyer
[`lɔjɚ]

名 律師

例句 I want to see my lawyer. ／我要見我的律師。

1087
☐☐☐

lay
[le]

(laid, laid) 動 [及物] 放，擺；產卵
動 [不及物] 產卵，下蛋

例句 He laid the book on the book shelf. ／他把書放在書架上。

片語 lay aside ①把…擱置一旁 ②留存，儲存 ‖ lay down 放下 ‖ lay off（暫時）解雇，資遣

第三週

lazy
[`lezɪ]

形 懶惰的，不努力的

例句 His teacher thought he was lazy. ／他的老師認為他不努力。

衍生 lazily 副 懶惰地；laziness 名 懶惰

1089

lead
[lid]

動 (led, led) 領導，帶領；導致，造成

例句 She led a blind man across the street. ／她帶領一位盲人過馬路。

片語 lead a...life 過…的生活 ‖ lead to 導致

辨析 lead, guide, direct
(1) lead 意為「帶路，牽引」，走在前頭，引到目的地。
(2) guide 意為「帶領，引導」，一直陪在一旁，邊走邊談。
(3) direct 意為「指路」，指出方向，不陪同去。

lead (在前) 領 (路)　　guide 帶領，引導　　direct 指 (路)

1090

leader
[`lidɚ]

名 領袖，領導者，首領；領先者

例句 He is a born leader.
／他生來就適合當領導者。

1091

leadership
[`lidɚˌʃɪp]

名 領導，領導力

巧記 leader(領導)+-ship(名詞尾碼)

片語 under the leadership of sb. 在某人的領導下

例句 Under his leadership, many problems were smoothly solved.
／在他的領導下，許多問題都迎刃而解了。

1092

leaf
[lif]

名 (pl.leaves) 葉，葉子；(書刊等的) 張，頁

巧記 圖解 leaf 的一詞多義：

葉　　　　頁

例句 A leaf is falling. ／一片葉子落了下來。

1093
□□□

learn
[lɝn]

動 [及物] (learned, learned; learnt, learnt) 學會，記住；得知
動 [不及物] 學，學習

例句 It is never too late to learn. ／學習永遠不嫌晚。
片語 learn about 得知 ‖ learn...by heart 記住… ‖ learn...by oneself 自學… ‖ learn to do sth. 學做某事

1094
□□□

least
[list]

形 最小的，最少的
副 最小，最少

例句 Which shirt costs the least money?
／哪件襯衫最便宜？
片語 at least 至少，起碼
反義 most **形** 最多的 **副** 最多
辨析 little 的最高級

1095
□□□

leave
[liv]

動 [不及物] (left, left) 去，出發
動 [及物] 離開；死後留下；遺忘

例句 The train will leave the station in five minutes.
／火車將於五分鐘後離站。
片語 leave behind ①留下，忘記帶走 ②遺留 ‖ leave for 動身到 ‖ leave out 省去 ‖ ask for leave 請假 ‖ on leave 休假
用法 (1) leave 的過去分詞 left 常用作後置限定詞，表示「剩下的」：After the robbery there was nothing left for the man. 遭到搶劫之後，這個人身無一物。
(2) leave+ 受詞 + 受詞補足語，表示「使…處於…狀態，聽任，讓」：Leave the door open. 不要關門。

1096
□□□

left
[lɛft]

形 左邊的 **副** 向左，在左側
名 (the ~) 左邊

例句 The company is on the left side of the street.
／這家公司在馬路左邊。

1097
□□□

left
[lɛft]

〔 leave 的過去式、過去分詞〕

例句 If he left immediately, he'd catch the 7:30 train.
／如果他馬上出發，就能趕上 7 點 30 分的火車。

1098
□□□

leg
[lɛg]

名 (人或動物的) 腿；(傢俱的) 腳

例句 He crossed his legs.
／他兩腿交叉著。

1099 □□□	**legal** [ˈligl]	形 法律（上）的；合法的，法定的

例句 In many parts of America, it is legal to carry a gun.
／在美國很多地方，攜帶槍枝是合法的。

1100 □□□	**lemon** [ˈlɛmən]	名 檸檬（樹）；檸檬汁；檸檬綠

巧記 諧音：〔英〕lemon —音譯→〔漢〕檸檬
例句 I'd like a cup of tea with lemon.
／我要一杯檸檬茶。

Group 3

1101 □□□ 59	**lend** [lɛnd]	動 [及物]（lent, lent）借出，借給

例句 He lent his umbrella to me yesterday, so I didn't get wet.
／昨天他把他的傘借我，所以我沒淋濕。
辨析 borrow 表示「借進」，與 from 連用表示「從⋯借來」；lend 表示「借出」，與 to 連用表示「把某物借給⋯」。
　※ You'd better not lend him the books borrowed from the library. 你最好不要把從圖書館借來的書借給他。
反義 borrow 動 借，借用

1102 □□□	**length** [lɛŋθ]	名〔long 的名詞〕長，長度

例句 The length of the bridge is 200 meters.
／那座橋長 200 公尺。
片語 at length ①最終，最後 ②長時間地

1103 □□□	**less** [lɛs]	形 更少的；〔用於比較級〕少於 副 較少

例句 We have less trouble now than before.
／我們現在的麻煩比以前少了。
片語 even less 更不用說，更談不上 ‖ less than 不到，少於
辨析 little 的比較級

1104 □□□	**lesson** [ˈlɛsn̩]	名 課，功課；教訓

例句 This experience will be a good lesson to you.
／這個經驗對你將是很好的教訓。
片語 draw/learn a lesson from... 從⋯中吸取教訓 ‖ give lessons 教課，上課 ‖ give/teach sb. a lesson 給某人一個教訓

1105 let
[lɛt]

動 [及物] (let, let) 讓，允許

例句 Her father will not let her go to the dance.
／她爸爸不會讓她去跳舞的。

片語 let down ①使失望，辜負 ②把…放下來 ‖ let go 放開，釋放 ‖ let in 讓…
進來，放進 ‖ Let me see. 讓我想想。

辨異 Let us, Let's
Let us 和 Let's 的區別在於：前者包括說話對方在內；而後者不包括對方
在內。例如：
(a) Let us go, will you? 讓我們走，行嗎？
(b) Let's go, shall we? 我們走吧，好嗎？

1106 letter
[ˋlɛtɚ]

名 信，函；字母

例句 She folded the letter and put it in an envelope.
／她把信折起來放進信封裡。

1107 lettuce
[ˋlɛtɪs]

名 萵苣，生菜

例句 Get some lettuce and tomatoes so I can make a salad.
／買一些萵苣和番茄，我就能做沙拉。

1108 level
[ˋlɛvl̩]

名 水準（面），高度；程度

例句 Students at this level may have problems with basic grammar.
／這個程度的學生可能會有基本文法的問題。

片語 be on a level with 與…齊平

1109 library
[ˋlaɪˏbrɛrɪ]

名 圖書館，藏書室

例句 He owns a library of 1,000 volumes.
／他擁有一間藏有 1,000 冊圖書的藏書室。

1110 lick
[lɪk]

動 [及物] 名 舔，舔吃

例句 The cat cleaned its fur by licking it.
／那隻貓用舔的方法清理身上的毛。

1111 lid
[lɪd]

名 蓋，蓋子；眼瞼

例句 She took off the lid of the box. ／她打開盒蓋。

1112 ☐☐☐ **lie** [laɪ]　　動 [不及物] (lay, lain) 臥，躺，鋪放；在…位置

片語 lie down ①躺下 ②屈服 ‖ lie in 在於…

例句 Walter lay in the grass enjoying the sunshine.
／華特躺在草地上享受著陽光。

辨析 lay, lie
(1) lay 常作及物動詞用，意思是「放，擺，鋪」等。
(2) lie 常作不及物動詞用，意思是「躺，位於」等。

lay 鋪放　　lie 躺

1113 ☐☐☐ **lie** [laɪ]　　動 [不及物] (lied, lied) 說謊
名 謊話，謊言

例句 Don't believe her because she always lies.
／不要相信她，因為她總是說謊。

片語 tell a lie 撒謊

1114 ☐☐☐ **life** [laɪf]　　名 (pl.lives) 生命，生物；(個人的) 壽命；人生，生活

例句 There is no life on Mars. ／火星上沒有生命。

片語 all one's life 終身，一生 ‖ for life 一生，終生 ‖ live a...life 過著…的生活

復合 nightlife 名 夜生活

1115 ☐☐☐ **lift** [lɪft]　　動 [及物] 舉起，提升，搬起
名 電梯；(汽車等) 搭便車

例句 The box was so heavy that I couldn't lift it.
／這個箱子太重，我提不動。

片語 give sb. a lift 讓某人搭便車

1116 ☐☐☐ **light** [laɪt]　　名 光，光亮；電燈
形 光亮的，明亮的

例句 Turn off the lights when you leave. ／離開時把燈關掉。

1117 ☐☐☐ **light** [laɪt]　　形 淡 (色) 的；輕的 副 輕快地；淡地

巧記 圖解 light 的不同詞義：

燈 / 光亮 ─ 名 ─ light ─ 形 ─ 輕的 ⟷ 重的 / 亮的 ⟷ 暗的 / 淺的 ⟷ 深的

例句 Is the parcel light or heavy?
／ 這個包裹是輕還是重？

反義 heavy 形 重的；dark 形 暗的；深的

1118 ☐☐☐ **lightning**
[ˋlaɪtnɪŋ]

名 閃電

例句 A lightning flashed across the dark sky.
／黑暗的天空中有一道閃電劃過。

Group 4

1119 ☐☐☐ **like**
[laɪk]

介 像，跟⋯一樣

60

例句 I wish I could swim like a fish.
／我希望我能像魚一樣游泳。

1120 ☐☐☐ **like**
[laɪk]

動 [及物] 喜歡，喜愛
介 和⋯一樣

例句 I like tea better than coffee.
／我喜歡茶勝過咖啡。

辨析 like doing sth. 意為「喜歡做某事」，表示習慣性的動作；like to do sth. 意為「喜歡去做某事」，表示一次性或特指的某一具體動作。
※ I like visiting friends on Sundays and I like to visit Joan this Sunday. 我喜歡星期天拜訪朋友，這星期天我想去拜訪瓊。

辨析 ▲後接 -ing 形式或動詞不定式作受補
反義 dislike 動 [及物] 不喜歡，討厭

1121 ☐☐☐ **likely**
[ˋlaɪklɪ]

形 可能的，有希望的
副 可能

例句 Are you likely to be in London this year?
／你今年可能去倫敦嗎？

1122 ☐☐☐ **limit**
[ˋlɪmɪt]

名 限度，限制
動 [及物] 限制，限定

巧記 〔數學〕lim 極限 →〔英文〕limit 極限，限度

例句 What is the speed limit?
／車輛限速是多少？

片語 go beyond/over the limit 超過限度 ‖ limit sb. to (doing) sth. 限制某人（做）某事

1123 ☐☐☐ **line**
[laɪn]

名 線；排，行列，皺紋
動 [及物] 沿⋯排成行

例句 The trees lined the river bank.
／樹木沿著河岸排成一排。

片語 wait in line 排隊等候

1124 ☐☐☐ **link**
[lɪŋk]

動 [及物] 連接，聯繫
名 環節，聯繫

例句 The new tunnel links Britain to France.
／新的隧道把英、法兩國連接起來。

片語 link up ①把…連接起來 ②匯合，碰頭

1125 ☐☐☐ **lion**
[`laɪən]

名 獅子

例句 A young lion is playing in the grass.
／一隻幼獅正在草地上玩耍。

衍生 lioness 名 母獅子

1126 ☐☐☐ **lip**
[lɪp]

名 嘴唇，嘴唇周圍部分

例句 He kissed her on the lips.
／他親吻了她的嘴唇。

1127 ☐☐☐ **liquid**
[`lɪkwɪd]

名 液體
形 液體的，液態的

例句 The liquid was red. ／那液體是紅色的。

1128 ☐☐☐ **list**
[lɪst]

名 清單，目錄，名單
動 [及物] 把…列表；列舉

例句 My name is not listed in the telephone directory.
／我的名字沒有列在電話簿上。

片語 a list of... 一張…的清單

1129 ☐☐☐ **listen**
[`lɪsn]

動 [不及物] 聽

例句 I was listening, but heard nothing.
／我在聽，但什麼也沒聽見。

辨析 listen, hear
(1) listen 是「仔細傾聽」，不一定聽見，指聽的過程，可有進行時態，一般與介系詞 to 連用。
(2) hear 是「聽見」，不一定都是有意的，有時是偶然聽見，指聽的結果，通常不用進行時態。

1130 ☐☐☐ **liter**
[`litə]

名 〔容量單位〕公升

例句 There are three liters of water in the bucket.
／桶子裡有三公升水。

1131 little
☐☐☐
[ˈlɪtl̩]

形 副 小的（地）；少的（地）
代 少許，少量

例句 Hurry up. There is little time left.
／快一點，只剩一點時間了。
片語 a little 少許，一點點 ‖ little by little 一點一點地，逐漸地 ‖ not a little 非常，十分

1132 live
☐☐☐
[lɪv]

動 居住；活著；生活

片語 live by 靠…過活 ‖ live on 以…為主食，靠…生活 ‖ live through 經受住
例句 He lived by begging instead of on government welfare.
／他靠乞討過活而不是政府的救濟金。

1133 loaf
☐☐☐
[lof]

名 (pl.loaves) 一條或一塊（麵包）；閒逛

例句 She bought three loaves of bread. ／她買了三條麵包。

1134 local
☐☐☐
[ˈlokl̩]

形 當地的，地方的，本地的；局部的

例句 We have some local wine. ／我們有一些本地的葡萄酒。

1135 lock
☐☐☐
[lɑk]

名 鎖
動 [及物] 鎖上 動 [不及物] 鎖得上，上鎖

例句 Don't forget to lock the door when you go out.
／出門時別忘了鎖門。

1136 London
☐☐☐
[ˈlʌndən]

名 倫敦（英國首都）

例句 He has two brothers, both of whom live in London.
／他有兩個兄弟，都住在倫敦。

1137 lonely
☐☐☐
[ˈlonlɪ]

形 孤獨的，寂寞的

例句 I was lonely without her. ／沒有她，我感到很孤獨。

1138 long
☐☐☐
[lɔŋ]

形（長度、距離、時間）長的，長久的；有…長
副 好久

例句 I was standing there for a long time. ／我在那裡站了很久。
片語 all day/night long 整日／夜 ‖ as/so long as 只要… ‖ before long 很快，不久 ‖ long before 很久以前
反義 short 形 短的

GEPT
Elementary

Week 4

第四週

1139 ☐☐☐ **look**
[lʊk]

🔊 61

動 [不及物] 看；看上去像，貌似
動 [及物] 打量

片語 look after 照顧，看管 ‖ look around 從四周看 ‖ look at 看 ‖ look down on/upon 瞧不起某人 ‖ look for 尋找 ‖ look out 當心，注意 ‖ look through 瀏覽 ‖ look up ①仰視 ②查詢

例句 She looked at me and smiled.
／她看了看我並且笑了。

1140 ☐☐☐ **lose**
[luz]

動 [及物] (lost, lost) 失去；輸，被打敗

例句 He lost interest in music.
／他對音樂失去興趣了。

片語 lose one's job 失業 ‖ lose one's life 犧牲 ‖ lose one's way 迷路

1141 ☐☐☐ **loser**
[`luzɚ]

名 失主，損失者；失敗者，輸者

例句 The guy was a born loser.
／這傢伙天生是個失敗者。

反義 winner 名 獲勝者，贏家

1142 ☐☐☐ **loss**
[lɔs]

名 丟掉，喪失；損失；輸，失敗

例句 The loss of his job worries him.
／他為失去工作而感到焦慮。

片語 at a loss 茫然不知所措
辨析 lose 的名詞

1143 ☐☐☐ **lot**
[lɑt]

代 副 許多，大量
名 一塊地，場地

片語 a lot 很，非常，很多 ‖ a lot of (=lots of) 大量的，許多的〔▲修飾可數與不可數名詞皆可〕

例句 He earned a lot of money.
／他賺了很多錢。

1144 ☐☐☐ **loud**
[laʊd]

形 大聲的，吵鬧的
副 (談笑) 大聲地

例句 He has a loud voice.
／他的嗓門很大。

第四週

1145 love
[lʌv]

名 摯愛，鍾愛；心愛的人
動 [及物] 愛，深愛，熱愛；喜歡

例句 I love my job very much.
／我非常熱愛我的工作。

片語 be in love (with sb.) (與某人)戀愛，愛上(某人) ‖ fall in love (with sb.) 愛上(某人)

用法 love 後面既可跟動詞 -ing 形式也可以跟動詞不定式作受詞，但含義不同：love doing sth. 表示一般傾向性或一貫的行為(指經常性的動作)；love to do sth. 則表示特定或具體的某種行為(指一次性的動作)。

辨析 love, like, enjoy
(1) love「熱愛」(反義詞 hate)，指引起深厚的、強烈的感情，並有依附感。
(2) like「喜歡」(反義詞 dislike)，指不反感，但不引起強烈感情和迫切願望。
(3) enjoy「喜愛，享受…樂趣」，具有滿足感。

1146 lovely
[ˈlʌvlɪ]

形 動人的，可愛的；令人愉快的

例句 The calm sea is a lovely sight.
／平靜的海面景色宜人。

1147 lover
[ˈlʌvɚ]

名 愛好者；情人

例句 We are all animal lovers.
／我們都是動物愛好者。

1148 low
[lo]

形 矮的；(價格等)低廉的，(數量、程度等)少的，小的

例句 This house has a low ceiling.
／這房屋的天花板很低。

反義 high 形 高的

1149 lucky
[ˈlʌkɪ]

形 幸運的，僥倖的

例句 I was lucky enough to get a job.
／我幸運地得到了一份工作。

1150 lunch
[lʌntʃ]

名 午餐，午飯

片語 be at lunch 在吃午飯 ‖ have lunch 吃午飯
例句 He usually has lunch at the little restaurant.
／他通常在那家小餐廳吃午餐。

1151 machine [məˋʃin]
名 機器

例句 The washing machine has gone wrong.
／洗衣機壞了。

1152 mad [mæd]
形 瘋狂的；著迷的；氣憤的

片語 be mad at sb. 生某人的氣 ‖ be mad with joy 欣喜若狂 ‖ go mad 瘋了
例句 Linda's teacher was so mad at her because she made lots of mistakes in the test.
／琳達的老師對她這麼氣，是因為她在考試中犯了許多錯誤。

1153 magazine [͵mægəˋzin]
名 雜誌，期刊

例句 I take this magazine every month.
／我每個月都買這本雜誌。

1154 magic [ˋmædʒɪk]
名 魔術；魔力
形 魔術的；有魔力的

例句 His words had a magic effect on us.
／他的話對我們有種魔力般的影響。

1155 magician [məˋdʒɪʃən]
名 魔術師

例句 Liu Qian is a famous magician.
／劉謙是個著名的魔術師。

1156 mail [mel]
名 郵件，信件，郵包
動 [及物] 郵寄

例句 He mailed the parcel last Monday.
／他上星期一寄出這個包裹。
片語 by mail 通過郵寄方式

1157 □□□

62

mailman
[ˋmel͵mæn]

名〔美〕郵差

例句 The mailman always comes at 9 o'clock.
／郵差總是九點鐘來。

同義 postman n.〔英〕郵遞員

1158 □□□

main
[men]

形 主要的；首要的

例句 What is the main purpose of your visit?
／ 你來拜訪的主要目的是什麼？

1159 □□□

maintain
[menˋten]

動 [及物] 維持，保持；維修，保養

例句 We should maintain our friendly relations with other teams.
／我們應該要和其他隊伍保持友好關係。

1160 □□□

major
[ˋmedʒɚ]

形〔無比較級〕較大的；主要的

例句 Tom played a major part in the improvement of teaching.
／湯姆把主要的部分擺在改進教學。

1161 □□□

major
[ˋmedʒɚ]

名 主修科目，專業；某專業的學生；少校

例句 He is an English major.
／他是主修英語的學生。

1162 □□□

major
[ˋmedʒɚ]

動 [不及物] 主修，專研

片語 major in 主修
例句 I want to major in physics at college.
／我想要在大學主修物理。

1163 □□□

make
[mek]

動 [及物] (made, made) 製造，製作；使

例句 If you see the cartoon film, it will make you laugh.
／如果你看這部卡通，它將使你大笑。

用法 在 make, let, have, see, watch, notice, hear, feel 等動詞後面可接不帶 to 的動詞不定式作受詞補語，表示動作的全過程，但在被動語態中應帶 to。

辨析 be made of, be made from, be made into
　(1) be made of「由…製成」，後接材料，但是不改變材料的性質。
　(2) be made from「由…製成」，後接材料，改變了材料的性質。
　(3) be made into「製成…」，後接成品。

  from   of

1164 □□□

male
[mel]

形 男 (性) 的
名 男子，雄性動植物

巧記 sex(性別) ⎡male (男)〔略作 M〕
　　　　　　　　⎣female (女)〔略作 F〕

例句 He is a member of the male chorus.
／他是男聲合唱團中的一員。

1165 □□□

mall
[mɔl]

名 購物中心

例句 I bought some clothes at the mall.
／我在購物中心買了一些衣服。

1166 □□□

man
[mæn]

名 (pl.men) 男人；人類

例句 I saw a tall man with dark hair.
／我看見一個黑頭髮的高個男子。

1167 □□□

manager
[`mænɪdʒɚ]

名 經理，管理人員

例句 When the manager went on holiday, his assistant took his place for a short while.
／當經理休假時，他的助理暫代其職。

1168 □□□

Mandarin
[`mændərɪn]

名 國語，華語；高官；柑橘

例句 The foreigner can speak good Mandarin.
／這老外國語說得很好。

1169 □□□

mango
[`mæŋgo]

名 芒果 (樹)

例句 Do you like eating mango? ／你喜歡吃芒果嗎？
例句 Taiwan mangos are my favorite fruit. ／台灣芒果是我的最愛。

第四週

1170 ☐☐☐
manner
[`mænɚ]
名 (常 sing.) 方法；(sing.) 態度；(pl.) 禮貌

例句 What is the best manner of doing it?
／做這件事的最佳方法是什麼？
片語 in a...manner 用…方式 ‖ table manners 用餐禮儀

1171 ☐☐☐
many
[`mɛnɪ]
形 (more, most) 許多的
代 許多

例句 Does the singer have many fans?
／ 那個歌手有很多歌迷嗎？
片語 a great/good many 許許多多 ‖ how many 多少 ‖ many a 不止一個，一個又一個的 ‖ so many ①這麼多的 ②同樣多的

1172 ☐☐☐
map
[mæp]
名 圖，地圖

例句 There was a map on the wall.
／牆上有幅地圖。

1173 ☐☐☐
March
[mɑrtʃ]
名 三月 (=Mar.)

例句 The date has been put back to March.
／約會已延到三月。

1174 ☐☐☐
mark
[mɑrk]
名 痕跡；記號，標記；分數
動 [及物] 做記號；打分數

例句 The exit sign was marked with an arrow.
／出口符號用箭頭做記號。

1175 ☐☐☐
marker
[`mɑrkɚ]
名 書籤；標誌；水彩筆，麥克筆

例句 Draw your child's outline with a heavy black marker.
／用深黑色的麥克筆畫出你孩子的輪廓。

Ⓖroup 3

1176 ☐☐☐
market
[`mɑrkɪt]
名 市場，市集

track **63**

例句 My father went to the market to buy some vegetables.
／我爸爸到市場買了一些蔬菜。
片語 bring...to market 把…推上市 ‖ come into the market 上市 ‖ on the market (市場上) 有售，能買到

1177
☐☐☐

marriage
[ˈmærɪdʒ]

名 結婚；婚姻

例句 They have a very happy marriage.
／他們有一個非常美滿的婚姻。

1178
☐☐☐

married
[ˈmærɪd]

形 已婚的，婚姻的；結婚的，夫婦的

例句 He is a married man.
／他是已婚男士。

1179
☐☐☐

marry
[ˈmærɪ]

動 [及物] 與…結婚，嫁，娶；把…嫁出
動 [不及物] 結婚

例句 She wants to marry her daughter to a rich man.
／她想把女兒嫁給有錢人。

片語 be married to〔表狀態〕與…結婚 ‖ get married to〔表動作〕與…結婚

用法 在表示「和某人結婚」時，常用 be/get married to sb. 結構，但 be married to sb. 可以和表示一段時間的副詞連用，get married to sb. 則不能。

注意 「與…結婚」為 marry sb. (NOT marry with sb.)

1180
☐☐☐

marvelous
[ˈmɑrvələs]

形 驚人的，不可思議的，非凡的

例句 I had a marvelous holiday.
／我過了一個非凡的假期。

1181
☐☐☐

mask
[mæsk]

名 面具，面罩，口罩；假面具；(常 sing.) 偽裝

例句 The thieves were wearing masks.
／那些小偷都戴著面具。

片語 under the mask of... 在…掩蓋下

1182
☐☐☐

mass
[mæs]

名 (聚成一體的) 塊，堆；眾多，大量；
(the -es) 群眾，民眾

巧記 圖解 mass 的一詞多義：

mass
團，塊，堆 ──→ 眾多，大量 ──→ the masses 群眾

片語 a mass of 眾多，大量 ‖ in the mass 總體上，大致上

例句 She has a mass of things to do.
／她有一大堆事要做。

1183 □□□
master
[`mæstɚ]
名 主人，雇主；大師；(M-) 碩士

例句 As a master he gave us a warm welcome at his home.
／作為主人，他在家裡給我們熱情的歡迎。
片語 be one's own master 自己做主
同義 host 名 主人

1184 □□□
mat
[mæt]
名 草蓆，墊子

例句 Wipe your shoes on the mat.
／在墊子上擦乾淨你的鞋子。

1185 □□□
match
[mætʃ]
名 火柴；比賽；對手，敵手
動 [及物] 是…的對手 動 相配；相似

例句 I saw the boxing match on television.
／我在電視上看到了那場拳擊賽。
片語 have a match 舉行一場比賽
用法 match 作「和…匹配，是…的對手，與…相配」之義時，是及物動詞，即 match sb./sth.。
辨析 game, match
(1) game〔美〕，指「比賽」，也可用以指比賽中的局、場次。
(2) match〔英〕，指 tennis（網球），boxing（拳擊）等的「比賽」。

1186 □□□
material
[mə`tɪrɪəl]
名 材料，原料；素材；(衣服的) 布料

例句 Plastic is a widely-used material.
／塑膠是一種廣泛使用的原料。

1187 □□□
math
[mæθ]
名 〔口〕數學 (=mathematics)

例句 Math is my favorite subject.
／數學是我最喜歡的科目。

1188 □□□
matter
[`mætɚ]
名 事情；問題
動 [不及物] 要緊；有關係

片語 It doesn't matter. 沒關係。‖ no matter (who, what, when, etc.) 無論，不管（誰，什麼，什麼時候等）
例句 No matter how hard it was, he would never give up.
／不管多困難，他決不放棄。

1189 ☐☐☐ **maximum**
[ˋmæksəməm]

图 頂點，最大量
彤〔作限定詞〕最大值的

巧記
數學
┌ max 最大值 →〔英〕maximum 图 最大值
└ min 最小值 →〔英〕minimum 图 最小值

▲上兩詞的複數是變 um 為 a 或直接加 s。

例句 Lucy can borrow a maximum of ten books from the library.
／露西最多可以從圖書館借 10 本書。

1190 ☐☐☐ **may**
[me]

勔 或許，也許；可以

例句 May I go to see a movie?
／ 我可以去看電影嗎？

用法 「may...but」表示「可以…但是…」的意思。

1191 ☐☐☐ **May**
[me]

图 五月

例句 They made an appointment for the second day of May.
／他們在 5 月 2 號有個約會。

1192 ☐☐☐ **maybe**
[ˋmebɪ]

副 或許，大概

例句 Maybe you have put the book in your desk.
／也許你把書放在書桌裡了。

She | may | be | angry.

Maybe | she is angry.

用法 maybe 是副詞，常用在句子開頭。意思是「也許、可能」。表示一種可能性。may be 是由情態動詞 may，和動詞原形 be 所組成的述語形式，和主詞形成系表結構，意思是「也許是、可能是」。

1193 ☐☐☐ **me**
[mi]

代〔I 的受格〕我

例句 Please let me try once more. ／請讓我再試一次。

Group 4

1194 ☐☐☐ **meal**
[mil]

图 進餐，一餐

64

例句 He had only two meals a day.
／他一天只吃兩餐。

片語 at meals 在用餐 ‖ have a good meal 一頓豐盛的飯

1195 ☐☐☐
mean
[min]

動 [及物] (meant, meant) 表示…的意思；故意

例句 The sign means that the road is blocked.
／這個標誌表示此路不通。

1196 ☐☐☐
meaning
[`minɪŋ]

名 意思，含義

例句 He has grasped my meaning.
／他領會到我的意思了。

衍生 meaningful 形 有意義的；淺顯易懂的

1197 ☐☐☐
means
[minz]

名〔單同複〕方法，手段，工具

例句 Driving is the quickest means of getting there.
／開車是去那裡最快的方法。

片語 by all means 當然可以，一定 ‖ by no means 絕不 ‖ by this means (=in this way) 透過這種方式

用法 (1) by no means 用在句首，主句倒裝。
(2) means 單複數相同，若作主詞，一定看清楚數。

1198 ☐☐☐
measure
[`mɛʒɚ]

名 措施，方法；計量單位
動 [及物] 丈量，測量

例句 She measured her daughter for a new dress.
／她為女兒量身做新衣服。

片語 beyond measure 無可估計，極度，過分 ‖ take measures to do... 採取措施…

1199 ☐☐☐
meat
[mit]

名 肉類，食用肉

例句 I gave up eating meat a few months ago.
／我幾個月前就不吃肉了。

辨析 ▲不包括魚肉、鳥肉

1200 ☐☐☐
mechanic
[mə`kænɪk]

名 技工，修理工

巧記〔熟〕machine 機械 →〔根〕mechan 機械 →〔生〕mechanic 技工，機修工

例句 The mechanic repaired my car.
／這個修理工修好了我的車。

1201 medicine
[`mɛdəsn̩]
名（內服）藥；醫學

例句 A good medicine tastes bitter.
／〔諺〕良藥苦口。
片語 take medicine 吃藥

1202 medium
[`midɪəm]
名 中間；媒體
形（肉）中等熟度的；中等的，適中的

例句 He is of medium height.
／他的身高中等。
片語 by/through the medium of... 以…為媒介，通過…

1203 meet
[mit]
動 [及物](met, met) 碰面；遇見

例句 I met your sister on the way.
／我在路上遇見了你妹妹。

1204 meeting
[`mitɪŋ]
名 集會，會議

片語 have/attend a meeting 開會 ‖ hold a meeting 召開會議
例句 We're having a meeting next week to discuss the matter.
／我們下周將開會討論此事。

1205 melon
[`mɛlən]
名 瓜，甜瓜，西瓜

例句 This kind of melon is very sweet.
／這種瓜很甜。

1206 member
[`mɛmbɚ]
名 成員，會員

例句 I am a member of the basketball team.
／我是籃球隊的一員。

1207 memory
[`mɛmərɪ]
名 記憶（力）；記憶體

片語 in memory of... 為紀念…
例句 This library was built in memory of the scientist.
／這個圖書館是為了紀念那位科學家而建的。

1208 □□□ **menu**
['mɛnju]

图（餐廳的）菜單；（電腦上的）功能表

例句 You can choose any food listed on the menu.
／你可以挑選菜單上列的任何食物。

1209 □□□ **message**
['mɛsɪdʒ]

图（書面或口頭的）消息；（手機或電子郵件）訊息

例句 I'll send my son to you with my message.
／我會讓我兒子把我的消息帶給你。

片語 leave a message 留言 ‖ send messages 傳送簡訊 ‖ take a message for sb. 傳訊息給某人

1210 □□□ **metal**
['mɛtl]

图 金屬

例句 This tool can cut metals like copper and silver.
／這種工具可以切開像銅和銀之類的金屬。

辨析 作物質名詞用

1211 □□□ **meter**
['mitɚ]

图 公尺 (=m)；計量器，儀表

巧記 諧音：〔英〕meter 一音譯→〔漢〕米

例句 The river is 10 meters across.
／這條河寬 10 公尺。

1212 □□□ **method**
['mɛθəd]

图 方法，方式；（思考、行為的）條理

例句 He invented a new method of teaching English.
／他發明了一種新的英語教學方法。

M

Lesson 2

1213
□□□

microwave
[`maɪkrəˌwev]

名 微波；微波爐

🔊65

例句 Mum has just won a microwave cooker.
　　／媽媽剛剛贏得一台微波爐。

1214
□□□

middle
[`mɪdl̩]

形 中間的；中等的
名 中間，中央

片語 in the middle of... 在…的中間 ‖ middle school 中學
例句 Joe is standing in the middle of the room.
　　／喬正站在房間中間。
辨析 middle, center
　　(1) middle 指長形物體、道路、一段時間的「中間」。
　　(2) center 指圓形、球形或市區等的「中心」。

1215
□□□

midnight
[`mɪdˌnaɪt]

名 午夜，半夜

片語 at midnight 在午夜
例句 At midnight you will hear the clock strike twelve.
　　／你可能會發現火車裡有點冷。

1216
□□□

might
[maɪt]

動 助 或許，可能

例句 You might find it is a little cold in the train.
　　／你也許會發現在火車裡有點兒冷。
用法 might 表示可能性，有「或許，可能」的意思，表示語氣比 may 更加不
　　肯定。在請求對方許可時，可用「Might I...」代替「May I...」，表示語
　　氣更加委婉，顯得更有禮貌。

1217
□□□

mile
[maɪl]

名 英哩

例句 My home is about a mile away from here.
　　／我家距離這裡大約一英哩。

1218
□□□

military
[`mɪləˌtɛrɪ]

形 軍事的，軍用的
名 (the ～) 軍隊，武裝力量

例句 My friend is in the military. ／我朋友在軍隊裡。

1219
□□□

milk
[mɪlk]

名 乳，牛奶

例句 It is no use crying over spilt milk.
　　／〔諺〕牛奶翻倒哭也沒用／覆水難收。

第四週

1220 □□□ **million** [ˋmɪljən]
代 百萬
名 百萬元；(pl.) 無數

例句 The population of that city is about eight million.
／那個城市的人口約有八百萬。

片語 millions of 數百萬

1221 □□□ **mind** [maɪnd]
名 想法；精神；頭腦
動 [及物] 在乎，介意

例句 Do you mind me smoking?
／你介意我抽煙嗎？

用法 mind 作「介意」講時，後面可接動詞 -ing 形式、從句，不能接動詞不定式。

片語 keep in mind 記在心裡 ‖ make up one's mind 下定決心 ‖ never mind 沒關係

1222 □□□ **mine** [maɪn]
代〔I 的代名詞〕我的

例句 He is an old friend of mine.
／他是我的一位老朋友。

1223 □□□ **minor** [ˋmaɪnə]
形 較小的，較少的；年幼的

例句 He'll not be content with a minor share of profit.
／他不會滿足於較少的利潤分紅。

1224 □□□ **minor** [ˋmaɪnə]
名 未成年人；輔修科目

例句 This film contains material unsuitable for minors.
／這部電影有些內容不適合未成年人觀看。

1225 □□□ **minor** [ˋmaɪnə]
動（大學裡）輔修（某課程）

例句 He majored in sociology and minored in political science.
／他主修社會學，輔修政治學。

1226 □□□ **minus** [ˋmaɪnəs]
介 減（去）
名 負數；減號

例句 Now the temperature is minus five degrees.
／現在氣溫是零下五度。

1227 ☐☐☐
minute
[ˋmɪnɪt]
图 分鐘;一會兒

片語 in a minute 立刻 ‖ just a minute 等一下
例句 You go on and I'll catch up with you in a minute.
╱你先走,我馬上就趕上來。

1228 ☐☐☐
mirror
[ˋmɪrɚ]
图 鏡子

例句 He looked at himself in the mirror.
╱他照了照鏡子。
片語 look in/into the mirror 照鏡子

1229 ☐☐☐
Miss
[mɪs]
图 小姐

例句 Miss Green is my English teacher.
╱格林小姐是我的英文老師。

1230 ☐☐☐
miss
[mɪs]
動 [及物] 失去,錯過;想念,懷念

巧記 圖解 miss 的一詞多義:

miss her parents
想念父母

miss the school bus
錯過校車

Miss Rose
羅絲小姐

例句 I ran fast but missed the bus.
╱我跑得很快,但還是錯過了公共汽車。
辨析 miss, lose(丟失)
miss 意為「發現丟失,覺得不在」;lose 意為「丟失,失」。在本質上,miss 是一種主觀感覺,而 lose 是一種客觀結果。miss 作「懷念」講,也是「發覺…不在,因…不在而覺得寂寞」的引申。

1231 ☐☐☐
missing
[ˋmɪsɪŋ]
形 失蹤的,找不到的;缺少的,不見的

例句 The last page of the diary was missing.
╱日記的最後一頁不見了。

1232 ☐☐☐
mistake
[mɪˋstek]

🎵66

名 錯誤，過失
動 [及物] (mistook, mistaken) 弄錯

片語 by mistake 錯誤地 ‖ make a mistake 犯錯誤
例句 I made three mistakes in my English examination.
／我在英語考試中犯了三個錯誤。

1233 ☐☐☐
mix
[mɪks]

動 (使) 混合
動 [及物] 使結合 名 混合 (體)

片語 mix...with... 把…和…混合 ‖ mix up ①攪和 ②混淆，搞混
例句 The teacher always mixes me up with another student.
／老師總是把我和另一個學生搞混。

1234 ☐☐☐
model
[ˋmɑdl]

名 模型；模特兒；樣式
形 模範的

例句 She is a good model for painters.
／她是一個很好的繪畫模特兒。

1235 ☐☐☐
modern
[ˋmɑdɚn]

形 現代的；現代化的，新式的

例句 There are a lot of modern buildings in our city.
／我們都市裡有許多現代化建築。

1236 ☐☐☐
moment
[ˋmomənt]

名 片刻，瞬間；時刻

例句 What's the most exciting moment in your life?
／你一生中最激動的時刻是什麼？
片語 a moment ago 剛剛，剛才 ‖ at the moment 此刻，目前 ‖ in a moment 很快，立刻 ‖ just a moment 等一下 ‖ wait (for) a moment 等一下

1237 ☐☐☐
Monday
[ˋmʌnde]

名 星期一 (=Mon.)

例句 The museum is open to the public except on Monday.
／這個博物館除了星期一外都對外開放。

1238 ☐☐☐
money
[ˋmʌnɪ]

名 金錢，貨幣；財產，財富

例句 He lost his money at last.
／他最後把錢輸掉了。
片語 make/earn money 賺錢 ‖ pocket money 零用錢 ‖ raise money 籌款／募捐

1239 □□□
monkey
[ˋmʌŋkɪ]

名 猴子；淘氣鬼，頑童

例句 My monkey doesn't bite.
／我的猴子不會咬人。

1240 □□□
monster
[ˋmɑnstɚ]

名 巨獸，龐然大物；怪獸，妖怪

例句 The moving van is a monster of a truck.
／這輛傢俱搬運車是卡車中的巨獸。

1241 □□□
month
[mʌnθ]

名 月，月份

例句 My exams start at the end of the month.
／我月底開始考試。

片語 by the month 按月

1242 □□□
monthly
[ˋmʌnθlɪ]

形 副 每月的（地），每月一次的（地）
名 月刊

例句 They meet monthly to discuss progress.
／他們每個月碰一次面討論進展。

1243 □□□
moon
[mun]

名 (the ～) 月球，月亮；衛星

例句 We usually eat moon cakes on Mid-Autumn Festival.
／我們通常會在中秋節吃月餅。

片語 cry for the moon 不切實際的願望 ‖ promise sb. a moon 向某人承諾做不到的事

1244 □□□
mop
[mɑp]

名 拖把
動 拖地；擦，拭

例句 We always clean the floor with a mop.
／我們總是用拖把清潔地板。

片語 mop up 用拖把擦

1245 □□□
more
[mor]

形 (much 或 many 的比較級) 更多的
副 (much 的比較級) 更

例句 I've some more questions to ask you.
／我有更多的問題要問你。

片語 more and more 越來越多 ‖ more than 多於，比…更 ‖ no more (=not any more) 不再 ‖ no more than 不過，只有 ‖ not more than 至多，不超過 ‖ what's more 而且

辨析 no more than, not more than

(1) no more than 後接基數詞相當於 only，意為「僅僅，只有」。

(2) not more than 後跟基數詞，相當於 at most，意為「至多，不超過」，含有「至多或許還會少於此數目」之義。

※ He worked no more than a week, so he could get not more than 5,000 dollars. 他只做了一個星期，因此他最多能得到 5,000 元。

1246 □□□

morning
[ˈmɔrnɪŋ]

名 早晨，上午

例句 I'll see you tomorrow morning.
／我明天早上會來看你。

片語 at dawn (在黎明) → in the morning (在早晨) → at noon (在中午) → in the afternoon (在下午) → at dusk (在傍晚) → in the evening (晚上) → at night (在夜裡) → at midnight (在半夜)

1247 □□□

mosquito
[məsˈkito]

名 蚊子

例句 I was bitten by a mosquito.
／我被蚊子叮了。

1248 □□□

most
[most]

形 (much 或 many 的最高級) 最多的；大多數
副 (much 的最高級) 最　**代** 大部分

例句 This is the most I can do.
／這是我所能做的最大限度／我已經盡力了。

片語 at (the) most 至多，大不了

用法
Most of ＋ ┌ 單數名詞→接單數述語動詞
　　　　　└ 複數名詞→接複數述語動詞

(a) Most of the apples were rotten.
大部分的蘋果是爛的。〔主述用複數〕

(b) Most of the apple was eaten by a rat.
這蘋果的大半被老鼠吃掉了。〔主述用單數〕

 are

Most of the apples

 is

Most of the apple

1249 □□□

mother
[ˈmʌðə-]

名 母親，媽媽 (=mommy=mom=momma=mamma)

例句 I, along with my mother, am going to go shopping.
／我和媽媽兩人準備去購物。

1250 □□□ **Mother's Day** [ˋmʌðɚˌde] 名 母親節

例句 The second Sunday of May is Mother's Day.
／五月的第二個星期天是母親節。

Group 3

1251 □□□ **motion** [ˋmoʃən] 名（物體的）運動；動作 動（向…）打手勢，示意

67

例句 He motioned to her to come nearer.
／他招手示意她靠近一些。

片語 in motion 運動中 ‖ motion picture 電影

1252 □□□ **motorcycle** [ˋmotɚˌsaɪkl] 名〔美〕摩托車

例句 She can ride a motorcycle, to say nothing of a bicycle.
／她會騎摩托車，更別說是腳踏車了。

同義 motorbike 名〔英〕摩托車

1253 □□□ **mountain** [ˋmaʊntn] 名 山，山嶽；(pl.) 山脈；大堆

例句 The mountains were covered with snow.
／這座山被雪覆蓋了。

1254 □□□ **mouse** [maʊs] 名 (pl.mice) 老鼠；(pl. -s)（電腦）滑鼠

例句 Mickey Mouse is very popular with the children.
／米老鼠很受孩子們的歡迎。

1255 □□□ **mouth** [maʊθ] 名 (pl.mouths) 嘴，口，口腔

例句 Don't speak with your mouth full.
／滿嘴食物時不要說話。

片語 from mouth to mouth 口口相傳 ‖ keep one's mouth shut 緘口不言

1256 □□□ **move** [muv] 動（使）移動；搬家
動 [及物] 打動

例句 The speech moved them to tears.
／這場演說讓他們感動落淚。

片語 move about/around 到處走動 ‖ move away 離開，搬走 ‖ move in 遷入
‖ move on 繼續向前移動

第四週

1257 ☐☐☐ **movement** [ˈmuvmənt]　名 活動，移動，動作，遷移

例句 He stood there without movement.
／他一動不動地站在那裡。

1258 ☐☐☐ **movie** [ˈmuvɪ]　名〔美〕電影；(the -s) 電影院

巧記 movie 源於 moving picture〔活動的圖畫→〕電影
例句 Let's go to see a movie!
／我們去看電影吧！
片語 go to the movies 去看電影
同義 film 名〔英〕電影

1259 ☐☐☐ **Mr.** [ˈmɪstɚ]　名 先生〔▲用於姓名或職稱前 =Mr〕

例句 Mr. Parker walked at a quick pace, so I couldn't keep pace with him.
／派克先生走得很快，所以我跟不上他。

1260 ☐☐☐ **Mrs.** [ˈmɪsɪz]　名 夫人〔▲用於已婚女子的夫姓前 =Mrs〕

例句 Mrs. Martin invited three students to have dinner at home.
／馬丁太太邀請了三位學生到她家吃飯。
※ Mr. A misses Mrs. B, but I miss Miss C.A 先生想念 B 夫人，而我想念 C 小姐。(miss 動 想念)

1261 ☐☐☐ **MRT** [ˌɛmˈɑr ti]　名 捷運，地鐵

例句 You'd better take the MRT to the station.
／你最好搭捷運去車站。

1262 ☐☐☐ **Ms.** [mɪz]　名 女士〔▲用在婚姻狀況不明的女子姓名前，=Ms〕

例句 Ms. Smith has made Switzerland her home.
／史密斯女士的家在瑞士。

1263 ☐☐☐ **MTV** [ˈɛmˈtiˈvi]　名 包廂式視聽中心，音樂電視台

例句 Do you want to go to the MTV center?
／你想去 MTV 中心嗎？

1264 much [mʌtʃ]

副 非常，很
形 代 許多 (的)，大量 (的)

例句 The students were much too tired after they finished too much homework.
／做完這麼多家庭作業後，學生們太疲倦了。

辨析 too much, much too
(1) too much 意為「太多」，可用作名詞短語，也可用作形容詞短語，修飾不可數名詞，或者用作副詞短語，修飾不及物動詞。
(2) much too 意為「太，非常」，用作副詞短語，修飾形容詞、副詞，但不可修飾動詞。

1265 mud [mʌd]

名 泥，泥漿

例句 The car was stuck in the mud.
／那輛車陷在泥中。

1266 museum [mjuˋzɪəm]

名 博物館，博物院

巧記 Muse (「繆斯」女神) +um (表示地點)；原是「繆斯」女神的廟宇
例句 The museum is a long way from here.
／博物館離這裡很遠。

1267 music [ˋmjuzɪk]

名 音樂，樂曲；樂譜

例句 I often listen to music when I'm in the car.
／我在車上經常聽音樂。

1268 musician [mjuˋzɪʃən]

名 音樂家，樂師，作曲家

例句 Some famous musicians have little or no sight.
／有些知名的音樂家視力很差或失明。

1269 must [mʌst]

動 助 必須；〔表示推測〕很可能，一定會

例句 You must be tired after your long journey.
／經過這麼長的旅程你一定很累。

用法 (1) mustn't 表示「不准許，一定不要」。
(2) must 提問的句子，否定回答用 needn't。
(3) must 表示推測，只用於肯定句，否定句用 can't 或 couldn't。

第四週

辨析 1 圖解 have to 與 must：

have to 不得不

I have to study hard.
我不得不努力學習

must 必須

I must study hard.
我必須努力學習

辨析 2 can, may, must

(1) can 表猜測時，多用於疑問句、否定句，肯定句中表示「有時會」，can't 表示「不可能」。

(2) may 用於肯定句、否定句，表示不太有把握的猜測，may not 表示「可能不」。

(3) must 只用於肯定句，表示很有把握的猜測，must not 表示「強令禁止」。

Group 4

1270
☐☐☐

my
[maɪ]

代〔I 的形容詞性物主代詞〕我的

例句 You've spelt my name wrong.
／你把我的名字拼錯了。

1271
☐☐☐

myself
[maɪˋsɛlf]

代〔反身代名詞〕我自己；〔表示強調〕我自己

例句 I'm going to get myself a new suit.
／我要幫自己買一套新衣服。

1272
☐☐☐

nail
[nel]

名 釘子；指甲
動〔及物〕釘，將…釘牢

例句 He hammered a nail into the wall and hung a picture on it.
／他將釘子釘在牆上，並掛上一幅畫。

片語 drive/knock in a nail 把釘子敲進去 ‖ finger nails 指甲

1273
☐☐☐

name
[nem]

名 名字，姓名；名聲
動〔及物〕取名；提名

例句 Can you name the following things in English?
／ 你能用英語說出這些東西的名稱嗎？

片語 be named after... 根據…命名 ‖ call sb.'s name 謾罵某人 ‖ in the name of... 以…的名義

1274
□□□
napkin
[`næpkɪn]

名 餐巾

例句 She handed him a napkin.
／她遞給他一條餐巾。

1275
□□□
narrow
[`næro]

形 窄的，狹窄的；心胸狹窄的

例句 They all went up some narrow steps into a large room.
／他們都走上幾個狹窄的臺階，進入一個大房間。

片語 in a narrow sense 在狹義上

反義 broad 形 寬的，闊的；wide 形 寬的

1276
□□□
nation
[`neʃən]

名 民族；國家；〔集體用法〕國民

例句 The Chinese nation is brave and hardworking.
／中華民族是勇敢勤勞的。

片語 the United Nations 聯合國

1277
□□□
national
[`næʃənḷ]

形 國家的；民族的；國際的

例句 This is the national dress of that country.
／這是那個國家的民族服裝。

片語 National Day 國慶日 ‖ national flag 國旗

1278
□□□
natural
[`nætʃərəl]

形 自然的，天然的；天生的

例句 It is natural that we should strive to improve our standard of living, but not at any cost.
／我們自然要努力提高生活水準，但不能不惜任何代價。

用法 It is natural 之後的 that 從句中，述語動詞須用「(should+) 動詞原形」。

1279
□□□
nature
[`netʃɚ]

名 大自然；本性，天性

片語 by nature 生性 ‖ in nature 本質上

例句 That man is proud by nature.
／那個人本性驕傲。

1280 naughty
[`nɔtɪ]
形 頑皮的，淘氣的

例句 He is a naughty boy.
／他是個頑皮的男孩。

1281 near
[nɪr]
介 靠近，在…附近　形 副 接近的
動 [及物] 靠近

例句 My office is quite near. ／我的辦公室就在這附近。

用法 nearby（附近的）既可作前置限定詞，又可作後置限定詞，而 near by 只能作後置限定詞 :a nearby hotel ≒ a hotel nearby/near by 附近的旅館。

1282 nearly
[`nɪrlɪ]
副 將近，幾乎

例句 She was nearly as tall as he was.
／她幾乎和他一樣高。

用法 nearly 一般用來修飾表示肯定意思的詞，不能與 never, nobody, none, nothing, nowhere, no 等否定意義的詞連用。

1283 necessary
[`nɛsəˌsɛrɪ]
形 必須的，必要的

例句 It is necessary that he should come here every Sunday.
／他必須每個星期日都到這裡來。

用法 It's necessary that... 從句中述語用「(should+) 動詞原形」形式。

1284 neck
[nɛk]
名 (頭) 頸，脖子；頸圈；物體的頸狀部分

例句 He had a sharp pain in the neck.
／他的頸部劇痛。

片語 break one's neck ①折斷頸骨 ②盡最大努力，用最快速度 ‖ neck and neck 並駕齊驅，不分上下

1285 necklace
[`nɛklɪs]
名 項鍊

例句 She lost her necklace.
／她把項鍊弄丟了。

1286 need
[nid]
動 需要　動 助 必須〔▲無時態和人稱變化〕
名 需要

例句 This job needs skills and experience.
／這份工作需要技術和經驗。

片語 be in need of 需要 ‖ fill one's need 滿足需要

1287 □□□ **needle**
[`nidl]

图 針，縫針；注射針
働 [及物]（用話）刺激，激怒

例句 She is threading a needle.
／她正在穿針線。

片語 as sharp as a needle 非常機敏 ‖ look for a needle in a haystack 大海撈針

1288 □□□ **negative**
[`nɛɡətɪv]

形 否定的；負面的，消極的
图 否定，拒絕

例句 He gave a negative answer.
／他給了一個否定的回答。

1289
☐☐☐

neighbor
[ˋnebɚ]

🄐 鄰居；鄰國

🄑 The neighbors all admire the beauty of the Smiths' garden.
／鄰居們都羨慕史密斯家花園的美麗。

1290
☐☐☐

neither
[ˋniðɚ]

🄒 既不⋯也不⋯，任何一個⋯都不⋯

🄑 Neither he nor I am well-educated.
／他和我都沒受過良好的教育。

🄓 (1) neither...nor 連接並列分句且放在句首時，都要用倒裝：Neither is he clever, nor does he work hard. 他既不聰明也不努力。
(2) 若前面有一否定句，用「neither/nor+ 倒裝」，表示「也不⋯」；若前面有一肯定句，則用「so+ 倒裝」表示「也⋯」。
　(a) He can't speak French, neither/nor can I. 他不會講法語，我也不會。
　(b) He is a teacher, so am I. 他是老師，我也是。
(3) 連接兩個主詞時，neither...nor 的述語形式遵循「就近原則」。

1291
☐☐☐

nephew
[ˋnɛfju]

🄐 侄子，外甥

🄑 His nephew is an officer in the navy.
／他的侄子是位海軍軍官。

1292
☐☐☐

nervous
[ˋnɝvəs]

🄒 神經質的；緊張不安的

🄑 I got nervous on the stage.
／我在舞臺上很緊張不安。

1293
☐☐☐

nest
[nɛst]

🄐 巢，窩；舒適的地方
🄓 [不及物] 築巢

🄑 The swallows nested under the eaves.
／燕子在屋簷下築巢。

1294
☐☐☐

never
[ˋnɛvɚ]

🄒 從不，決不

🄑 Cathy was born blind so she has never seen our beautiful world.
／凱西天生失明，所以她從來沒看過這個美麗的世界。

🄓 never 放到句首表示強調時句子要部分倒裝：Never shall I forget your kindness. 我永遠不會忘記你的好意。

1295 □□□
new
[nju]
形 新的，最近的；生疏的；新鮮的

例句 Is this computer new or secondhand?
／這台電腦是新的還是二手的？

片語 be new to sb./sth. 對某人 / 物不熟悉 ‖ make a new man of ①使…恢復健康 ②使…改過自新

1296 □□□
New Year's Day
[ˌnju jɪrz`de]
名 元旦，新年

例句 What are you going to do on New Year's Day?
／你元旦打算做什麼？

1297 □□□
New Year's Eve
[ˌnju jɪrz iv]
名 除夕，跨年夜

例句 My friend will arrive on New Year's Eve.
／我朋友將在跨年夜到達。

1298 □□□
New York
[nju`jork]
名 (美國) 紐約

例句 He took the ten o'clock flight to New York.
／他搭 10 點鐘的飛機去紐約。

1299 □□□
news
[njuz]
名 新聞；消息

巧記 news(新聞) 來自東西南北，請看它的結構：

East 東　　West 西
North 北 ←—NEWS—→ South 南

例句 He has got into the habit of listening to the news broadcast at 6:30 a. m.
／他養成了早上 6 點半聽新聞廣播的習慣。

用法 news 是不可數名詞，作主詞時述語動詞用單數形式；說「一條新聞」用 a piece of news。

1300 □□□
newspaper
[`njuzˌpepɚ]
名 報紙

例句 What newspaper do you take?
／ 你要訂什麼報紙？

用法 漢語說「報紙上」，英語則說 in the newspaper/paper。寫在紙上用 on paper，且不用 the。

1301
□□□
next
[`nɛkst]

形 緊接著的；下一個的
副 然後，接下去

片語 next to 在…的旁邊，緊靠
例句 It's next to the post office.
／它在郵局旁邊。

1302
□□□
nice
[naɪs]

形 美好的；友善的；好看的，漂亮的

例句 Some shoes are not good, but they look very nice.
／有些鞋子品質不好，但是很好看。
辨析 nice, good
(1) 修飾人或物時，nice 側重外表，指外觀的漂亮、好看 (帶有一定感情色彩)。
(2) good 側重於表示人的品質不錯或東西的品質好。

1303
□□□
niece
[nis]

名 侄女，外甥女

例句 He looked at his niece.
／他看著自己的侄女。

1304
□□□
night
[naɪt]

名 夜間，夜晚

例句 Some animals only come out at night.
／有些動物只在夜晚才出現。
片語 all night 整夜 ‖ at night 在夜裡 ‖ have a good night 睡得好

1305
□□□
nine
[naɪn]

名 形 九 (的)

例句 The first swimming session is at nine o'clock.
／第一段游泳時間是在 9 點鐘。
片語 nine cases out of ten 十之八九

1306
□□□
nineteen
[`naɪn`tin]

名 形 十九 (的)

例句 He keeps nineteen dogs.
／他養了 19 條狗。

1307
□□□
ninety
[`naɪntɪ]

名 形 九十 (的)

例句 Ninety percent of the new seeds are good.
／ 90% 的新種子是好的。

1308 □□□ **no** [no]
形 沒有；禁止
副 不，不是

70 例句 The room has no windows.
／那個房間沒有窗戶。

1309 □□□ **nobody** [ˋnobadɪ]
代 沒有人
名 無足輕重的人

例句 I knocked on the door several times but nobody answered, so I left.
／我敲了幾次門沒人回應，所以我就離開了。

用法 nobody 作主詞時，其述語動詞要用單數形式。

1310 □□□ **nod** [nɑd]
名 動 [不及物] 點頭

例句 I nodded to show that I agreed.
／我點頭以表示我同意了。

1311 □□□ **noise** [nɔɪz]
名 吵鬧聲，噪音

例句 Oh, my god! The kids are making too much noise here. I can't do anything.
／天啊！孩子們在這裡這麼吵鬧，我什麼事也不能做。

1312 □□□ **noisy** [ˋnɔɪzɪ]
形 喧鬧的，嘈雜的

例句 We went along the noisy street.
／我們沿著那條嘈雜的街道走。

反義 quiet 形 安靜的

1313 □□□ **none** [nʌn]
代 沒有一個
副 一點也不，絕不

例句 They were all very tired, but none of them took a rest.
／他們都很疲憊，但是沒有一個人休息。

辨析❶ none, no one
(1) none 用以指人或物，可以與 of 連用，可以用來回答以 how many/ much 開頭的問句。
(2) no one 只能指人，其後不跟 of 短語，作主詞時述語動詞用單數形式， 只能回答以 who 開頭的問句。

第四週

辨析2 neither, none

　　(1) neither 否定兩個人或物。

　　(2) none 否定三個及多個人或物。

　　〔譯〕這四個學生都沒及格。

　　〔誤〕Neither of the four pupils passed.

　　〔正〕None of the four pupils passed.

1314
☐☐☐
noodle
[`nudl]

名 麵條，麵

例句 Do you like noodles?

／你喜歡吃麵條嗎？

1315
☐☐☐
noon
[nun]

名 中午，正午

例句 He usually sleeps until noon.

／他常常睡到中午才起床。

片語 at noon 正午 ‖ at the noon of one's life 在人生全盛期，在壯年期

1316
☐☐☐
nor
[nɔr]

連 也不

例句 The story was long, nor have I heard it out.

／這個故事很長，我從來沒聽完過。

用法 nor 常與 neither, not 連用，有時也與 no, never 等表示否定意義的詞連用。

1317
☐☐☐
north
[nɔrθ]

名 (sing.) 北，北方；副 向 / 在 / 從北方
形 北的，朝北的

例句 There is a north window in my room.

／我房間有一個朝北的窗戶。

片語 in the north 在北方 ‖ North China 華北 ‖ North Pole 北極

反義 south 名 南，南方，南部

1318
☐☐☐
northern
[`nɔrðən]

形 北部的，北方；朝北的，來自北方的

例句 Do you know what is the population of Northern Europe?

／你知道北歐的人口數是多少嗎？

反義 southern 形 南部的；來自南方的

辨析 north, northern

　　(1) north 作形容詞，泛指北的；也可作名詞，表示「北方，北部」。

　　(2) northern 只能作形容詞，常指一個國家、地區或世界的北面，常用大寫。

　　※ The north half of the Earth is called the Northern Hemisphere.

　　　地球的北半部分稱為北半球。

注意 注意音變

1319 □□□

nose
[noz]

名 鼻子；嗅覺

例句 A dog has a good nose.
／狗有靈敏的嗅覺。

片語 blow one's nose 擤鼻涕 ‖ nose to nose 面對面

1320 □□□

not
[nɑt]

副 不

例句 The man told me not to move.
／那個人叫我別動。

片語 not a (=no) 沒有 ‖ not at all... 一點兒也不⋯

用法 (1) no 可以用在不可數名詞前，也可用在可數名詞單數和複數前。

(2) no 和 not a, not any 的意義稍有不同：no 更強調否定含義，常有「絕不是，絕沒有」之義。

1321 □□□

note
[not]

名 便條；鈔票；筆記
動 [及物] 注意；記下

例句 The policeman noted some footprints.
／警察注意到一些腳印。

片語 take notes 做筆記

1322 □□□

notebook
[`not͵bʊk]

名 筆記本；筆記型電腦

例句 I wrote down her telephone number in my notebook.
／我在筆記本上記下了她的電話號碼。

1323 □□□

nothing
[`nʌθɪŋ]

名 代 沒有東西，沒有什麼

片語 nothing but... 除了⋯外，只有⋯
例句 We could see nothing but fog.
／除了霧之外，我們什麼也看不見。

1324 □□□

notice
[`notɪs]

動 [及物] 注意到
名 佈告；通知；注意

片語 notice sb. do sth. 注意到某人做過某事 ‖ notice sb. doing sth. 注意到某人正在做某事
例句 Have you noticed her cry?
／你有注意到她哭嗎？

1325 □□□ **novel**
[ˈnɑvl̩]
名 (長篇) 小說

例句 Dickens wrote many novels.
／狄更斯寫了許多小說。

1326 □□□ **novel**
[ˈnɑvl̩]
形 新穎的，新奇的

例句 He always has novel ideas.
／他總是有新奇的想法。

Ⓖroup 3

1327 □□□ **November**
[noˈvɛmbɚ]
名 十一月 (=Nov.)

71
例句 He started work here last November.
／他去年 11 月開始在這裡工作。

1328 □□□ **now**
[naʊ]
副 現在，此刻；立刻，馬上

例句 I can't do it now, you'll have to wait.
／我不能馬上做這件事，你必須等一下。

片語 by now 到現在，此時 ‖ from now on 從現在起 ‖ now and then 不時 ‖ right now 立刻 ‖ up to now 到現在為止

1329 □□□ **number**
[ˈnʌmbɚ]
名 數字；號碼 動 編號；總計

例句 The cards were numbered from 1 to 50.
／這些卡片從 1 號編到 50 號。

辨析 a number of, the number of
(1) a number of 意為「許多的，大量的」，當「a number of+ 可數名詞複數」作主詞時，述語動詞用複數形式。
(2) the number of 意為「…的數目」，當「the number of+ 可數名詞複數」作主詞時，述語動詞用單數形式。

1330 □□□ **nurse**
[nɝs]
名 護士
動 [及物] 護理，看護，照料

例句 She nursed the sick boy back to health.
／她照顧著生病的孩子直到他康復。

1331 ☐☐☐ obey
[ə`be]

動 服從，遵守

例句 Everyone must obey the rules.
／人人都要遵守規則。

1332 ☐☐☐ object
[`abdʒɪkt]

名 物品，物體

例句 Tell me the names of the objects in this room.
／告訴我這房間裡的物品名稱。

1333 ☐☐☐ object
[əb`dʒɛkt]

動 [不及物] 反對，不贊成

片語 object to 反對〔▲ to 為介系詞〕
例句 We objected to leaving him alone.
／我們反對丟下他一個人。

1334 ☐☐☐ occur
[ə`kɝ]

動 [不及物] (occurred, occurred) 出現；浮現，想起；發生

巧記 圖解 occur 的一詞多義：

（突然）出現
↓
（偶然）想起

occur

片語 occur to sb. (主意或想法突然) 浮現於某人腦中
例句 An excellent idea occurred to me when I woke up this morning.
／今天早上起床時，我突然想到一個很棒的點子。

辨析 occur, happen, take place
(1) occur 多用來指具體事情的「發生」，雖也可指偶然性，但與 happen 相比程度較弱。
(2) happen 常用來表示「偶然，碰巧」，而且多指整個情況，這時不能用 occur/take place 代替。
(3) take place 作「發生」解時較為正式，不帶有偶然之義，並經常用來指經事先安排的事情。

1335 ☐☐☐ ocean
[`oʃən]

名 海洋，大洋

例句 I like to swim in the ocean when it's warm enough.
／天氣足夠暖和的時候，我喜歡在海裡游泳。

1336 □□□ **o'clock** [ə`klɑk]　　副 點鐘

例句 "What time is it? " "It is just eight o'clock. "
／「現在幾點鐘？」「正好八點。」

1337 □□□ **October** [ɑk`tobə-]　　名 十月 (=Oct.)

例句 I was born in Taipei on October 22, 1981.
／我於 1981 年 10 月 22 日在台北出生。

1338 □□□ **of** [ɑv]　　介 …的

例句 There is a picture of my family on the wall.
／牆上有一張我家人的相片。

1339 □□□ **off** [ɔf]　　副 離開；下（公車、飛機等）；距離；關掉
　　介 從…離開，從…下來

例句 The school is 500 meters off.
／學校距離這裡 500 公尺。

1340 □□□ **offer** [`ɔfə-]　　動 [及物] 名 提供；提議；出價

片語 offer sb. sth.(=offer sth. to sb.) 向某人提供某物 ‖ offer to do sth. 提出要做某事
例句 The little girl offered her seat to an old man on the bus.
／小女孩在公車上把她的座位讓給一位老人。

1341 □□□ **office** [`ɔfɪs]　　名 辦公室；公職；部，局

例句 Will you come into my office for a moment, please?
／請你到我的辦公室來一下好嗎？

1342 □□□ **officer** [`ɔfəsə-]　　名 公務員，官員；警官

例句 "Move along, please! " said a police officer.
／「請往前走！」一位警官說道。

1343 □□□ **official** [ə`fɪʃəl]　　形 官方的
　　名 官員

片語 official language 官方語言
例句 There are two official languages, French and English, in
Canada. ／在加拿大有兩種官方語言：法語和英語。

1344
☐☐☐

often
[`ɔfən]

副 經常，常常

例句 She often works on the weekend.
／她周末經常要上班。

片語 how often 多久時間一次

1345
☐☐☐

oil
[ɔɪl]

名 植物油，食用油
動 [及物] 幫…加潤滑油

例句 She cooked the fish in oil in a pan.
／她在平底鍋裡用油煎魚。

片語 pour oil on the flames 火上加油

Group 4

1346
☐☐☐

72

OK
[`o`ke]

副 （口）好，不錯
形 很好的；還不錯的

例句 The computer is working OK.
／這台電腦運作起來還不錯。

1347
☐☐☐

old
[old]

形 老的，年老的；舊的；（年齡）…歲的

例句 The old are taken good care of in that country.
／那個國家的老人都得到很好的照顧。

用法 the old 表示「老人，老年人」，作主詞時述語動詞用複數形式。

反義 young 形 年輕的；new 形 新的

1348
☐☐☐

omit
[o`mɪt]

動 [及物] 省略，刪節；遺漏，疏忽

例句 You can omit the last chapter of the book.
／你可以省略這本書的最後一章。

1349
☐☐☐

on
[ɑn]

介 在…之上
副 （電燈等）開著

例句 The book is lying on the table.
／這本書放在桌子上。

辨析 on, in, at
(1) on 表示日、周日或特定某日中的一段時間：on Thursday morning 在星期四上午。
(2) in 表示一日中的上午、下午、晚上或周、月、季、年：in the afternoon 在下午。
(3) at 表示鐘點、一日中的黎明、中午、黃昏、半夜等：at dawn 在黎明。

1350 □□□

once
[wʌns]

副 曾經；一次
連 一旦⋯（就⋯）

例句 Once the sun had set, the air turned cold.
／太陽一旦下山，空氣就變冷了。

片語 at once 馬上，立刻 ‖ once again/more 再一次，重新 ‖ once upon a time 從前，很久很久以前

1351 □□□

one
[wʌn]

名 一（個）
形〔強調數目，常重讀以加強語氣〕一個的

例句 I have one orange and he has two oranges.
／我有一顆橘子，他有兩顆橘子。

片語 all in one 合為一體，連身服 ‖ in one word 總之 ‖ one by one 依序
辨析 one, it, that
(1) one 表示泛指。
(2) it 表示特指，與所指名詞為同一個。
(3) that 表示特指，與所指名詞為同類，但不是同一個。

1352 □□□

onion
[ˋʌnjən]

名 洋蔥（頭）

例句 I like onions.
／我喜歡吃洋蔥。

onion 與 union

▲你瞧！洋蔥 (onion) 多團結 (union)，片片相擁，抱成一體 (one)。

onion（洋蔥） ←→ union（團結）

1353 □□□

only
[ˋonlɪ]

副 才；只有
形 唯一的

例句 Don't judge a thing from the outside only.
／不要只從外表判斷事情。

用法 「only+ 副詞」放在句首時，句子用部分倒裝結構；not only...but also... 「不但⋯而且⋯」是並列連詞，其連接的部分作主詞時，述語動詞遵循就近原則。

1354 □□□

open
[ˋopən]

形 開著的；開闊的
動 [及物] 打開 動 [不及物] 開幕

例句 Leave the windows open.
／讓窗戶保持開著。

片語 be open to... 對⋯開放的 ‖ in the open air 在戶外，在野外
反義 closed 形 關閉的；(商店、公共建築等) 關門的，不開放的

1355 operate
[`ɑpə‚ret]

動 [不及物] 運轉；對…動手術
動 [及物] 經營；操作

例句 This machine doesn't operate smoothly.
／這台機器運轉不順。

片語 operate on sb. (for some disease) 幫某人動手術 (治某病)

1356 operation
[‚ɑpə`reʃən]

名 運轉；操作；手術

片語 come into operation 生效，實施 ‖ in operation 運轉中，操作中 ‖ put into operation 使實施

例句 The new system came into operation last month.
／這套新系統於上個月開始運作。

1357 opinion
[ə`pɪnjən]

名 看法；意見

例句 My opinions about education have changed.
／我對教育的看法改變了。

片語 in one's opinion(=in the opinion of sb.) 在某人看來 ‖ give/express one's opinion on/upon... 對…發表意見

1358 opportunity
[‚ɑpɚ`tjunətɪ]

名 時機，機會

例句 I nearly lost the opportunity.
／我差一點錯過這個機會。

1359 or
[ɔr]

連 否則；或者

例句 Jenny, put on your coat or you will catch a cold.
／珍妮，穿上妳的外套，否則妳會感冒。

1360 orange
[`ɔrɪndʒ]

名 柳橙，柳丁
形 橙色的

例句 The jacket is orange.
／這件夾克是橘色的。

1361 order
[`ɔrdɚ]

名 次序；秩序；訂購，訂單；狀況

片語 in order 按順序 ‖ in order to 為了 (做某事)〔後接動詞原形〕‖ out of order 不按順序，故障

例句 The public telephone is out of order.
／公用電話故障了。

辨析 book, order

book 和 order 都表示「預訂」，但 book 一般指預訂票、座、房間等；而 order 主要指預訂貨物、菜、衣服等。

1362
□□□

order
[`ɔrdɚ]

動 [及物] 命令，指示
動 訂，點（菜）；向…訂購

例句 She ordered me away.
／她命令我走開。

用法 三個「命令」(order, command, direct) 用 that 從句作受詞時，從句中的述語動詞要用「(should+) 動詞原形」。

片語 order sb. to do sth. 命令某人做某事

1363
□□□

ordinary
[`ɔrdn͵ɛrɪ]

形 通常的，正常的，平常的

例句 Simon was wearing a suit, but I was in my ordinary clothes.
／賽門穿了套裝，但是我穿著平常的衣服。

1364
□□□

organization
[͵ɔrgənə`zeʃən]

名 團體，機構，組織

例句 Only with organization can the wisdom of the collective be given full play.
／只有組織可以讓集體的智慧充分發揮。

1365 ☐☐☐

organize
[`ɔrgə,naɪz]

動[及物]，組織；(使建立系統)組織，安排
動[不及物]組織起來

73

例句 They organized a new team.
／他們組織了一個新團隊。

1366 ☐☐☐

other
[`ʌðə·]

形 其他的，另外的
代 (兩個中)另一個(人或事物)

片語 every other... 每隔一… ‖ one...the other...(兩個人或物中)一個…另一個…

例句 New Zealand has two islands. One is North Island and the
other is South Island.
／紐西蘭有兩座島，一個是北島，另一個是南島。

辨析 other, else
(1) other 只用於名詞前作限定詞。
(2) else 常用於疑問句中，修飾不定代詞或疑問詞，並置於這些詞之後。

1367 ☐☐☐

our
[`aʊr]

形 我們的

例句 We put our books in our bags.
／我們把我們的書放進書包裡。

1368 ☐☐☐

ours
[`aʊrz]

代 我們的(東西)

例句 The house opposite ours was burnt down last week.
／我們家對面的房子上個星期燒毀了。

1369 ☐☐☐

out
[aʊt]

副 (位置及運動的方向)出去，外出；
介 從…出去

例句 The fishing boats are all out at sea.
／所有的漁船都出海了。

片語 out of... ①在…外 ②從…離開

1370 ☐☐☐

outside
[`aʊt`saɪd]

名 外部(面)，外表
副 向(在)外面　形 外部的

例句 They stood outside the door.
／他們站在門外。

反義 inside 副 在內，往裡面

1371 ☐☐☐

oven
[`ʌvən]

名 烤箱，爐灶

例句 This bread is fresh from the oven.
／這些麵包剛出爐。

O

Lesson 4

第四週

1372 □□□ **over**
[ˋovɚ]

形 在那邊的；結束的
介 (表示數目、程度)超過；在⋯以上

例句 Hang that picture over the fireplace.
／請把那幅畫掛在壁爐上方。

片語 all over 到處，各處 ‖ all over the world 遍及全球 ‖ over and over (again) 反覆不斷地，再三

辨析 above, over, on
(1) above 表示位置高於某物，並不一定垂直，反義詞是 below。
(2) over 表示在某物垂直的上方，反義詞是 under。
(3) on 表示和某物表面有接觸的上方，反義詞是 beneath。

```
        above                      over
         ↑↑↑                        ↑
          •          on             •
      ┌────────────────•─────────────────┐
      └──────────────────────────────────┘
         ↓↓↓        beneath            ↓
          •                            •
        below                       under
```

1373 □□□ **overpass**
[͵ovɚˋpæs]

名 天橋，高架道

例句 I walked through an overpass over the road.
／我走天橋穿過那條路。

1374 □□□ **overseas**
[ˋovɚˋsiz]

副 在海外，在國外
形 (在)海外的，(在)國外的

例句 My brother lives overseas.
／我哥哥住在國外。

1375 □□□ **own**
[on]

形 自己的 代 自己，本人
動 [及物] 擁有；承認

例句 He has a house of his own, and the house was built on his own last year.
／他有一間自己的房子，這間房子是去年他自己蓋的。

辨析 of one's own, on one's own
(1) of one's own 是「(某人)自己的」的意思，一般用作限定詞。
(2) on one's own 是「獨自地，獨立地」的意思，一般用作副詞。

1376 □□□ **owner**
[ˋonɚ]

名 物主；所有權人

例句 Who is the owner of this book?
／這本書的所有人是誰？

1377 ☐☐☐
ox
[ɑks]

名 (pl.oxen) 牛

例句 The ox had run away.
／那頭牛逃走了。

1378 ☐☐☐
P.M.
[ˋpiˋɛm]

副 下午 (=p.m.=PM)

例句 We will hold a meeting at 3 P. M.
／我們將在下午 3 點舉行會議。

1379 ☐☐☐
pack
[pæk]

名 包，背包；一包
動 [及物] 裝進，打包　動 [不及物] 打包

例句 Have you packed your things yet?
／你的東西打包好了嗎？

片語 pack away 把…裝起來 ‖ pack in 把…擠在裡面 ‖ pack off 打發走 ‖ pack up ①收拾行李，打包 ②放棄某事物

1380 ☐☐☐
package
[ˋpækɪdʒ]

名 包裹，包裝

例句 A bill came along with the package.
／帳單與包裹一起送來了

1381 ☐☐☐
page
[pedʒ]

名 (書、報紙等的)頁；電腦頁面

例句 Open your books to page 36.
／打開書本翻到第 36 頁。

片語 home page 主頁 ‖ the sports pages 體育專欄 ‖ turn the page over 翻頁

注意 縮寫為 p.，複數形式略為 pp.

1382 ☐☐☐
pain
[pen]

名 疼；痛苦

例句 He caused his parents a great deal of pain.
／他帶給父母極大的痛苦。

1383 ☐☐☐
painful
[ˋpenfəl]

形 令人疼痛的，使人痛苦的

例句 The cut was still painful. ／傷口還在痛。
辨析 painful, in pain
(1) painful 的準確含義是「引起疼痛的」(giving pain)。
(2) in pain 是「疼痛的」。

1384 □□□

paint
[pent]

74

動 塗以顏色；把…塗成；畫，繪畫
名 油漆

巧記 圖解 paint 的一詞多義：

paint 塗以顏色

paint 繪畫

例句 I painted the gate blue.
／我把大門漆成藍色。

1385 □□□

painter
[`pentɚ]

名 畫家；油漆匠

例句 Rembrandt was a famous painter in Holland.
／林布蘭特是一位著名的荷蘭畫家。

1386 □□□

painting
[`pentɪŋ]

名（一幅）畫；繪畫；（上）油漆

例句 There is a painting on the wall.
／牆上掛著一幅畫。

用法 a painting of Jim 指「別人為吉姆畫的一幅肖像畫」；a painting by Jim 指「吉姆畫的一幅作品」。

1387 □□□

pair
[pɛr]

名 一對，一雙

例句 I found a couple of socks in the room but they did not make a pair.
／我在房間裡找到兩隻襪子，但它們不是一雙的。

片語 a pair of 一對，一雙 ‖ in pairs 成對的

辨析 pair, couple
pair 與 couple 都可指「一雙，一對」，但 pair 指兩部分有機結合，缺一不可，而任何兩個同樣的東西，都可稱為 couple，可分可合。

1388 □□□

pajamas
[pə`dʒæməz]

名〔美〕睡衣；（回教徒穿的）寬長褲

例句 At bedtime, I take off my clothes and put on my pajamas.
／睡覺時，我脫掉衣服換上睡衣。

同義 pyjamas 名〔英〕睡衣

1389 ☐☐☐
pale
[pel]
形 (臉色)蒼白的;淺的,淡的

例句 Are you ill? You look pale.
／你生病了嗎?你臉色蒼白。

1390 ☐☐☐
pan
[pæn]
名 平底鍋

例句 First turn off the gas and cover the pan.
／先關掉瓦斯爐,然後把平底鍋蓋起來。

1391 ☐☐☐
panda
[`pændə]
名 貓熊,熊貓

例句 The panda is a native of China.
／貓熊產於中國。

1392 ☐☐☐
pants
[pænts]
名 〔美〕(pl.) 長褲

例句 She was wearing dark blue pants and a white sweater.
／她穿著深藍色長褲和白色毛衣。
同義 trousers 名 〔英〕長褲

1393 ☐☐☐
papaya
[pə`paɪə]
名 木瓜

例句 I want to buy a papaya milk.
／我要買木瓜牛奶。

1394 ☐☐☐
paper
[`pepɚ]
名 紙;考卷;(pl.) 文件;論文,報告

巧記 圖解 paper 的一詞多義:

a ⎰ sheet ⎱ of paper
  ⎱ piece ⎰

papers
(複數形式)
a paper, two papers

例句 The English paper was very easy.
／這份英語考卷很容易。
片語 on paper ①以書面形式 ②理論上 ‖ paper cut 剪紙

1395 ☐☐☐
pardon
[`pardn]
名 動 [及物] 原諒,寬恕

例句 Please pardon me for waking you.
／請原諒我吵醒了你。

用法 I beg your pardon./Beg your pardon. 在會話中常簡稱為 Pardon，其含義根據上下文可以理解為：①請原諒。②對不起，我沒聽清楚，請再說一遍。③對不起，我不敢苟同。

1396 □□□
parent
[`pɛrənt]
名 父母，爸媽

例句 My parents are very understanding.
／我父母很明理。

用法 parent 作單數名詞時，只指「父母中的一個」；當表示「雙親」時，要用複數 parents。

1397 □□□
Paris
[`pærɪs]
名 巴黎

例句 I flew from London to Paris last Sunday.
／我上星期天從倫敦飛到巴黎。

1398 □□□
park
[pɑrk]
名 公園

例句 Let's go for a walk in the park.
／我們去公園散步吧！

1399 □□□
park
[pɑrk]
動 停車

例句 You can't park your car in this street.
／你不能把車子停在這條街上。

1400 □□□
parrot
[`pærət]
名 鸚鵡

例句 A parrot can talk like a person.
／鸚鵡可以像人一樣說話。

1401 □□□
part
[pɑrt]
名 參加；部分；角色

片語 play a part in 對…有影響，參與 ‖ take (an active) part in... (積極) 參加…
例句 How many countries took part in the last Olympic Games?
／有多少個國家參加上一屆的奧運會？

1402 □□□
particular
[pə`tɪkjələ]
形 特定的，特有的；特別的；講究的

例句 Language is particular to mankind. ／語言是人類特有的。
片語 in particular 特別 (的)，尤其 (的)

1403 partner
[ˋpɑrtnɚ]
名 配偶；夥伴，合夥人，搭檔

Track 75

巧記 漢語的「伴」中有「半」字，英語的「partner」中有「part」。

例句 They are good partners.
／他們是好搭檔。

1404 party
[ˋpɑrtɪ]
名 聚會，派對

例句 We held a farewell party for him.
／我們為他舉辦了一場歡送會。

注意 常指在某人家中吃喝或跳舞

1405 pass
[pæs]
動 [及物] 通過；超過；傳遞（用具等）
名 通行證

例句 After the students passed their exams, they celebrated by having a party.
／學生們通過考試後，他們舉行聚會慶祝。

片語 pass away 去世 ‖ pass by ①（時間）過去 ②從旁邊經過 ‖ pass down 傳下來

1406 passenger
[ˋpæsndʒɚ]
名 旅客，乘客，過路人

例句 There were many passengers in the train.
／火車上有許多乘客。

1407 past
[pæst]
副 經過，超過
介（時間等）過…

例句 I saw Li Zhen hurry past.
／我看到李珍匆匆經過。

1408 past
[pæst]
形 過去的
名 過去

片語 in the past 在過去 ‖ in/during/over the past few days 在過去的幾天裡

例句 In the past, 30,000 people lived in the town.
／在過去，這個鎮上住了三萬人。

1409 paste
[pest]
名 漿糊；麵糰；醬，膏
動 [及物] 黏，貼上

例句 A notice had been pasted to the door.
／門上貼了一張公告。

1410 □□□ **path** [pæθ]　名 小路；路線；〔喻〕途徑，道路

例句 An old lady was taking a walk along a path in the park.
／一位老太太沿著公園的小路散步。

1411 □□□ **patient** [`peʃənt]　形 有耐心的，能容忍的

片語 be patient of sth. 容忍某事 ‖ be patient with sb. 對某人有耐心
例句 You will have to be patient with my grandma—she is getting rather deaf.
／你對我奶奶要容忍一點，她的耳朵相當重聽。

1412 □□□ **patient** [`peʃənt]　名 病人

例句 Be patient when you examine patients.
／幫病人檢查時要有耐心。

1413 □□□ **pattern** [`pætɚn]　名 模式，方式；花樣，圖案；榜樣

例句 These behavior patterns are typical of this age group.
／這些行為模式是這個年齡層的典型。

1414 □□□ **pause** [pɔz]　動 [不及物] 中止，暫停　名 中止，暫停
動 [及物]（按暫停鍵）暫停放音（放影像）

例句 He paused for a moment to rest.
／他停下來休息一下。
片語 without pause 不停地

1415 □□□ **pay** [pe]　動 (paid, paid) 付錢，支付
名 工資，薪金

片語 pay back 償還 ‖ pay for ①付⋯的錢 ②為⋯付出代價 ‖ pay off 還清 ‖ pay sb. for sth. 為某事付給某人報酬
例句 In order to protect the environment, people have to pay for their trash.
／為了保護環境，人們為他們的垃圾付費。

1416 □□□ **PE** [ˌpi `i]　名 體育 (=physical education)

例句 His uncle is a PE teacher.
／他叔叔是一位體育老師。

1417 ☐☐☐ **peace**
[pis]
图 和平;安靜

例句 He wants to work for world peace.
／他想為世界和平而努力。

片語 at peace 處於和平狀態 ‖ in peace 安靜地,平安地

1418 ☐☐☐ **peaceful**
['pisfəl]
形 和平的,太平的;安靜的,平靜的

例句 We had a peaceful afternoon without the children.
／我們度過了一個沒有小孩的平靜午後。

1419 ☐☐☐ **peach**
[pitʃ]
图 桃子

例句 There is a peach tree near the house.
／房子旁邊有一棵桃樹。

1420 ☐☐☐ **pear**
[pɛr]
图 梨子

例句 The pear is a delicious fruit and I like it very much.
／梨子是美味的水果,我很喜歡它。

1421 ☐☐☐ **pen**
[pɛn]
图 筆,鋼筆;〔喻〕文筆

例句 The pen is mightier than the sword.
／〔諺〕文筆勝於刀劍。/ 文勝於武。

Ⓖroup 4

1422 ☐☐☐ **pencil**
['pɛnsl̩]
图 鉛筆

76

例句 Can you buy a pencil for me?
／你可以買一枝鉛筆給我嗎?

1423 ☐☐☐ **people**
['pipl̩]
图 人們;種族;(the ～) 人民;民族

巧記 圖解 people 的一詞多義:

three people
三個人

four peoples 四個民族

第四週

例句 America is made up of many peoples.
／美國由很多種族所構成。
※ People say that the Chinese are a great people, and the Chinese people are very hardworking. 人們都說中華民族是一個偉大的民族，中國人是非常勤勞的。

1424 □□□ pepper
[`pɛpɚ]

名 胡椒粉，胡椒，辣椒

例句 This kind of pepper is not hot.
／這種辣椒不會辣。

1425 □□□ perfect
[`pɝ-fɪkt]

形 完美的，理想的；精通的，嫻熟的

例句 Her English was perfect.
／她的英語很精通。

辨析 perfect, complete
perfect 不但指各個組成部分「完整無缺」(complete)，而且還「盡善盡美」。所以，一個東西可以是 complete，但並不一定是 perfect；而一個東西如果是 perfect，則一定是 complete。

1426 □□□ perhaps
[pɚ`hæps]

副 可能，大概，也許

例句 I don't know where she is—perhaps she's still at work.
／我不知道她在哪裡，大概還在工作吧！

1427 □□□ period
[`pɪrɪəd]

名 一段時間；時期，時代

例句 During that period many people moved from the countryside to the towns.
／那個時期有很多人從鄉下搬到城裡。

辨析 period, age
(1) period 是最普通用詞，概念廣泛，時間長短不限，既可指任何一個歷史時期，又可指個人或自然界的一個發展階段。
(2) age 指歷史上具有顯著特徵的大時代或考古學上的大時代，持續時間往往較長。

1428 □□□ person
[`pɝ-sn̩]

名 人，人物；人身；外表

例句 I think she's the best person for the job.
／我認為她是這份工作最合適的人選。

片語 in person 親自，本人
注意 「一個人」可以說 a person，但不能說 a people。

1429 □□□

personal
[`pɝ-sn̩l]

形 個人的，私人的

例句 This letter is personal, and I don't want anyone else to read it.
／這是一封私人信件，我不想讓任何人看。

1430 □□□

pet
[pɛt]

名 寵物；受寵愛的人，寶貝，寵兒

例句 She's the teacher's pet.
／她是老師的寶貝學生。

1431 □□□

Philippines
[`fɪlə,pinz]

名 菲律賓

例句 The Philippines has just 6,000 square kilometers of forest left.
／菲律賓只剩下 6,000 平方公里的森林了。

1432 □□□

phone
[fon]

名 電話，電話機
動 打電話 (給)(=telephone)

例句 I phoned him last night.
／我昨天晚上打電話給他。
片語 on the phone 通電話，在電話裡 ‖ phone book 電話簿 ‖ phone card 電話卡 ‖ phone number 電話號碼

1433 □□□

photo
[`foto]

名 照片，相片 (=photograph)

例句 This photo is not sharp enough.
／這張照片不夠清晰。
片語 family photo 全家福 ‖ take photos 照相

1434 □□□

photograph
[`fotə,græf]

名 照片，相片 (=photo)

例句 He doesn't like to have his photograph taken.
／我被這位知名的攝影師拍過照。

1435 □□□

photographer
[fə`tɑgrəfɚ]

名 攝影師

例句 I had a photo taken with the famous photographer.
／我和這位著名的攝影師合過影。

1436 □□□ **physics**
[ˋfɪzɪks]

名 物理，物理學

例句 I don't like physics.
／我不喜歡物理。

1437 □□□ **piano**
[pɪˋæno]

名 鋼琴

片語 play the piano 彈鋼琴〔▲樂器前加定冠詞 the〕
例句 He often plays the piano after supper.
／他常在晚飯後彈奏鋼琴。

1438 □□□ **pick**
[pɪk]

動 [及物] 採，摘；挑選

片語 pick out 選出，選拔 ‖ pick up ①拾起，撿起 ②搭載
例句 If you see any litter on the school playground, you'd better pick it up.
／如果你在學校操場上看見垃圾，你最好把它撿起來。
辨析 choose, pick
(1) choose「選擇，挑選」，是最普通的用語。
(2) pick「挑選，挑揀」，是仔細挑選和苛刻選擇，多指挑選有形的東西。

1439 □□□ **picnic**
[ˋpɪknɪk]

動 [不及物] (picnicked, picnicked) 去野餐，去郊遊
名 野餐（食物）

例句 We picnicked in the forest last week.
／上個星期我們去森林野餐。
片語 take/have a picnic 去野餐

1440 □□□ **picture**
[ˋpɪktʃɚ]

名 圖畫；照片
動 [及物] 畫，繪；描繪，描述

例句 The room had several pictures on the walls.
／那個房間牆上有幾幅畫。
片語 take a picture 拍照

P

Lesson 5

1441 □□□
pie
[paɪ]
名（西點）派，餡餅

77

巧記 諧音：〔英〕pie 一音譯→〔漢〕派

例句 Do you like apple pie?
／你喜歡蘋果派嗎？

片語 pie in the sky 遙不可及的夢想

1442 □□□
piece
[pis]
名一件（片，張，塊…）

片語 a piece of 一條／張／片／塊 ‖ in pieces 零碎地，粉碎地

例句 I'm so hungry. Please give me three pieces of bread to eat.
／我太餓了，請給我三塊麵包吃。

1443 □□□
pig
[pɪg]
名豬

例句 He keeps pigs.
／他養豬。

1444 □□□
pigeon
[ˈpɪdʒɪn]
名鴿子

例句 An old man sat on the park bench feeding the pigeons.
／一位老人坐在公園的長凳上餵鴿子。

1445 □□□
pile
[paɪl]
名堆；〔口〕大量
動 [及物] 堆放

例句 He piled the truck with vegetables. / He piled vegetables on the truck.
／他把蔬菜堆放在卡車上。

片語 a pile of 一堆 ‖ pile up 堆積，積聚

1446 □□□
pillow
[ˈpɪlo]
名枕頭

例句 She lay with her face in the pillow.
／她把臉埋在枕頭裡。

1447 □□□
pin
[pɪn]
名大頭針，別針；釘；胸針
動 [及物]（用別針）別在一起

例句 She pinned the materials together.
／她把材料釘在了一起。

片語 not care a pin 毫不在乎 ‖ not worth a pin 一文不值 ‖ (sit) on pins and needles 如坐針氈，坐立不安，急得要命

第四週

1448 □□□ **pineapple**
[ˋpaɪnˌæpl]

名 鳳梨

例句 She drank a cup of pineapple juice.
／她喝了一杯鳳梨汁。

1449 □□□ **pink**
[pɪŋk]

形 粉紅色的
名 粉紅色

例句 She was dressed in pink.
／她穿著粉紅色的衣服。

1450 □□□ **pipe**
[paɪp]

名 管子；煙斗；管樂器

例句 The pipe behind the store is for the gas.
／商店後面的管子是瓦斯管。

1451 □□□ **pizza**
[ˋpitsə]

名 比薩餅，義大利烤餡餅

巧記 諧音：〔英〕pizza 一音譯→〔漢〕比薩
例句 She ate a slice of pizza.
／她吃了一片比薩。

1452 □□□ **place**
[ples]

名 地點；位置
動 [及物] 放置

片語 a place of interest 名勝 ‖ take place 發生 ‖ take the place of 代替
例句 Great changes have taken place in Shanghai in the past
five years.
／在過去的五年裡，上海發生了巨大的變化。

1453 □□□ **plain**
[plen]

名 平原

例句 Is the plain good for growing crops?
／這個平原適合種植農作物嗎？

1454 □□□ **plain**
[plen]

形 簡單的，平易的；清楚的；坦率的；平凡的
名 草原

例句 The story is written in plain English.
／這個故事是用簡單的英文所寫。
片語 to be plain with you 坦白對你說

1455 □□□ **plan**
[plæn]

名 動 [及物] **計畫；規畫**

例句 We're planning to visit London this summer.
／我們計畫今年夏天要去倫敦旅行。

1456 □□□ **plane**
[plen]

名 **飛機；平面，水平面**

片語 by plane (=by air, in a plane) 搭飛機
例句 It's much quicker to go by plane.
／搭飛機去會快很多。

1457 □□□ **planet**
[ˋplænɪt]

名 **行星**

例句 A planet is a heavenly body that moves around the sun.
／行星是圍繞太陽運轉的天體。

1458 □□□ **plant**
[plænt]

動 [及物] **栽種（植物）**

例句 We're going to plant trees around the house.
／我們打算在房子周圍種樹。

1459 □□□ **plant**
[plænt]

名 **植物，農作物；工廠**

例句 Don't forget to water the plants.
／別忘記幫植物澆水。

Group 2

1460 □□□ **plate**
[plet]

名 **盤子，碟子**

(78) 例句 The plates were piled high with rice.
／盤子裡盛滿了米飯。

辨析 dish, plate
dish 是裝西餐的「大盤子」，用餐者從那裡撥一些菜，放在自己的碟子 (plate) 上；此外，平常盛菜的盤子常用 plate。

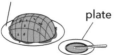

dish

plate

1461 ☐☐☐ **platform**
[`plæt͵fɔrm]

名 台，平臺，講臺；月臺

巧記 plat(平) + form(形狀)

例句 A hall has a platform for speakers.
／禮堂有為演講者設置的講臺。

1462 ☐☐☐ **play**
[ple]

動 玩耍；打、踢(球)；演奏；播放

片語 play basketball/football/ping-pong 打籃球／踢足球／打乒乓球 ‖ play with 以…為消遣，玩弄

例句 The children were playing in the room and one of them was playing with a toy dog.
／孩子們在房間裡玩，其中一個在玩玩具狗。

辨析 play, play with
(1) play 意為「玩」。
(2) play with 意為「玩弄」、「玩耍」、「玩火，玩玩具」等。

1463 ☐☐☐ **play**
[ple]

名 戲劇；劇本；表演；玩耍

例句 The play was damned by the reviewers.
／這齣戲被評論家們批評得一無是處。

1464 ☐☐☐ **player**
[`pleɚ]

名 運動員，選手，遊戲者

巧記 play(玩)+-er(…人)

例句 He is a good chess player. ／他是一名好棋手。

1465 ☐☐☐ **playground**
[`ple͵graʊnd]

名 運動場，操場，遊樂場

例句 The children were playing baseball in the playground.
／孩子們在操場上打棒球。

1466 ☐☐☐ **pleasant**
[`plɛzənt]

形 令人愉快的；舒適的

例句 We had a pleasant time.
／我們度過了一段愉快的時光。

1467 ☐☐☐ **please**
[pliz]

動 取悅；使高興；使滿意

例句 The film pleased the children very much.
／電影讓孩子們非常高興。

1468 please
[pliz]
動 請，請求

例句 Could you please clean up the living room?
／可以請你打掃一下客廳嗎？

1469 pleased
[plizd]
形 高興的，樂意的

片語 be pleased to do... 樂於做… ‖ be pleased with oneself 洋洋得意
例句 He will be pleased to help you.
／他會很樂意幫助你。

1470 pleasure
[ˋplɛʒɚ]
名 愉快；滿足

例句 It's a pleasure to meet you here.
／在這裡碰到你真是令人高興。
用法 pleasure 本身為不可數名詞，但指代具體的某件事時，用作可數名詞，
類似用法的詞還有：failure, success, surprise 等。
片語 to one's pleasure 使某人高興 / 滿意的是 ‖ with pleasure 樂意

1471 plus
[plʌs]
形 正數的；外加的，額外的 介 加，加上
名 加號，正數；好處

例句 The temperature was plus fifteen degrees.
／氣溫是正 15 度。

1472 pocket
[ˋpakɪt]
名 口袋 動 [及物] 把…放進口袋
形 袖珍型的

例句 He put the key into his pocket.
／他把鑰匙放進口袋裡。
片語 in sb.'s pocket 在某人掌握之中，受制於某人 ‖ out of pocket 損失錢財
的 ‖ pick a pocket 扒竊

1473 poem
[ˋpoɪm]
名 詩，韻文

例句 Tom has written a poem.
／湯姆寫了一首詩。

1474 point
[pɔɪnt]
動 [不及物] 指，指向；指出
動 [及物] 指出

例句 She pointed in the direction of the parking lot.
／她指著停車場的方向。
片語 point at (含有惡意地) 指著 ‖ point out 指出，強調 ‖ point to 指向

1475 □□□ **point**
[pɔɪnt]

名 點；小數點；要點；尖端；分數

例句 Our team scored six points.
／我們隊獲得了 6 分。

1476 □□□ **poison**
[ˋpɔɪzn]

名 毒，毒物，毒藥
動 [及物] 使中毒；毒害

例句 He swallowed some type of poison.
／他吞下了某種毒藥。

1477 □□□ **police**
[pəˋlis]

名（常用 the～，視為複數）警察，警方

例句 The police are going to question everyone in the house.
／警察將詢問屋裡的每個人。

用法 police 是集體名詞，作主詞時述語動詞用複數。類例：cattle, people, youth 等。

1478 □□□ **policeman**
[pəˋlismən]

名 (pl.policemen) 警員，警察 (=cop)

例句 The policeman chased and arrested the thief.
／那名警員追逐並逮捕了小偷。

Ⓖroup 3

1479 □□□ **policy**
[ˋpaləsɪ]

名 政策，方針

79

例句 Honesty is the best policy.
／〔諺〕誠實為上策。

1480 □□□ **polite**
[pəˋlaɪt]

形 有禮貌的

例句 She is a polite girl.
／她是個有禮貌的女孩。

片語 be polite to sb. 對某人有禮貌

反義 impolite 形 無禮的；rude 形 粗魯的，無禮的

1481 □□□ **pollute**
[pəˋlut]

動 [及物] 污染，弄髒

例句 The river has been polluted by the factory waste.
／這條河已經被工廠的垃圾污染了。

1482
☐☐☐

pollution
[pə`luʃən]

名 污染；污染物

例句 We must stop the pollution of our beaches.
／我們必須制止對海灘的污染。

片語 air pollution 空氣污染 ‖ water pollution 水污染

1483
☐☐☐

pond
[pɑnd]

名 池塘

例句 There is a pond in front of our court.
／我們院子前面有一座池塘。

1484
☐☐☐

pool
[pul]

名 水池；游泳池；液體的一灘

例句 There were pools of water all over the house after the pipe burst.
／水管破裂後，屋子裡淹成了水池。

1485
☐☐☐

poor
[pʊr]

形 貧困的，窮的；可憐的；貧乏的，

例句 She was too poor to buy clothes for her children.
／她窮得沒錢買衣服給孩子。

片語 be poor in...(=be low in...) 在…方面很差或含量低

反義 rich 形 富裕的

1486
☐☐☐

popcorn
[`pɑp,kɔrn]

名 爆米花

巧記 pop(爆)+corn(玉米)

例句 I am fond of popcorn. ／我很愛吃爆米花。

1487
☐☐☐

popular
[`pɑpjələ]

形 大眾的；流行的；受歡迎的

片語 be popular with... 受…喜愛

例句 The Old Town of Tainan is popular with tourists for its beautiful old buildings.
／台南因為有漂亮的古建築，非常受到遊客喜愛。

1488
☐☐☐

population
[,pɑpjə`leʃən]

名 人口

例句 What was the population of Europe in 1990?
／ 1990 年歐洲的人口是多少 ?

用法 表示人口「多、少」時要用 large 或 small；提問人口數量多少要用 what。

1489 ☐☐☐ **pork**
[pork]
  名 豬肉

例句 Her mother is frying pork in the pan.
／她媽媽正在用平底鍋煎豬肉。

1490 ☐☐☐ **position**
[pə`zɪʃən]
  名 位置；職位；姿勢；立場
  動 [及物] 放置

例句 What's your position on this problem?
／你對這個問題的立場是什麼？
片語 in position 在適當的位置　out of position 不在適當的位置

1491 ☐☐☐ **positive**
[`pazətɪv]
  形 表示贊同的；積極樂觀的

例句 We've had a very positive response to the idea.
／我們對這個想法十分贊同。
反義 negative 形 消極的

1492 ☐☐☐ **possible**
[`pasəbl]
  形 可能的

例句 It is possible for us to finish the work in two days.
／我們兩天之內完成這個工作是有可能的。
片語 as...as possible 盡可能… ‖ if possible 如有可能
反義 impossible 形 不可能的

1493 ☐☐☐ **post**
[post]
  動 [及物] 郵寄；張貼（佈告等）
  名 郵件；職位

例句 The exam results were posted on the blackboard yesterday.
／考試成績昨天張貼在黑板上了。
同義 mail 動 [及物] 郵寄　名 郵件

1494 ☐☐☐ **post**
[post]
  名 柱，杆，樁

例句 He fixed the post firmly in the ground.
／他把柱子牢牢地固定在地上。

1495 ☐☐☐ **postcard**
[`post͵kard]
  名 明信片

例句 A postcard bridges the relationship between us.
／一張明信片拉近了我們之間的關係。

1496
□□□
pot
[pɑt]

名 罐，壺，鍋

例句 Little pot is soon hot.
／〔諺〕小壺易熱。／人窮志短。

1497
□□□
potato
[pə`teto]

名 (pl.potatoes) 馬鈴薯

例句 Will you clean the potatoes?
／請你洗馬鈴薯好嗎？

Ⓖroup 4

1498
□□□
pound
[paʊnd]

名〔英〕英鎊（符號為£）；磅

80

巧記 諧音：〔英〕pound 一音譯→〔漢〕磅

例句 Sugar is sold by the pound.
／糖以磅為單位出售。

注意 重量單位，約454克

1499
□□□
powder
[`paʊdɚ]

名 粉，粉末
動〔及物〕灑粉於，（用粉狀物）覆蓋

例句 The leaves were powdered with dust.
／樹葉被塵土覆蓋住。

辨析 powder, flour
(1) powder「粉」，指香粉、藥粉、火藥粉等。
(2) flour「細粉」，通常指小麥粉。

1500
□□□
power
[`paʊɚ]

名 力量，能力；影響力，勢力；權力

例句 I did everything in my power to help her.
／我盡我所能幫助她。

片語 come into power 當權 ‖ have power over 控制，支配

1501
□□□
powerful
[`paʊɚ-fəl]

形 強大的，有力的；強壯的；（藥）有特效的

例句 The headmaster is a powerful man.
／這位校長是個有力人士。

1502
□□□
practice/-ise
[`præktɪs]

名 實習；練習
動 練習，實踐

例句 Practice makes perfect. ／〔諺〕熟能生巧。

片語 in practice 在實踐中，實際上 ‖ put in/into practice 實行，實施 ‖ practice teacher 實習教師

1503 □□□
praise
[prez]
動 [及物] 名 稱讚

例句 The book received much praise. ／這本書深受歡迎。

片語 in praise of... 為了表揚… ‖ praise sb. for... 因…而讚揚某人 ‖ sing high praise for 高度讚揚

1504 □□□
pray
[pre]
動 請求，懇求；禱告，祈求

例句 She prayed to God to help her. ／她祈求上帝能幫助她。

1505 □□□
precious
[`prɛʃəs]
形 珍貴的，貴重的

巧記 〔熟〕price —i 變 e → 〔根〕prec(i)(價格，價值) → 〔生〕precious 珍貴的，貴重的

例句 Diamonds are precious stones. ／鑽石是一種貴重的石材。

1506 □□□
prefer
[prɪ`fɝ]
動 [及物] 更喜歡，寧可，寧願 (選擇)

巧記 pre-(前，先) + fer(取，拿)

例句 Do you prefer rice or bread? ／你喜歡米飯還是麵包？

片語 prefer doing/to do... 更喜歡做… ‖ prefer sth. to sth. 與…相比更喜歡…

1507 □□□
prepare
[prɪ`pɛr]
動 準備；籌備，(為…) 作準備

片語 prepare for (=get ready for) 為…作準備 ‖ prepare to do sth. 準備去做某事

例句 The students are preparing for the final examination.
／學生們正在為期末考試作準備。

1508 □□□
present
[`prɛznt]
形 在場的；出席的；現在的

例句 How many people were present at the meeting?
／這次會議有多少人出席？

片語 at present 目前，現在 ‖ for the present 暫時

反義 absent 形 缺席的，不在的

1509 □□□
present
[`prɛznt]
名 禮物；(the ～) 現在

例句 He gave his mother a present. ／他送給他母親一份禮物。

1510 □□□ **president**
[ˈprɛzədənt]

图 總統，主席；校長，會長；董事長

例句 In 1896, Abraham Lincoln was elected President of the United States. ／1896 年，亞伯拉罕 · 林肯獲選為美國總統。

1511 □□□ **press**
[prɛs]

图 按，壓，熨；印刷機

例句 Give the doorbell a press. ／按一下門鈴。

1512 □□□ **press**
[prɛs]

動 [及物] 按，壓，熨

例句 She pressed her face against the window.
／她把臉貼在窗戶上。

片語 press sth. into service 強迫徵用 ‖ press sth. on sb. 把⋯強加於人

1513 □□□ **pretty**
[ˈprɪtɪ]

形 動人的，漂亮的，標緻的

例句 She is a pretty girl. ／她是個漂亮的女孩。

1514 □□□ **pretty**
[ˈprɪtɪ]

副 相當地，很，頗

例句 The movie was pretty good. ／那相當不錯。

1515 □□□ **price**
[praɪs]

图 價格；代價
動 [及物] 給⋯定價

例句 Prices are rising. ／物價正在上漲。

用法 (1) 問價錢，英文習慣用「What is the price?」而不用「How much is the price?」

(2) 說價格高或低只能用形容詞 high 或 low，而不能用 expensive 或 cheap。只有在商品作主詞時才能用 expensive 或 cheap。

物品

expensive　　　cheap

昂貴　　　　　　　　便宜

high　　　　　low

價格

1516 □□□ **priest**
[prist]

图 神父，牧師

例句 The priest made the sign of the cross over him.
／神父在他上方畫了個十字。

GEPT
Elementary

Week 5

第五週

P

Lesson **1**

1517 ☐☐☐
🔊**81**

primary
[ˋpraɪˌmɛrɪ]

形 基本的；初級的；小學的；主要的
名 小學

例句 Personal safety is of primary importance.
／人身安全至關重要。

片語 primary school 小學

1518 ☐☐☐

prince
[prɪns]

名 王子，親王

例句 The prince was changed into a frog by magic.
／王子被魔法變成青蛙。

1519 ☐☐☐

princess
[ˋprɪnsɪs]

名 公主，王妃

巧記 prince+-ess(表示陰性)
例句 She was like a princess in a fairy tale.
／她就像童話裡的公主。

1520 ☐☐☐

principal
[ˋprɪnsəpl̩]

名 負責人，校長；資本；主角
形 主要的

例句 The principal allowed the parents to look around the school.
／校長同意家長們參觀學校。

1521 ☐☐☐

principle
[ˋprɪnsəpl̩]

名 原理，規則；原則，信條

例句 It is against my principle to tell a lie.
／說謊違背我的原則。

片語 in principle 原則上，大致上 ‖ on principle 根據原則

1522 ☐☐☐

print
[prɪnt]

動 [及物]列印；印刷
名 指紋；印刷物

例句 They printed 30,000 copies of the book.
／這本書他們印了三萬冊。

第五週

1523 ☐☐☐

printer
[ˋprɪntɚ]

名 印表機；印刷工人

巧記 print+-er(…人)
例句 The printer needs paper.
／印表機需要補充紙了。

1524 □□□ **prison** [ˋprɪzn̩]　　名 監獄；監禁

例句 Peter was sentenced to three years in prison.
／彼得被判監禁三年。

片語 break (out of) prison 越獄 ‖ put/throw sb. in/into prison 把某人關進監獄

用法 表示「監禁」時，prison 前不加冠詞，如 in prison 坐牢，put sb.into prison 將某人關進監獄；表示「監獄」的建築時，prison 前常加冠詞，如 go to the prison to visit him 去監獄探望他。

1525 □□□ **prisoner** [ˋprɪznɚ]　　名 囚犯，犯人；俘虜

例句 She was kept prisoner in a locked room.
／她被關在一間上鎖的房間裡。

1526 □□□ **private** [ˋpraɪvɪt]　　形 私人的，個人的
　　　　　名 私下

例句 The car is his private property.
／這輛汽車是他的私人財產。

片語 in private 私下，祕密地

反義 public 形 公眾的，公共的

1527 □□□ **prize** [praɪz]　　名 獎品；獎金；獎賞

例句 World peace is the greatest prize of all.
／世界和平是最有價值的東西。

1528 □□□ **probably** [ˋprɑbəblɪ]　　副 很可能，大概

例句 It will probably rain tonight.
／今晚很可能會下雨。

1529 □□□ **problem** [ˋprɑbləm]　　名 問題

例句 I can't solve this problem.
／我無法解決這個問題。

片語 no problem 沒問題 ‖ settle/work out a problem 解決問題

1530 □□□ **produce** [prəˋdjus]　　動 [及物] 生產，製造；引起

例句 His hard work produced good results.
／他的努力得到了好成績。

1531 □□□ **product** [ˈprɑdəkt]　名 產品;作品,創作

例句 Coffee is Brazil's main product.
／咖啡是巴西的主要產品。

1532 □□□ **production** [prəˈdʌkʃən]　名 生產,製造;產量

例句 The company is famous for the production of small cars.
／那家公司以生產小型汽車聞名。

1533 □□□ **professor** [prəˈfɛsə-]　名 大學教授

例句 He is a professor of history at the university.
／他是這所大學的歷史教授。

1534 □□□ **program** [ˈprogræm]　名 節目;計畫;程式
動 [及物] 為電腦設計程式;安排

例句 What is your program for tomorrow?
／你明天有什麼安排?

辨析 list, menu, program
(1) list 可泛指任何「單子」。
(2) menu 專指餐館裡的「功能表」,在電腦用語中被引申為「菜單」。
(3) program 是「節目單」,在電腦用語中指「程式」。

1535 □□□ **progress** [prəˈgrɛs]　動 前進;進展
名 進步

片語 in progress 進行中 ‖ make progress in... 在…取得進步
例句 You've made great progress in speaking English.
／你說英語已大有進步。

辨析 progress, advance
(1) progress「進步」,指不斷的進步,是很生動的用語,常被用作抽象意義。
(2) advance「前進,進步」,側重向前達到某目的,再回看出發點,感覺
到 a great advance。

Group 2

1536 □□□ **project** [prəˈdʒɛkt]　名 計畫,方案;專案

82 例句 They formed a project to build a new school building.
／他們計畫蓋一棟新的校舍。

1537 □□□ **promise**
[ˋprɑmɪs]

名 諾言
動 [及物] 答應；允諾

例句 My father has made a promise that he will take me to Dubai next month.
／我父親承諾下個月要帶我去杜拜。

片語 break one's promise 違背諾言　keep one's promise 遵守諾言

1538 □□□ **pronounce**
[prəˋnaʊns]

動 發音；宣佈，宣告

例句 The doctor pronounced the patient to be dead.
／醫生宣告那個病人已經死亡。

衍生 pronunciation〔注意拼寫〕名 發音，讀音

1539 □□□ **propose**
[prəˋpoz]

動 [及物] 提議，建議；提名，推薦；打算

例句 I propose we should have another meeting.
／我建議我們再開一次會。

用法 propose 作「提議，建議」講時，後接受詞從句一般用 (should+) 動詞原形表示虛擬語氣。

1540 □□□ **protect**
[prəˋtɛkt]

動 [及物] 保護

例句 He protected his hands from the cold with gloves.
／他戴手套保護手不受凍。

用法 protect...from/against... 指「保護…不受…的損害或侵犯」。但對於較大的事情 (如火災) 通常用 against，對於較小的事情用 from。

1541 □□□ **protection**
[prəˋtɛkʃən]

名 保護，防護；防護物

例句 The trees were a good protection against the wind.
／樹木是很好的防風屏障。

片語 under the protection of... 在…的保護下

1542 □□□ **proud**
[praʊd]

形 自豪的；驕傲的

片語 be proud of... 為…而感到驕傲 ‖ be proud to do sth. 自豪地做某事
例句 She is proud of herself for not giving up easily.
／她對自己沒有輕易放棄感到驕傲。

1543 prove
[pruv]
勔 證明，證實；檢驗，查驗

例句 You needn't prove① the truth of the news, which has proved②(to be) true.
／你不必查驗這項消息的真實性，它已被證實是真的了。

用法 prove ①「證明」，後接名詞或 that 從句；prove ②「(結果) 表明」，後接 (to be+) 形容詞，主動式表被動意義。

1544 provide
[prə`vaɪd]
勔 提供，供應；(法律等) 規定

片語 provide against 作準備，預防短缺 ‖ provide for 贍養，供養 ‖ provide sb.with sth.(provide sth.to/for) sb. 提供某人某物

例句 The sun provides us with light and heat. / The sun provides light and heat for us.
／太陽提供我們光和熱。

1545 public
[`pʌblɪk]
形 公共的；公開的；公用的
名 公眾

片語 in public 公開地

例句 Praise your friends in public.
／在公開場合讚揚朋友。

反義 private 形 個人的，私有的

1546 pull
[pʊl]
勔 拉；拖；拔
名 拉，拖，扯；力，引力

例句 The horse was pulling a cart. ／那匹馬拉著馬車。

片語 pull away 開走，(使) 離開 ‖ pull down 拆毀 ‖ pull in (車) 停下，(車) 進站，(船) 到岸 ‖ pull out ①拔出，抽出，取出 ②(車、船) 駛出 ③擺脫困境

反義 push 動 推 名 推 (力)

1547 pump
[pʌmp]
名 泵；幫浦，抽水機
勔 用抽水機抽…

例句 Every village used to have a pump from which everyone drew their water.
／過去每個村莊都有抽水機供人們抽水用。

片語 pump...from... 從…裡面抽…

1548 pumpkin
[`pʌmpkɪn]
名 南瓜，南瓜藤

例句 Pumpkin pie is a traditional American dish served on Thanksgiving. ／南瓜派是美國傳統的感恩節食物。

1549 □□□ **punish** [`pʌnɪʃ]
動 [及物] 處罰，懲罰

例句 Anybody who breaks the rules will be punished.
／任何人破壞了規矩，都要受到懲罰。

1550 □□□ **puppy** [`pʌpɪ]
名 小狗，幼犬；幼小的動物

例句 The puppy was lying on the grass.
／那隻小狗正躺在草地上。

1551 □□□ **purchase** [`pɝtʃəs]
動 [及物] 買，購買，訂購（▲比 buy 正式）
名 購買，購買的物品

例句 I purchased this book at the store.
／我在這家店裡買了這本書。

1552 □□□ **purple** [`pɝpl]
形 紫的
名 紫色

例句 She wore purple and green silk.
／她穿紫綠相間的綢衣。

1553 □□□ **purpose** [`pɝpəs]
名 目的，意圖

例句 The purpose of this meeting is to protect our environment.
／這次會議的目的是保護我們的環境。
片語 on purpose 故意

1554 □□□ **purse** [pɝs]
名（女式）錢包；（女用）手提包

例句 I kept my money in a leather purse.
／我把錢放在皮包裡。

Group 3

1555 □□□ **push** [pʊʃ]
動 推；督促
名 推，推力；促進

Track 83

例句 The rise in interest rates will push prices up.
／利率提高將促使物價上揚。
片語 push...in 把…擠進 ‖ push over 推倒
反義 pull 動 拉

1556 □□□
put
[pʊt]

動 [及物] (put, put) 放；擺；裝

片語 put away 放好 ‖ put down ①記下，寫下 ②放下 ③鎮壓 ‖ put off 延遲，拖延 ‖ put on 穿上，戴上 ‖ put out 熄滅，撲滅 ‖ put up ①掛起，舉起 ②建造，搭建 ③張貼

例句 Never put off till tomorrow what you can do today.
／〔諺〕今日事今日畢。

1557 □□□
puzzle
[`pʌzl]

名 猜謎；難題；迷惑
動 [及物] 使迷惑，使為難

例句 Do you know the key to the puzzle?
／你知道謎底嗎？

1558 □□□
quality
[`kwɑlətɪ]

名 品質；品德，品性；性質

例句 This cloth is good in quality.
／這匹布的品質很好。

1559 □□□
quarter
[`kwɔrtɚ]

名 四分之一；一刻（十五分鐘）；一季

例句 I'll meet you in a quarter of an hour.
／我們十五分鐘後見。

1560 □□□
queen
[`kwin]

名 女王；（樸克牌或西洋棋中的）王后

巧記 圖解 queen 的一詞多義：

| the queen of chess 棋后 | the queen bee 蜂后 | the queen of hearts 紅桃皇后 | queen 女王 |

例句 People bow to the Queen as a mark of respect.
／人們向女王鞠躬以示敬意。

1561 □□□
question
[`kwɛstʃən]

名 問題
動 [及物] 詢問，審問；懷疑

例句 He was questioned by the police.
／他被警方審問。

片語 out of question 毫無疑問 ‖ out of the question 不可能的
辨析 problem, question
二者都可作「問題」解，有時可通用。
(1) problem 著重指難以解決 (solve) 的「問題，難題」。
(2) question 指提出 (ask) 並有待回答 (answer) 的「問題，疑問」。

1562 ☐☐☐
quick
[kwɪk]

形 快的，迅速的

例句 Be quick! The train will leave in five minutes!
／快一點！再五分鐘火車就要開了！

1563 ☐☐☐
quiet
[`kwaɪət]

形 安靜的；寧靜的

例句 It is very beautiful and quiet here, but it rains a lot.
／這裡很漂亮也很安靜，只是經常下雨。

反義 noisy 形 喧鬧的

1564 ☐☐☐
quit
[kwɪt]

動 (quitted, quitted; quit, quit) 停止，放棄；
離開，辭 (職)；戒 (煙)

例句 Quit smoking in this room, please.
／在這房間裡請勿吸煙。

用法 quit 接動名詞作受詞，接不定式作目的副詞。

1565 ☐☐☐
quite
[kwaɪt]

副 很；十分；相當

例句 You have done it quite well.
／你做得相當好。

1566 ☐☐☐
quiz
[kwɪz]

名 小測驗；問答比賽，益智競賽

例句 We had a quiz in English yesterday.
／我們昨天英文小考。

1567 ☐☐☐
rabbit
[`ræbɪt]

名 兔子；兔肉，兔毛

片語 as timid as a rabbit 害羞的，膽怯的，膽小如鼠
例句 This boy is as timid as a rabbit.
／這個男孩膽小如鼠。

1568 ☐☐☐ **race**
[res]

名 人種，種族；家族；競賽；賽跑
動 賽跑

例句 There are many races of people in the world.
／世界上有許多人種。

1569 ☐☐☐ **radio**
[ˋredɪˌo]

名 無線廣播電台；(pl. radios) 收音機

例句 Tom studied English on the radio when he was young.
／湯姆年輕時透過收音機學英語。

注意 限定詞名詞，當形容詞用

1570 ☐☐☐ **railroad**
[ˋrelˌrod]

名〔美〕鐵路；鐵路系統

例句 Could you direct me to the railroad station?
／你能告訴我到火車站怎麼走嗎？

同義 railway 名〔英〕鐵路

1571 ☐☐☐ **rain**
[ren]

名 雨；雨天；雨季
動〔不及物〕下雨〔▲主詞是 it〕

例句 The rains began in April.
／雨季從四月開始。

1572 ☐☐☐ **rainbow**
[ˋrenˌbo]

名 彩虹

例句 We saw a beautiful rainbow across the sky.
／我們看見一道美麗的彩虹橫跨天空。

bow 弓 ──→ rainbow 彩虹

1573 ☐☐☐ **rainy**
[ˋrenɪ]

形 陰雨的，多雨的

例句 It will be rainy tomorrow.
／明天有雨。

片語 for a rainy day 未雨綢繆

1574 raise
[rez]

動 [及物] 提高，舉起；飼養；籌（款）；招（兵）
名 舉起；升起；加薪

例句 They are raising funds to help the poor.
／他們正在籌款幫助窮人。

片語 raise a question 提出一個問題 ‖ raise money for... 為…籌錢 ‖ raise one's hand 舉手 ‖ raise one's voice 提高聲音

1575 range
[rendʒ]

名 區域，範圍
動 [及物] 包括；在某個範圍之內

例句 This is beyond my range of knowledge.
／這超出我的知識範圍。

片語 range from...to... 在…範圍內變化，範圍包括從…到…

1576 rapid
[`ræpɪd]

形 快的，迅速的

例句 The patient made a rapid recovery. ／病人的復原迅速。

反義 slow **形** 慢的，緩慢的

1577 rare
[rɛr]

形 稀有的，罕見的；（空氣等）稀薄的

例句 Snow is quite rare in this district.
／這個地區下雪是十分罕見的。

1578 rat
[ræt]

名 老鼠

例句 A rat crossing the street is chased by all.
／〔諺〕老鼠過街，人人喊打。

注意 體型比 mouse 大

1579 rather
[`ræðɚ]

副 寧願；相當

片語 rather than 而不 ‖ would rather do ...than do... 寧願…，而不願…

例句 I would rather watch TV at home than play soccer outside.
／我寧願在家裡看電視，也不要去外面踢足球。

1580 reach
[ritʃ]

動 到達；達到
名 手臂展開的長度

例句 We didn't reach London before dark.
／天黑前我們還沒到達倫敦。

片語 beyond/out of sb.'s reach 某人能力不及的　within sb.'s reach/within reach of sb. 某人能力所及的

1581 □□□ **read**
[rid]

動 (read, read) 讀，閱讀；了解

例句 While reading today's newspaper, I read about the traffic accident.
／看到今天的報紙時，我了解了那起交通事故。

1582 □□□ **ready**
['rɛdɪ]

形 準備好的；有準備的

片語 be ready to do sth. 願意做某事 ‖ get ready for sth. 為…作準備
例句 Are you getting ready for the Spring Festival?
／你們正在為春節作準備嗎？

1583 □□□ **real**
['riəl]

形 真實的，真正的；衷心的

例句 That is not her real name.
／那不是她的真名。

1584 □□□ **realize/-ise**
['riə,laɪz]

動 [及物] 認識到；實現

例句 His dream has been realized.
／他的夢想實現了。

1585 □□□ **really**
['riəlɪ]

副 〔表明事實或真相〕真正地，實際上；〔強調觀點等〕確實，的確

例句 Tell me what really happened.
／告訴我究竟發生了什麼事。

1586 □□□ **reason**
['rizn̩]

名 理由，原因

例句 I'd like to know the reason why she didn't accept the job.
／我想知道她不接受這份工作的原因。

用法 reason 後面的限定詞從句可由 why 引導，why 也可以省略。
片語 by reason of 由於，因為 ‖ for reasons of... 因…的理由 ‖ in reason 合理的，正當的，理所當然的

1587 □□□ **receive**
[rɪ'siv]

動 [及物] 收到；接到

例句 Did you receive my presents on your birthday?
／你生日那天收到我的禮物了嗎？

辨析 receive, accept

receive 指客觀上「收到」，accept 指主觀上 (願意)「接受」。客觀上 receive，主觀上不一定 accept。

※ He received a gift, but he didn't accept it. 他收到了一件禮物，但他沒有接受。

receive　accept

1588
☐☐☐
recent
[ˈrisn̩t]

形 最近的，新的，近代的

例句 The situation has improved in recent years.
／最近幾年形勢有所好轉。

反義 early 形 早期的；old 形 年代久遠的

1589
☐☐☐
recently
[ˈrisn̩tlɪ]

副 最近，近來

例句 She's been working hard recently. ／她最近工作很努力。

用法 recently 可與過去時或現在完成時連用，但通常不與現在時連用。

同義 lately 副 近來，最近

1590
☐☐☐
record
[rɪˈkɔrd]

名 紀錄；唱片
動 記錄；錄音 (影)

例句 I've recorded the whole concert.
／我把整場音樂會錄下了。

片語 break the record 打破紀錄 ‖ keep the record 保持紀錄 ‖ set the record 創造紀錄

1591
☐☐☐
recover
[rɪˈkʌvɚ]

動 [不及物] 恢復，痊癒
動 [及物] 重新得到；使復原，使康復

例句 The patient had recovered from his illness.
／病人已經康復了。

片語 recover oneself ①恢復健康，痊癒 ②清醒過來

1592
☐☐☐
rectangle
[rɛkˈtæŋgl̩]

名 長方形

巧記 rect(=right 垂直)+angle(角度)

例句 The width of the rectangle is seven meters.
／這個長方形七公尺寬。

1593
recycle
[ri`saɪk!]

動 [及物] 回收，再利用

85

巧記 re-(= again 又，再)+cycle(迴圈)；再迴圈

例句 Glass, plastic and paper can all be recycled.
／玻璃、塑膠和紙類都可以回收。

1594
red
[rɛd]

形 紅的，紅色的；漲紅的
名 紅色

例句 Tom was red in the face with anger.
／湯姆氣得滿臉通紅。

1595
refrigerator
[rɪ`frɪdʒə͵retə]

名 冰箱 (=fridge=icebox)

例句 We have a refrigerator in our kitchen.
／我們廚房裡有一台冰箱。

1596
refuse
[rɪ`fjuz]

動 拒絕，回絕

例句 He refused to work for her.
／他拒絕為她工作。

用法 refuse 只接動詞不定式，不接動詞 -ing 形式。

1597
regard
[rɪ`gɑrd]

動 [及物] 看待；認為
名 尊重；問候

片語 regard...as... 把…當作…
例句 I regard him as a friend.
／我把他當作朋友。

1598
region
[`ridʒən]

名 地區，地帶，區域；行政區

例句 Our town is in an industrial region.
／我們的城鎮位於工業區。

1599
regret
[rɪ`grɛt]

名 動 遺憾；抱歉；悔恨

片語 regret doing/having done sth. 為做了某事表示後悔 ‖ regret to do sth.
對要做某事表示遺憾
例句 I regret to tell you that I have regretted lending you so
much money.
／我很抱歉告訴你，我很後悔借你這麼多錢。

第
五
週

1600 regular [ˈrɛgjələ]　形 有規律的，固定的；經常的，習慣性的

例句 He is a regular customer of that restaurant.
／他是那家餐廳的常客。

1601 reject [rɪˈdʒɛkt]　動 [及物] 拒絕；退回，摒棄

巧記 re-(=back)+ject(=throw)

例句 She rejected his offer of help.
／她拒絕了他提供的幫助。

同義 refuse 動 拒絕

反義 accept 動 接受

1602 relative [ˈrɛlətɪv]　名 親屬，親戚，同類
　　　　　　　　　　　形 有關的；比較的，相對的

片語 relative to... 和…比較起來，關於…的

例句 Supply is relative to demand. ／供給和需求是相對的。

1603 remember [rɪˈmɛmbə]　動 [及物] 記住，記得；想起

片語 remember doing sth. 記得曾做過某事 ‖ remember to do sth. 記得要做某事

例句 "Remember to return the bat to me." "But I remember having returned it to you."
／「記得把球拍還我。」「可是我記得已經還給你了。」

1604 remind [rɪˈmaɪnd]　動 [及物] 使想起，提醒

片語 remind sb. of... 使某人想起… ‖ remind sb. to do... 提醒某人做…

例句 Remind me to write to mother.
／提醒我要寫信給媽媽。

1605 rent [rɛnt]　動 [及物] (rent, rent) 出租，出借；租用
　　　　　　　名 租金

例句 Mr. Smith rents this flat to us.
／史密斯先生把公寓租給我們。

片語 for rent 出租的 ‖ rent out 把…租出去

辨析 rent, hire
出租房屋常用 rent，但租用設備用 hire。rent 表示「租出去」和「租借」兩種含義：
(1) rent...from... 向…租借…
(2) rent...to... 把…租給…

1606 repair
□□□
[rɪ`pɛr]

動 [及物] **名** 修理；修補

例句 I put my car into the garage for repairs.
／我把車子送到修車廠修理。

片語 in repair 修好的 ‖ under repair 在修理中

1607 repeat
□□□
[rɪ`pit]

動 重複

例句 Please repeat what I've just told you.
／請重複我剛才告訴你的事情。

用法 repeat 不可與 again 連用，因 repeat 本身已含有「重複」之義。

1608 reply
□□□
[rɪ`plaɪ]

動 名 回答，答覆

例句 Should I reply to his letter?
／我要回他的信嗎？

辨析 reply, answer
(1) reply 為正式用語，一般表示較正式或經過考慮的答覆，用作及物動詞
時，後接直接引語或 that 從句；用作不及物動詞時與介系詞 to 連用。
(2) answer 是普通用語，一般用作及物動詞。

1609 report
□□□
[rɪ`port]

名 動 報告；報導

例句 The policeman reported that he had not seen anybody.
／警察報告說他沒看見任何人。

片語 It is reported that... 據報導… ‖ make a report 作報告

1610 reporter
□□□
[rɪ`portɚ]

名 記者，報告人

例句 The newspaper reporters interviewed the minister.
／報社記者採訪了部長。

ⒼGroup 2

1611 require
□□□
86
[rɪ`kwaɪr]

動 [及物] 需要；要求，規定

例句 They require my appearance. / They require me to appear.
／他們要求我出面。

1612 □□□

respect
[rɪ`spɛkt]

動 [及物] 尊敬；重視，考慮
名 尊敬；關心

例句 Everyone should respect his teachers.
／每個人都應該尊敬老師。

片語 in/with respect to 關於 ‖ without respect to 不管，不論

1613 □□□

responsible
[rɪ`spɑnsəbl]

形 需負責任的，承擔責任的；責任重大的，重要的

例句 I will hold you personally responsible if anything goes wrong.
／如果有什麼差錯，我要你個人負起責任。

片語 be responsible for sth./to sb. 對…負責
▲如果主詞是人，表示「應負責的，有責任的」；如果主詞不是人，則表示造成事實的「原因」。

用法 responsible 作前置限定詞與作後置限定詞的意義不同:a responsible person 指「可信賴的人，可靠的人」；而 the person responsible 指「負責人，主管人」。

1614 □□□

rest
[rɛst]

名 休息；(the ～) 剩餘的部分
動 [不及物] 休息

片語 have/take a rest 休息一下
例句 I had an hour's rest after work.
／下班後我休息了一個小時。

用法 the rest 作主詞時，若代替可數名詞，句子述語用複數；代替不可數名詞，句子述語用單數。

1615 □□□

restaurant
[`rɛstərənt]

名 餐廳，飯店

例句 There is a new restaurant.
／有一家新餐廳。

1616 □□□

restroom
[`rɛst͵rum]

名 公共廁所，休息室 (=rest room)

例句 Do you know where the restroom is?
／你知道廁所在哪裡嗎？

1617 □□□

result
[rɪ`zʌlt]

名 結果；成果
動 [不及物] 結果，導致；起因於，因…而造成

片語 as a result 結果 ‖ as a result of 由於，作為…的結果 ‖ resulted from 起因於
例句 She died as a result of her injuries.
／她因為受傷而導致死亡。

1618 □□□ 辨析 result, effect, influence
(1) result「結果，影響」，指由某一行動、計畫或事件帶來的直接的後果等。
(2) effect「結果，影響」，指由一行動、計畫、事件帶來的間接的後果或某一事物產生的效應 (動詞為 affect)。
(3) influence「影響」，指對周圍一切或今後歷史等產生的影響，或指有影響、有勢力的人或有影響的事物。

1619 □□□

return
[rɪ`tɜ·n]

動 [不及物] 返回；恢復　動 [及物] 歸還
名 回來；回復

例句 Please return my book. ／請把我的書還我。
用法 return 不和 back, again 連用，因 return 自身已含「返回」之義。
辨析 圖解 borrow, lend, return 和 keep:

| lend the book | borrow the book | return the book | keep the book for a week |
| 借出書 | 借入書 | 歸還書 | 借書一週 |

1620 □□□

review
[rɪ`vju]

動 [及物] 複習；回顧
名 審查，檢查；(尤指為準備考試的) 複習

巧記 re-(=back)+view(看)；往回看 → 複習；回顧
例句 He reviewed the whole of his past life.
／他回顧了自己過去的所有生活。

1621 □□□

revise
[rɪ`vaɪz]

動 [及物] 複習；修訂，校訂

巧記 re-(=again)+vise(=see)；根義：再看，再閱 → 複習；修訂，修改
例句 This dictionary has been completely revised.
／這本字典已全部修訂過。

1622 □□□

rice
[raɪs]

名 米，飯

例句 She comes from the land of rice and fish.
／她來自魚米之鄉。

1623 □□□

rich
[rɪtʃ]

形 有錢的；富饒的，豐富

片語 be rich in 富於…
例句 Our country is rich in resources.
／我們國家的資源豐富。

1624 □□□
ride
[raɪd]

動 (rode, ridden) 騎（馬、腳踏車等）；乘（車、船）

例句 She was riding a bicycle.
／她在騎腳踏車。

1625 □□□
right
[raɪt]

副 正好；恰當地；立刻，馬上
形 正確的

例句 He was standing right here.
／他就站在這裡。

片語 right away 馬上，立刻 ‖ right now 現在
反義 wrong 形 錯誤的

1626 □□□
right
[raɪt]

副 向右，朝右
形 右邊的 名 右邊

巧記 圖解 right 的不同詞義：

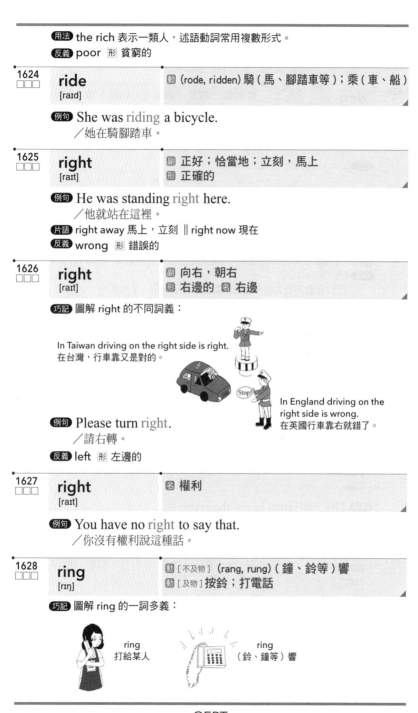

In Taiwan driving on the right side is right.
在台灣，行車靠右是對的。

Stop!

In England driving on the right side is wrong.
在英國行車靠右就錯了。

例句 Please turn right.
／請右轉。

反義 left 形 左邊的

1627 □□□
right
[raɪt]

名 權利

例句 You have no right to say that.
／你沒有權利說這種話。

1628 □□□
ring
[rɪŋ]

動 [不及物] (rang, rung)（鐘、鈴等）響
動 [及物] 按鈴；打電話

巧記 圖解 ring 的一詞多義：

ring
打給某人

ring
（鈴、鐘等）響

片語 ring back 回電 ‖ ring off 掛斷電話 ‖ ring (sb.) up 打電話給 (某人)
例句 We shall tell you the results after they ring us up.
／他們打電話來後，我們會告訴你結果。

1629
□□□

ring
[rɪŋ]

名 鈴聲，鐘聲；環形物 (如圈、環、戒指等)

例句 I gave three rings at the door.
／我在門口按了三次鈴。
片語 give sb. a ring 打電話給某人

1630
□□□

rise
[raɪz]

動 [不及物] (rose, risen) 名 上升；提高；增長

例句 Food prices are still rising.
／食品的價格仍在上漲。
片語 ive rise to 引起，使發生 ‖ rise to one's feet 站起來 ‖ rise up 升起，上升
辨析 lift, raise, rise
(1) lift 是用體力或機械力把某物從地面舉到一定高度。
(2) raise 強調抬高動作的姿勢。
(3) rise 意為「升起，站起來」，是不及物動詞，表示主詞由低到高的變化
過程，通常指日、月、星辰升起。

Group 3

1631
□□□

87

river
[ˈrɪvɚ]

名 江，河

例句 The longest river in Africa is the Nile.
／非洲最長的河流是尼羅河。

1632
□□□

road
[rod]

名 路，道路，公路；手段，方法

例句 The road runs along the river.
／那條道路沿著河流延伸。
片語 by road 經由公路 ‖ get out of the road ①讓路 (給某人) ②不妨礙 (某人)

1633
□□□

rob
[rɑb]

動 [及物] 搶劫，盜竊；(非法) 剝奪，使喪失

片語 rob sb. of sth. 搶走某人的東西
例句 Robbers robbed him of all his money.
／強盜搶走了他所有的錢。

1634 robot
[ˈrobət]
名 機器人；機器般工作的人

例句 They use robots to work in dangerous areas.
／他們在危險區域使用機器人工作。

1635 rock
[rak]
名 岩石；暗礁；巨石塊

例句 They climbed the steep rock.
／他們攀登了那塊陡峭的岩石。

1636 rock
[rak]
動 [及物] 搖動，搖晃；使震驚
動 [不及物] 搖晃，顛簸

例句 Mother rocked the baby to sleep.
／母親搖動嬰兒入睡。

1637 role
[rol]
名 角色；作用

片語 play an important role in... 在…中發揮重要作用
例句 Words play an important role in everyday life.
／文字在日常生活中發揮重要作用。

1638 roll
[rol]
動 滾動；（人、動物）打滾
名 麵包捲；蛋捲

巧記 圖解 roll 的一詞多義：

| a roll of wallpaper 一卷壁紙 | bread rolls 小圓麵包 | towel roll 毛巾滾軸 | toilet rolls 捲筒衛生紙 | a roll of film 一捲底片 |

例句 The puppy was rolling on the grass.
／那隻小狗在草地上打滾。
片語 roll back 倒帶 ‖ roll over 翻滾

1639 roof
[ruf]
名 屋頂，車頂，頂部

例句 The roofs of our school house are red.
／我們校舍的屋頂是紅色的。
片語 the roof of the world 世界屋脊

1640 room
[rum]
图 房間；空間；餘地

例句 This room has a fine view of the sea.
／從這房間可清楚地看到大海的景色。
片語 make room for 為⋯空出地方 ‖ room and board 食宿
辨析 room, place
(1) room 表示「位置，空間」，常指正在尋找或沒有被佔用的空間。
(2) place 表示「位置，地點」，指已經佔用或選用的單個的位置。

1641 root
[rut]
图 根（部）；起因，根源
動 （使）生根

例句 These plants produce a number of thin roots.
／這些植物會長出一些細根。
片語 take root ①生根，紮根 ②建立，確立

1642 rope
[rop]
图 繩子，繩索；一串（東西）

例句 Hold the rope tight and I'll pull you up.
／抓緊繩子，我會拉你上來。
片語 know the ropes 知道內情

1643 rose
[roz]
图 薔薇科植物，玫瑰花

例句 There are many red roses in her garden.
／她的花園裡有許多紅玫瑰。

1644 round
[raʊnd]
形 圓形的 副 圍繞地
介 在⋯周圍 图 （一）回合

例句 The earth moves round the sun.
／地球圍繞太陽運行。
片語 round about 周圍的，附近的
辨析 around，round
around 作「環繞，在四周，繞過，轉向」等義時，通常可用 round 代替，只是美國人較常用 around，英國人則較常用 round。作「大約，在附近」等義時，用 around 較合適。

1645 row
[ro]
图 排，行

例句 I'm in row two.
／我在第二排。
片語 in a row ①排成一列 ②接連不斷地

1646 □□□
row
[ro]

動 [不及物] 划船
動 [及物] 划 (船)

例句 Please row me across the river.
／請划船帶我過河。

1647 □□□
royal
[ˋrɔɪəl]

形 王室的，皇家的；堂皇的，高貴的，莊嚴的

例句 Henry was born of a royal family.
／亨利生於皇家。

1648 □□□
rub
[rʌb]

動 擦，摩擦

例句 The cat rubbed its head against my legs.
／貓把牠的頭靠在我腿上磨蹭。

1649 □□□
rubber
[ˋrʌbɚ]

名 橡皮擦；板擦；橡膠；(pl.) 膠鞋；本壘板
形 橡膠的

巧記 〔熟〕 rub(擦，摩擦)→ 〔生〕 rubber 橡皮擦
例句 You use a rubber to rub out pencil marks which are wrong.
／你用橡皮擦擦掉寫錯的鉛筆字跡。

Ⓖ roup 4

1650 □□□
88
rude
[rud]

形 粗魯的，不禮貌的；粗陋的；原始的

例句 He was punished because he was rude to his teacher.
／他因為對老師不禮貌，所以被處罰。

反義 polite 形 有禮貌的，客氣的

1651 □□□
ruin
[ˋrʊɪn]

動 (使) 毀滅，(使) 毀壞；(使) 破產
名 (pl.) 廢墟，遺跡

例句 The storm ruined the crops.
／暴風雨毀壞了農作物。

片語 be/lie in ruins ①倒塌 ②崩潰，垮掉 ‖ fall in/into ruin 衰落，敗落
辨析 ruin, destroy

ruin (逐漸地) 毀壞   destroy (徹底地) 破壞

1652 ☐☐☐ **rule**
[rul]

名 規則；規定
動 [及物] 統治

例句 We must obey the rules.
／我們必須遵守規定。

片語 as a rule 通常，一般來說

1653 ☐☐☐ **ruler**
[`rulɚ]

名 尺；統治者

例句 Do you need a ruler?
／你需要尺嗎？

1654 ☐☐☐ **run**
[rʌn]

動 (ran, run) 跑；工作，運轉，經營
名 跑步

例句 He ran down the road.
／他沿著街跑去。

片語 in the long run 從長期來看　in the short run 從短期來看 ‖ run across 偶然遇見 ‖ run after ①追趕，追捕 ②追求 ‖ run away 逃走 ‖ run into ①(開車) 撞上 ②偶然遇見 ‖ run out (of) 用完，耗盡

辨析 run out, run out of
(1) run out 是不及物短語動詞 (= become used up)，其主詞通常為時間、食物、金錢等名詞。
(2) run out of 是及物短語動詞，表示主動含義，主詞一般是人。

1655 ☐☐☐ **rush**
[rʌʃ]

動 [不及物]　名 衝，奔

例句 At the end of the film there was a rush for the exit.
／電影一結束，大家都湧向出口。

片語 rush hour 交通尖峰期 ‖ rush into 衝進

1656 ☐☐☐ **Russia**
[`rʌʃə]

名 俄羅斯，俄國

例句 She comes from Russia.
／她來自俄羅斯。

1657 ☐☐☐ **Russian**
[`rʌʃən]

形 俄國的；俄國人的；俄語的
名 俄國人；俄語

例句 After mastering English Marx went on to study Russian.
／精通了英語後，馬克思接著去學俄語。

1658 ☐☐☐ **sad**
[sæd]

形 悲哀的，傷心的；令人傷心的

例句 He is very sad about his cat's death.
／他的貓死了，他很傷心。

反義 glad 形 高興的；happy 形 高興的

1659 ☐☐☐ **safe**
[sef]

形 安全的；保險的；平安的

例句 The children returned safe.
／孩子們平安歸來。

片語 safe and sound 安然無恙

反義 dangerous 形 危險的

注意 不置於名詞之前，多與 come, arrive, return 等動詞連用

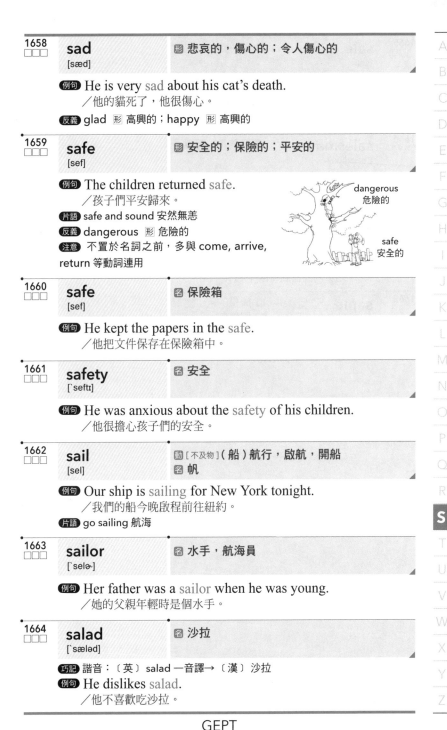

dangerous
危險的

safe
安全的

1660 ☐☐☐ **safe**
[sef]

名 保險箱

例句 He kept the papers in the safe.
／他把文件保存在保險箱中。

1661 ☐☐☐ **safety**
[`seftɪ]

名 安全

例句 He was anxious about the safety of his children.
／他很擔心孩子們的安全。

1662 ☐☐☐ **sail**
[sel]

動 [不及物]（船）航行，啟航，開船
名 帆

例句 Our ship is sailing for New York tonight.
／我們的船今晚啟程前往紐約。

片語 go sailing 航海

1663 ☐☐☐ **sailor**
[`selɚ]

名 水手，航海員

例句 Her father was a sailor when he was young.
／她的父親年輕時是個水手。

1664 ☐☐☐ **salad**
[`sæləd]

名 沙拉

巧記 諧音：〔英〕salad 一音譯→〔漢〕沙拉

例句 He dislikes salad.
／他不喜歡吃沙拉。

1665 □□□ **sale**
[sel]

名 賣；銷售；特價

片語 for sale 待售，供出售 ‖ on sale 上市，開賣；出售；特賣

例句 His new book will be on sale here next month.
／他的新書下個月將在這裡開賣。

1666 □□□ **salesman**
[`selzmən]

名 業務員，推銷員

例句 Do you know the salesman?
／你認識那個推銷員嗎？

1667 □□□ **salt**
[sɔlt]

名 食鹽，鹽狀物

例句 Too much salt is not good for your health.
／過量的食鹽對健康不利。

1668 □□□ **same**
[sem]

代 同樣的人 / 物
形 同樣的

例句 She was born on the same day as me.
／她和我同一天出生。

1669 ☐☐☐
89
sample
[`sæmpl]

名 樣品，樣本；試用品
形 例題 動[及物]從⋯抽樣；嘗試

巧記 〔熟〕example 例子，榜樣 → 〔生〕sample 樣品，標本
例句 I'd like to see some samples of your work.
／我想看看你做的一些樣品。

1670 ☐☐☐
sand
[sænd]

名 沙，沙子；沙灘，沙地

例句 There is some sand in the bottle.
／瓶子裡有些沙子。

1671 ☐☐☐
sandwich
[`sændwɪtʃ]

名 三明治

巧記 諧音：〔英〕sandwich 一音譯→〔漢〕三明治
▲詞源：18 世紀時英國的 Sandwich 伯爵嗜賭，為免於離開賭桌用餐而想出麵包加肉片的吃法，這種食品因此而得名。

例句 Would you like some sandwiches for lunch?
／你午餐要吃點三明治嗎？

1672 ☐☐☐
satisfy
[`sætɪsˌfaɪ]

動[及物]使滿足；使滿意

例句 That answer won't satisfy her.
／那個答案不能讓她滿意。

1673 ☐☐☐
Saturday
[`sætə-de]

名 星期六 (=Sat.)

例句 She will come on Saturday morning.
／她星期六早上要來。

1674 ☐☐☐
saucer
[`sɔsə-]

名 淺碟

例句 The flying saucer is yet an unsolved mystery.
／飛碟仍是個未解之謎。

注意 原是盛 sauce 的器具

a saucer

a cup and saucer
一組杯碟

1675 save
□□□
[sev]

動 [及物] 挽救；儲蓄；儲存；節省；保存

巧記 圖解 save 的一詞多義：

save a ball
救球

save a child from
drowning
救溺水的小孩

save
存錢

save a file
存檔

例句 If you save money now, you will be able to buy a car soon.
／如果你現在存錢，不久就能買一輛車了。

片語 save one's life 挽救某人的生命

1676 say
□□□
[se]

動 [及物] (said, said) 說，講

片語 It is said that... 據說…

例句 It is said that He is one of the richest people in the world.
／據說他是全世界最富有的人之一。

1677 scale
□□□
[skel]

名 刻度，尺度；等級；規模；(pl.) 天平，磅秤；
比例尺

例句 I step on the scales every morning.
／我每天早上都會量體重。

片語 on a...scale …規模地，在…規模上 ‖ scale down 按比例縮減

1678 scared
□□□
[skɛrd]

形 害怕的，對…感到恐懼

例句 I have always been scared of dogs. ／我一直很怕狗。

1679 scarf
□□□
[skɑrf]

名 (pl.scarfs 或 scarves) 頭巾，圍巾

例句 She reached up to loosen the scarf around her neck.
／她伸手鬆了鬆脖子上的圍巾。

1680 scene
□□□
[sin]

名 (戲劇、事件等) 背景，現場；景色

例句 The scenes of this film are beautiful and romantic.
／這部電影的場景美麗又浪漫。

片語 on the scene 現場，當場

1681 □□□
school
[skul]
名 學校

片語 go to school 去上學 ‖ go to the school 去學校 (辦事) ‖ leave school ① 放學 ②退學 ③畢業離校

例句 When do you usually go to school?
／你通常幾點去上學？

1682 □□□
science
[ˋsaɪəns]
名 科學

例句 He doesn't have much knowledge of science.
／他沒有太多科學知識。

1683 □□□
scientist
[ˋsaɪəntɪst]
名 科學家

例句 She is a professor and scientist.
／她是教授及科學家。

1684 □□□
scooter
[ˋskutɚ]
名 摩托車；(兒童的) 滑板車，踏板車

例句 The boy wants to have a scooter.
／那個男孩想要一台滑板車。

1685 □□□
score
[skor]
動 [及物] 得 (分)；幫…打分數
動 [不及物] 得分，記分 名 (比賽) 得分，比數；二十個

例句 The score is 2 to 1 in favor of our team.
／我們的隊以二比一的比數得勝。

片語 in scores 大量地，大批地 ‖ scores of 許多，大量

用法 (1) score 表示「二十」時，與具體數字連用不加 s：three score years 六十年。(2) scores of 後接可數名詞：I have scores of books. 我有許多書。

1686 □□□
screen
[skrin]
名 銀幕，螢幕；屏風，紗窗
動 [及物] 掩蔽；放映 (電影)

巧記 圖解 screen 的一詞多義：

screens 螢幕   screens 屏風

例句 This is her first appearance on the screen.
／這是她首次在螢光幕上亮相。

1687
☐☐☐
sea
[si]

名 (常 the ～)海，海洋；

例句 The sea was calm.
／海上風平浪靜。

片語 a sea of 大量 ‖ at sea ①在海上〔▲ at the sea 在海邊〕②茫然，不知所措
注意 用「a ～, -s」表示「大量、茫茫一片」

Group 2

1688
☐☐☐
90
search
[sɝtʃ]

名 動 搜尋；探索，搜查

例句 He searched every room in the house.
／他搜查了房子的每一個房間。

片語 search for 尋找，搜尋
辨析 search for, search
　　(1) search for 表示「尋找，搜尋」(=look for)。
　　(2) search 表示「搜查，檢查」(=examine)。

1689
☐☐☐
season
[ˈsizn̩]

名 季節，時節

例句 The four seasons are spring, summer, autumn and winter.
／四季為春、夏、秋、冬。

片語 at all seasons 一年四季，一年到頭 ‖ in season 當令的　out of season 不
合時令的 ‖ season ticket 季票，長期票
注意 也表示一年中開展某項活動的「旺季」

spring 春

summer 夏

autumn 秋

winter 冬

1690
☐☐☐
seat
[sit]

名 座位
動 (使)坐下；(使)就座

例句 Are there enough seats for everyone?
／每個人都有座位嗎？

片語 take a seat 坐下，就座

1691
☐☐☐
second
[ˈsɛkənd]

名 第二個，第二
名 秒，片刻，瞬間

例句 Every second counts.
／分秒必爭。

片語 in a second 立刻，馬上，一會兒

second
[ˋsɛkənd]

形 次級品
副 第二地，第二位地　名 次級品

巧記 圖解 second 的不同詞義：

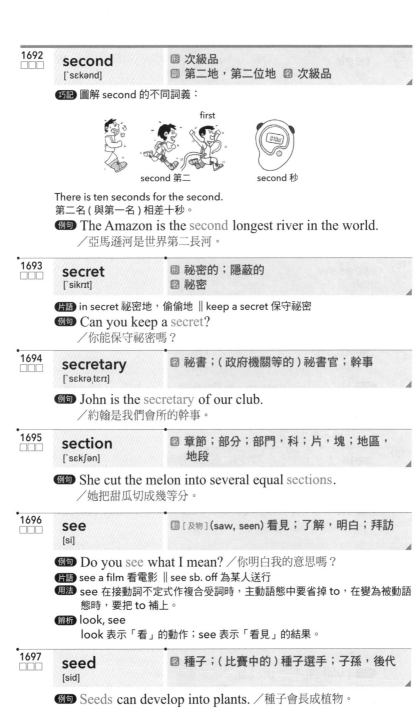

first

second 第二　　second 秒

There is ten seconds for the second.
第二名 (與第一名) 相差十秒。

例句 The Amazon is the second longest river in the world.
　　／亞馬遜河是世界第二長河。

1693

secret
[ˋsikrɪt]

形 祕密的；隱蔽的
名 祕密

片語 in secret 祕密地，偷偷地 ‖ keep a secret 保守祕密
例句 Can you keep a secret?
　　／你能保守祕密嗎？

1694

secretary
[ˋsɛkrəˌtɛrɪ]

名 祕書；(政府機關等的) 祕書官；幹事

例句 John is the secretary of our club.
　　／約翰是我們會所的幹事。

1695

section
[ˋsɛkʃən]

名 章節；部分；部門，科；片，塊；地區，地段

例句 She cut the melon into several equal sections.
　　／她把甜瓜切成幾等分。

1696

see
[si]

動 [及物](saw, seen) 看見；了解，明白；拜訪

例句 Do you see what I mean? ／你明白我的意思嗎？
片語 see a film 看電影 ‖ see sb. off 為某人送行
用法 see 在接動詞不定式作複合受詞時，主動語態中要省掉 to，在變為被動語態時，要把 to 補上。
辨析 look, see
　　look 表示「看」的動作；see 表示「看見」的結果。

1697

seed
[sid]

名 種子；(比賽中的) 種子選手；子孫，後代

例句 Seeds can develop into plants. ／種子會長成植物。

1698 □□□
seek
[sik]
🔢 (sought, sought) 尋找；試圖，設法；徵求（意見），請求（幫助）

例句 They were seeking employment.
／他們在找工作。

片語 seek after 尋求，追求 ‖ seek out 找出

1699 □□□
seem
[sim]
🔢[不及物] 好像，似乎

例句 It seems that they haven't known the news.
／他們似乎還不知道這個消息。

用法 seem 可用作連系動詞，主要結構有：seem+to do/be「似乎，好像」；
seem+ 形 名「看上去好像」；It seems/seemed that...「看來好像…」。

1700 □□□
seesaw
[ˈsiˌsɔ]
🔢 蹺蹺板

例句 Marriage is an emotional seesaw.
／婚姻是一塊感情的蹺蹺板。

1701 □□□
seldom
[ˈsɛldəm]
🔢 很少，不常

例句 He seldom goes to see the film, does he?
／他很少去看電影，是嗎？

用法 seldom 作副詞放在句首時，句子要部分倒裝；seldom 在反意疑問句中，
用肯定形式反問。

1702 □□□
select
[səˈlɛkt]
🔢[及物] 選擇，挑選

巧記〔熟〕elect 選舉 →〔根〕lect 選 →〔生〕select 精選
例句 He lets her daughter select her own birthday present.
／他讓她女兒挑選自己的生日禮物。

1703 □□□
selfish
[ˈsɛlfɪʃ]
🔢 自私的，利己的

例句 He is a selfish man. ／他是一個自私的人。
反義 selfless 形 無私的

1704 □□□
sell
[sɛl]
🔢 (sold, sold) 出售，賣

例句 I want to sell the car. ／我想賣掉這輛車。
片語 sell off 廉價出售 ‖ sell out 賣完，銷售一空 ‖ sell well 暢銷
反義 buy 動 買；purchase 動 購買

1705 □□□ **semester** [sə`mɛstə] 　名 一學期

例句 A student will probably take four or five courses during each semester.
／每個學生一學期可能要修四到五門課。

1706 □□□ **send** [sɛnd] 　動 [及物] (sent, sent) 送；派遣；發射

例句 I'll send her an e-mail tomorrow.
／我明天會傳一封電子郵件給她。
片語 send for 派人去叫 ‖ send out 發出，放出 ‖ send up 發射

Ｇroup 3

1707 □□□ **sense** [sɛns] 　動 [及物] 感覺到，意識到
　名 感官；感覺

91 例句 Dogs have a very good sense of hearing.
／狗有很好的聽覺。

1708 □□□ **separate** [`sɛpəˌret] 　動 [及物] 分隔；隔離　動 [不及物] 分開
　形 不同的；單獨的，各自的

例句 The boys were fighting, but the teacher separated them.
／男孩們在打架，不過老師把他們拉開了。
片語 separate...from... 使…和…分離

1709 □□□ **September** [sɛp`tɛmbə] 　名 九月 (=Sept.)

例句 They are going to marry in September.
／他們打算九月結婚。

1710 □□□ **serious** [`sɪrɪəs] 　形 嚴重的；嚴肅的

例句 That's a very serious problem.
／那是非常嚴重的問題。

1711 □□□ **servant** [`sɜˋvənt] 　名 僕人，傭人；公務員，公僕

例句 Money is a good servant but a bad master.
／金錢是善僕，但又是惡主。

A B C D E F G H I J K L M N O P Q R **S** T U V W X Y Z

1712 □□□
serve
[sɝv]
動（為…）服務；端上（飯菜等）

例句 The waiter served him a glass of beer.
／服務生為他端上一杯啤酒。

1713 □□□
service
[`sɝvɪs]
名 服務；招待

例句 The shop gives good service.
／這家商店服務周到。

片語 at sb.'s service 聽某人差遣 ‖ in service ①服勤中的 ②現職的

1714 □□□
set
[sɛt]
名 裝置；一套，一組

例句 The man bought a set of gardening tools.
／那個人買了一套園藝工具。

1715 □□□
set
[sɛt]
動 [不及物]（set, set）（日、月）落；下沉
動 [及物] 放置；安置；設定 形 規定的；準備好的

例句 She got to the park before the set time.
／她在規定的時間之前到達公園。

片語 set about (doing) sth. 開始、著手（做）某事 ‖ set out/off 動身，出發 ‖ set up 建立，創立

1716 □□□
seven
[`sɛvn]
代 名 形 七，七個，七點

例句 We close the store at seven. ／我們七點關店。

1717 □□□
seventeen
[sɛvn`tin]
代 名 形 十七，十七個

例句 I left home when I was seventeen. ／我 17 歲時離開了家。

1718 □□□
seventy
[`sɛvntɪ]
代 名 形 七十，七十個；(pl.) 七〇年代（的）

例句 We lost touch during the seventies.
／我們七〇年代失去了聯繫。

1719 □□□
several
[`sɛvərəl]
形 代 幾個

例句 I saw several of my classmates there.
／我在那邊看到幾個同學。

1720 □□□ **shake**
[ʃek]

動 (shook, shaken) 搖動；握手；(使)顫抖；震動
名 搖動

巧記 圖解 shake 的一詞多義：

shake hands
握手

shake one's head
搖頭

shake a bottle
搖瓶子

shake with fear
害怕得發抖

片語 shake hands with sb. 和某人握手

例句 Mary shook hands with her friends.
／瑪麗和她的朋友們握手。

1721 □□□ **shall**
[ʃæl]

動 助 (我，我們)將要；要不要…

例句 She says, "I shall marry Tom."
／她說：「我將要嫁給湯姆了。」

1722 □□□ **shape**
[ʃep]

名 外形，形狀
動 [及物] 製作；使成形

例句 New robots will have many different shapes.
／新型機器人會有許多不同的外形。

1723 □□□ **share**
[ʃɛr]

動 [及物] 分享；分擔
名 一份

片語 share sth. with sb. 與某人分享某物

例句 I shared my umbrella with her.
／我與她共撐一把傘。

1724 □□□ **shark**
[`ʃɑrk]

名 鯊魚

巧記 諧音：〔英〕shark 一音譯→〔漢〕鯊(魚)

例句 Sharks are circling around our boat.
／鯊魚繞著我們小船周圍游。

1725 □□□ **sharp**
[ʃɑrp]

形 鋒利的，尖的；(言辭等)尖酸的

例句 He cut down a tree with a sharp axe.
／他用鋒利的斧頭砍倒一棵樹。

A B C D E F G H I J K L M N O P Q R **S** T U V W X Y Z

S

Lesson ❸

1726 ☐☐☐ **she**
[ʃi]
🅰 她；她（雌性動物）

92 例句 She works hard.
／她努力工作。

1727 ☐☐☐ **sheep**
[ʃip]
🅰〔單同複〕羊，綿羊

例句 The man looks after about eighty sheep.
／這個人放牧大約八十頭羊。

片語 a black sheep 害 群 之 馬
‖ separate the sheep from
the goats 區別好壞／優劣

goat

sheep

1728 ☐☐☐ **sheet**
[ʃit]
🅰 被單；一張，一片，一塊

例句 I will put some clean sheets on the bed for you.
／我會幫你鋪上乾淨的床單。

片語 (as) white as a sheet〔口〕(臉)無血色的，蒼白的

1729 ☐☐☐ **shelf**
[ʃɛlf]
🅰 (pl.shelves) 架子，層板

例句 We'll have to put up some more shelves for all these books.
／我們得為這些書再釘一些層板。

片語 on the shelf 被擱置

1730 ☐☐☐ **shine**
[ʃaɪn]
🅱 (shone, shone) 照耀；(使)發光

例句 The moon shone brightly in the sky.
／月光照亮了天空。／皓月當空。

1731 ☐☐☐ **ship**
[ʃɪp]
🅰 船，輪船

例句 How many ships can you see in the picture?
／這幅在圖畫中裡你能看見幾艘輪船？

片語 by ship 搭船

1732 ☐☐☐ **ship**
[ʃɪp]
🅱〔及物〕把…裝上船，運送

例句 They shipped machines from Kaohsiung to Taipei.
／他們用船把機器從高雄運往台北。

第五週

1733 □□□

shirt
[ʃɝt]

名 (尤指男式) 襯衫

例句 I have to wear a shirt and tie to work.
／我上班必須穿襯衫打領帶。

辨析 blouse, shirt

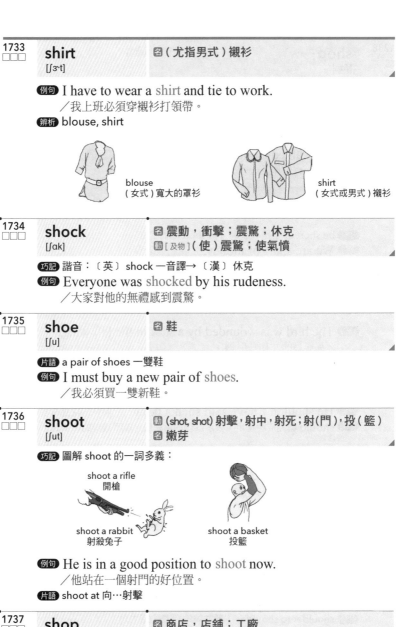

blouse
(女式) 寬大的罩衫

shirt
(女式或男式) 襯衫

1734 □□□

shock
[ʃɑk]

名 震動，衝擊；震驚；休克
動 [及物] (使) 震驚；使氣憤

巧記 諧音：〔英〕shock 一音譯→〔漢〕休克
例句 Everyone was shocked by his rudeness.
／大家對他的無禮感到震驚。

1735 □□□

shoe
[ʃu]

名 鞋

片語 a pair of shoes 一雙鞋
例句 I must buy a new pair of shoes.
／我必須買一雙新鞋。

1736 □□□

shoot
[ʃut]

動 (shot, shot) 射擊，射中，射死；射(門)，投(籃)
名 嫩芽

巧記 圖解 shoot 的一詞多義：

shoot a rifle
開槍

shoot a rabbit
射殺兔子

shoot a basket
投籃

例句 He is in a good position to shoot now.
／他站在一個射門的好位置。

片語 shoot at 向…射擊

1737 □□□

shop
[ʃɑp]

名 商店，店鋪；工廠

例句 We buy bread at the baker's shop.
／我們在麵包店買麵包。

1738 ☐☐☐
shop
[ʃɑp]

動 [不及物] 買東西，購物

例句 He always shops in that store. ／他總是在那間商店購物。

1739 ☐☐☐
shore
[ʃor]

名 海岸，海濱

例句 We walked along the shore. ／我們沿著海邊散步。
片語 on shore 在岸上 ⟷ off shore 離岸

1740 ☐☐☐
short
[ʃɔrt]

形 短的；矮的

片語 be short of 不足，缺乏 ‖ in short 總而言之
例句 We are short of money. ／我們缺乏資金。
反義 long 形 長的；tall 形 高的

1741 ☐☐☐
shot
[ʃɑt]

名 開槍，射擊；射門，投籃

例句 The bird was wounded by a shot in the left wing.
／那隻鳥的左翅被射傷。

1742 ☐☐☐
should
[ʃʊd]

動 助 應該

例句 He shouldn't have said such a thing. ／他不該說那種話。
用法 should 與完成時連用，表示該做的事未做，或不該做的事卻做了。

1743 ☐☐☐
shoulder
[`ʃoldɚ]

名 肩膀；衣服的肩部；(道路的) 路肩；山肩

巧記 圖解 shoulder 的一詞多義：

shoulder 肩膀　　shoulder pad 墊肩　　The shoulder of a T-shirt T恤的肩部　　shoulder 路肩

例句 He put his arm around her shoulders. ／他把手臂摟在她肩上。
片語 shoulder to shoulder ①肩並肩地 ②齊心協力地

1744 ☐☐☐
shout
[ʃaʊt]

名 動 呼喊，呼叫

例句 "Help!" she shouted. ／"救命啊！" 她大聲喊道。

1745 ☐☐☐

93

show
[ʃo]

動 [及物] (showed, shown) 給…看；出示
名 展覽

片語 on show 展覽 ‖ show off 炫耀，賣弄 ‖ show sb. around/round 帶某人參觀 ‖ show sb. sth.(=show sth. to sb.) 給某人看某物 ‖ show up 出席，露面

例句 Would you please show me your ID card?
／可以出示一下你的身份證嗎？

1746 ☐☐☐

shower
[ˈʃaʊɚ]

名 淋浴；淋浴間；蓮蓬頭；陣雨；一陣
動 [不及物] 洗淋浴；下陣雨

例句 We were caught in a shower on the way.
／我們在路上被一陣雨淋濕了。

片語 take a shower 淋浴，洗澡

1747 ☐☐☐

shrimp
[ʃrɪmp]

名 小蝦，蝦子

例句 I'm going to have shrimps for my supper.
／晚餐我要吃蝦子。

1748 ☐☐☐

shut
[ʃʌt]

動 (shut, shut) 關閉

例句 He shut himself in the room to do his homework.
／他把自己關在房間裡做作業。

片語 shut down 關閉，停止 ‖ shut off 切斷，關掉 ‖ shut up 〔口〕閉嘴

1749 ☐☐☐

shy
[ʃaɪ]

形 害羞的，靦腆的；膽怯的

例句 She was a shy girl.
／她是個害羞的女孩。

1750 ☐☐☐

sick
[sɪk]

形 生病的；不適的

片語 be/fall sick 生病 ‖ be sick of 厭惡，厭倦 ‖ be sick with 患…病

例句 She was sick in bed with a cold.
／她因感冒而臥病在床。

辨析 ill, sick
ill 和 sick 都可以作「生病的」、「有病的」解，但 ill 一般只能作主詞補語，而 sick 既可以作主詞補語，又可以作限定詞。

1751 □□□ **side**
[saɪd]
名 邊;面;身體側邊

例句 I got a pain in my left side.
／我的左肋疼痛。

片語 by the side of 在…旁邊 ‖ on one's side 和某人站在同一邊，支持某人 ‖ side by side 肩並肩地

1752 □□□ **sidewalk**
[`saɪd,wɔk]
名〔美〕人行道

例句 This sidewalk is made of stone.
／這條人行道是用石頭鋪成的。

同義 pavement 名〔英〕人行道

1753 □□□ **sight**
[saɪt]
名 視力;視覺

例句 The soldier lost his sight in a fight.
／那個士兵在戰爭中失明了。

1754 □□□ **sign**
[saɪn]
動 簽名;做手勢;(和…)簽約

例句 Sign your name here, please.
／請在這裡簽上您的大名。

片語 sign for 簽收 ‖ sign in 簽到 ‖ sign out ①簽退 ②登記攜出(某物)

1755 □□□ **sign**
[saɪn]
名 符號，標記;招牌，指示牌，標誌;徵兆;手勢

巧記 圖解 sign 的一詞多義：

road sign 路標　minus sign 減號　plus sign 加號　V sign 勝利手勢

例句 Look at the sign—"No entry."
／看看這個指示牌—「禁止進入」。

片語 give sb. a sign 示意某人

1756 □□□ **silence**
[`saɪləns]
名 寂靜;沉默

例句 There was dead silence all around.
／周圍一片沉寂。

片語 in silence 靜靜地 ‖ keep silence 保持沉默

1757 silent
[`saɪlənt]
形 沉默的

例句 He was silent for a moment.
／他沉默了一會兒。

1758 silly
[`sɪlɪ]
形 愚蠢的，糊塗的

例句 It's silly of you to trust him.
／你會相信他真是愚蠢。

1759 silver
[`sɪlvɚ]
名 銀，銀器，銀幣
形 銀色的

例句 The old man took out some silver from his pocket.
／那位老人從口袋裡掏出一些銀幣。

1760 similar
[`sɪmələ]
形 相似的，類似的

例句 Jenny and her sister look very similar.
／珍妮跟她姐姐長得很像。

片語 be similar to 與…類似

1761 simple
[`sɪmpl]
形 簡單的；樸素的，單純的

例句 This book is written in simple English.
／這本書是以簡單的英文寫成的。

1762 simply
[`sɪmplɪ]
副 簡單地；樸素地；只不過；完全，簡直

例句 Please explain it simply.
／請簡單地說明此事。

1763 since
[sɪns]
介 連 副 自從

例句 Where have you been since I last saw you?
／自從上次見面之後，你去哪裡了？

片語 ever since 從那以後一直

用法 (1)「since+ 時間點」常與完成時連用。
(2)「It is+ 時間段 +since...」指「自從…已經…時間了」。

1764 □□□
sincere
[sɪn`sɪr]

🔊**94**

形 誠摯的，真誠的，誠懇的

例句 Please accept my sincere apologies.
／請接受我誠摯的道歉。

1765 □□□
sing
[sɪŋ]

動 [不及物] (sang, sung) 唱，演唱
動 [及物] 唱，演唱

例句 The birds are singing in the tree. ／鳥兒在樹上歌唱。

1766 □□□
Singapore
[`sɪŋə,por]

名 新加坡

例句 They will arrive in Singapore three days later.
／三天後他們將抵達新加坡。

1767 □□□
singer
[`sɪŋɚ]

名 歌星，歌手，聲樂歌唱家

例句 His mother was an opera singer. ／他的母親是一位歌劇演唱家。

1768 □□□
single
[`sɪŋɡl]

形 單一的；單身的
名 單人房；單打

例句 Are you married or single? ／你是已婚還是單身？

反義 return 名 雙程票，往返票；doubles 名 雙打（比賽）

1769 □□□
sink
[sɪŋk]

名 水槽，洗臉槽

例句 My husband was washing dishes in the sink.
／我先生在洗水槽裡的盤子。

1770 □□□
sink
[sɪŋk]

動 (sank, sunk) 下沉，沉沒

例句 A big wave sank the boat.
／一個大浪讓船沉了。

float 浮起　　　　　　　rise 聳立

sink 沉沒　　　　　　　sink 下沉

1771 □□□
sir
[sɝ]

名 先生，閣下，老師，長官

例句 "Can I help you, sir? " asked the shop assistant.
／店員問：「先生，需要幫忙嗎？」

注意 表示「先生」時，指對上級和長輩的尊稱，或商業信件中對男子的稱呼。

反義 ma'am 夫人，女士 ※May I help you ma'am? 女士有需要我服務的嗎？

1772 ☐☐☐ **sister** [ˋsɪstɚ]　　名 姐妹，姐姐，妹妹

例句 She has been like a sister to me.
／她待我親如姐妹。

1773 ☐☐☐ **sit** [sɪt]　　動 (sat, sat) 坐；使就座；位於

例句 The minibus will sit ten people.
／這輛小巴可以乘坐十個人。
片語 sit down 坐下 ‖ sit up ①坐正，坐起 ②熬夜
辨析 sit, seat
(1) sit 意為「坐，就座」，通常作不及物動詞。
(2) seat 意為「使坐下」，作及物動詞，可與反身代詞連用，或用 be seated 這一形式。

1774 ☐☐☐ **six** [sɪks]　　代 名 形 六，六個

例句 I've been working for six hours. ／我已經工作六個小時了。

1775 ☐☐☐ **sixteen** [ˋsɪksˋtin]　　代 名 形 十六，十六個

例句 My brother is sixteen years of age. ／我弟弟 16 歲。

1776 ☐☐☐ **sixty** [ˋsɪkstɪ]　　代 名 形 六十，六十個；(pl.) 六〇年代

例句 Sixty people were killed in the plane crash.
／這場墜機造成 60 人喪生。

1777 ☐☐☐ **size** [saɪz]　　名 尺寸；大小

片語 be of a size 同樣大小 ‖ take the size of 量…的尺寸
例句 Your bag is of a size with mine. ／你的包包和我的一樣大。

1778 ☐☐☐ **skate** [sket]　　名 溜冰鞋
動 溜冰，滑冰

例句 Would you like to go skating with me?
／你要和我一起去滑冰嗎？

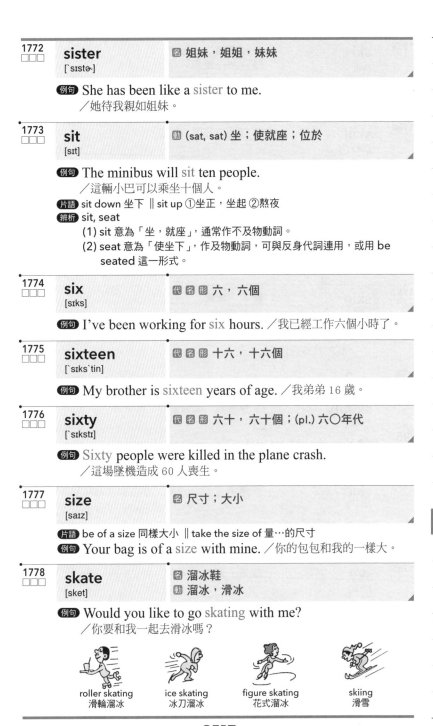

roller skating 滑輪溜冰　　ice skating 冰刀溜冰　　figure skating 花式溜冰　　skiing 滑雪

| 1779 □□□ | **ski**
[ski] | 图 滑雪板
動 [不及物] 滑雪 |

例句 The students often go skiing during winter vacation.
／學生們常在寒假去滑雪。

| 1780 □□□ | **skill**
[`skɪl] | 图 技巧；技術，技能 |

例句 Reading and writing are different skills.
／閱讀和寫作是不同的技能。

| 1781 □□□ | **skillful**
[`skɪlfəl] | 形 靈巧的，熟練的，擅長的 |

例句 She is skillful at painting.
／她擅長繪畫。

| 1782 □□□ | **skin**
[skɪn] | 图 皮，皮膚 |

例句 He has dark skin.
／他的皮膚黝黑。

Group 3

| 1783 □□□ track 95 | **skinny**
[`skɪnɪ] | 形 極瘦的，皮包骨的；吝嗇的 |

例句 You should eat more. You are too skinny.
／你要吃多一點，你太瘦了。

| 1784 □□□ | **skirt**
[skɝt] | 图 裙子 |

例句 She is in a white skirt.
／她穿著一條白裙子。

| 1785 □□□ | **sky**
[skaɪ] | 图 天，天空 |

例句 The sky was blue and cloudless.
／天空蔚藍無雲。
片語 in the sky 在天空中

1786 □□□ **sleep**
[slip]

動 [不及物] 名 (slept, slept) 睡，睡覺

例句 I went to bed at ten last night, but I didn't go to sleep at twelve.
／昨晚我十點就上床了，但是到了十二點還沒睡著。

辨析 go to bed, go to sleep, sleep
(1) go to bed 表示「上床」，與 get up(起床) 相對。
(2) go to sleep 表示「入睡」，與 wake (up) (醒來) 相對，二者都是表示瞬間動作。
(3) sleep 表示「睡眠」的持續狀態。

1787 □□□ **sleepy**
[`slipɪ]

形 想睡的，睏倦的，瞌睡的

例句 I felt sleepy all day.
／我一整天都覺得愛睏。

辨析 asleep, sleepy
(1) asleep 指「已睡著的」。
(2) sleepy 指「困倦的，想睡的」。

1788 □□□ **slender**
[`slɛndɚ]

形 苗條的，修長的；微薄的，微小的

例句 His chances of winning are extremely slender.
／他獲勝的機會極為渺茫。

同義 slim 形 苗條的

1789 □□□ **slide**
[slaɪd]

動 (slid, slid) 滑動，下滑，滑行
名 溜滑梯；滑動，下滑；山崩；投影片

例句 The book slid off my knees.
／書從我的膝蓋上滑落。

1790 □□□ **slim**
[slɪm]

形 苗條的

例句 She eats very little in order to keep slim.
／為了保持身材苗條，她吃得很少。

同義 slender 形 苗條的

1791 □□□ **slip**
[slɪp]

動 [不及物] 滑行，滑落；溜走；失足
名 滑，滑倒

例句 His foot slipped and he fell down the stairs.
／他失足摔下樓梯。

1792
□□□

slipper
[`slɪpə-]

名 拖鞋，便鞋

例句 Slippers are usually worn indoors.
／拖鞋通常是在室內穿的。

1793
□□□

slow
[slo]

形 緩慢的　副 緩慢地
動（使）放慢，變慢

例句 Please drive much slower.
／請開得再慢一點。

反義 fast 形 快的；quick 形 快的

1794
□□□

small
[smɔl]

形 小的；少的；小規模的，微小的

例句 She drives a small car.
／她開著一輛小車。

反義 big 形 大的

1795
□□□

smart
[smɑrt]

形 漂亮的，時髦的；聰明的，伶俐的，精明的

巧記 諧音：〔英〕smart 一音譯→〔漢〕時髦
例句 He is a smart businessman.
／他是個精明的生意人。

同義 clever 形 聰明的

1796
□□□

smell
[smɛl]

名 氣味
動 (smelt, smelt) 聞；聞起來；發出氣味

例句 You'd better smell① the fish to find out whether it smells② bad.
／你最好聞一下這條魚，看牠聞起來臭不臭。

用法 smell ①「聞」，是及物動詞，後接名詞等；smell ②「聞起來」，是連系動詞，後接形容詞。

1797
□□□

smile
[smaɪl]

動 [不及物] 微笑　動 [及物] 用微笑表示…
名 微笑

例句 She smiled at me, and laughed at my jokes.
／她對我微笑，並大笑我的笑話。

辨析 laugh, smile
(1) laugh 指出聲地「笑」，常伴有動作，表示高興、快樂、嘲笑等。
(2) smile「微笑」，指無聲地笑，重在笑容，表示愉快、親切、友好等。

1798 □□□ **smoke** [smok]
名 煙
動 冒煙；吸煙

例句 Children mustn't smoke.
／小孩絕對不可以抽煙。

1799 □□□ **snack** [snæk]
名 小吃，點心
動 [不及物] 吃點心，吃零食

例句 I had a snack on the train.
／我在火車上吃點心。

1800 □□□ **snail** [snel]
名 蝸牛

例句 Snails are eating our lettuce.
／蝸牛在吃我們的萵苣。

1801 □□□ **snake** [snek]
名 蛇

例句 Snakes usually live on small animals, birds and insects.
／蛇通常吃小動物、小鳥和昆蟲。

Ⓖroup 4

1802 □□□ **sneakers** [`snikɚs]
名 (pl.) 運動鞋

96

例句 Mark bought a pair of sneakers.
／馬克買了一雙運動鞋。

1803 □□□ **sneaky** [`snikɪ]
形 偷偷摸摸的，鬼鬼祟祟的

例句 His sneaky behavior aroused our suspicion.
／他鬼鬼祟祟的行為造成我們懷疑。

1804 □□□ **snow** [sno]
名 雪，雪花，積雪
動 [不及物] 下雪

例句 It is snowing hard.
／雪下得很大。

1805 □□□ **snowy** [`snoɪ]
形 雪白的，下雪的，積雪的

例句 The snowy tops of the mountains are beautiful.
／有積雪的山頂很美。

S

1806 □□□ **so**
[so]

副 這麼，那麼；非常

例句 The weather isn't so hot as yesterday.
／天氣沒有昨天那麼熱。

片語 or so 大約 ‖ so...that... 如此…以至於…

1807 □□□ **so**
[so]

連 因此，所以；為了，以便

例句 I was tired, so I went to bed.
／我累了，所以我去睡覺了。

片語 so as to 為了 ‖ so that ①所以，因此 ②以便，為了
辨析 so that, so...that...
(1) so that 引導目的副詞從句時，表示「以便，為了」，從句中常使用
can/could 等情態動詞；引導結果副詞從句時，從句中一般不用 can
和 may 等詞，在 so that 前可以用逗號，意思是「因此，所以」。
(2) so...that... 意為「如此…以至於…」，引導結果副詞從句，so 後接形
容詞或副詞原形。

1808 □□□ **soap**
[sop]

名 肥皂，香皂
動 [及物] 用肥皂洗，抹肥皂

例句 He soaped himself all over.
／他全身都抹了肥皂。

1809 □□□ **soccer**
[ˈsɑkɚ]

名 英式足球

例句 He's playing soccer.
／他正在踢足球。

1810 □□□ **social**
[ˈsoʃəl]

形 社會的；社交的

例句 Mary has a busy social life.
／瑪麗忙於社交活動。

1811 □□□ **society**
[səˈsaɪətɪ]

名 社會；社團

例句 I'm a member of the school Art Society.
／我是學校藝術社團的成員。

1812 □□□ **socks**
[saks]

名 短襪，半統襪

例句 Are these socks yours?
／這些短襪是你的嗎？

1813 □□□ **soda**
[`sodə]

名 蘇打水，汽水；蘇打，碳酸鈉

巧記 諧音：〔英〕soda 一音譯→〔漢〕蘇打
例句 She doesn't like drinking chocolate soda.
／她不喜歡喝巧克力汽水。

1814 □□□ **sofa**
[`sofə]

名 長沙發，沙發

巧記 諧音：〔英〕sofa 一音譯→〔漢〕沙發
例句 Please sit on the sofa.
／請坐在沙發上。

1815 □□□ **soft**
[sɔft]

形 柔軟的；光滑的；心軟的；(飲料) 不含酒精成分的

例句 This kind of paper is very soft.
／這種紙非常柔軟。
片語 soft drink 不含酒精的飲料
反義 hard 形 硬的

1816 □□□ **soldier**
[`soldʒɚ]

名 士兵，軍人

例句 He wants to be a soldier.
／他想成為一名軍人。

1817 □□□ **solution**
[sə`luʃən]

名 答案，謎底；解決辦法

例句 I hope you can come up with a better solution than this.
／我希望你能想出一個比這更好的解決辦法。

1818 □□□ **solve**
[salv]

動 [及物] 解決

例句 Students should learn how to solve problems.
／學生們應該學會如何解決問題。

1819 □□□	**some** [sʌm]	形 代 一些，若干

例句 Won't you have some cake?
／你不吃一點蛋糕嗎？

用法 some 既可修飾可數名詞複數，也可修飾不可數名詞。some 多用於肯定句，有時也可用於疑問句或條件句，表示請求、建議並期望得到對方的肯定回答。

1820 □□□	**somebody** [ˋsʌmˌbɑdɪ]	代 某人，有人；重要人物，大人物

例句 You can ask somebody wise for help.
／你可以向某個聰明的人求助。

1821 □□□

someone
[`sʌm,wʌn]

代 某人，有人；重要人物

97

例句 Can someone answer the question?
／有人能回答這個問題嗎？

同義 somebody 代 某人；重要人物，大人物

1822 □□□

something
[`sʌmθɪŋ]

代 某事／物，某種東西；多少，相當，若干

例句 There's something wrong here.
／這兒有一點錯誤。

片語 have something to do with 與…有關 ‖ something else 別的東西
‖ something like ①有點像 ②大約

1823 □□□

sometimes
[`sʌm,taɪmz]

副 有時，不時

例句 He sometimes writes to me.
／他有時候會寫信給我。

辨析 sometimes, sometime, some time, some times
(1) sometimes 表示「有時」，用來描述現在或過去常發生的事。
(2) sometime 表示「(將來或過去的)某個時候」。
(3) some time 名詞短語，常用來表示「一段時間」。
(4) some times 名詞短語，表示「幾次」。

1824 □□□

somewhere
[`sʌm,hwɛr]

副 某處，在某處；在附近，前後

例句 I have left my watch somewhere.
／我把手錶丟在某個地方了。

1825 □□□

son
[sʌn]

名 兒子

例句 They have two sons and one daughter.
／他們有兩個兒子和一個女兒。

1826 □□□

song
[sɔŋ]

名〔sing 的名詞〕歌，歌曲，唱歌

例句 They sat around, singing songs.
／他們圍坐在一起唱著歌。

1827 ☐☐☐
soon
[sun]

圈 不久，很快

例句 No sooner had he arrived than he was asked to leave again.
/He had no sooner arrived than he was asked to leave again.
/他剛來不久後就被叫走了。

用法 no sooner 若放在句首，則句子用倒裝結構，不放句首則用正常語序，than 引導的從句常用一般過去時，主句常用過去完成時。

片語 as soon as 一…就… ‖ as soon as possible 盡快 ‖ sooner or later 遲早

1828 ☐☐☐
sore
[sor]

圈 疼痛的，痛苦的；劇烈的
名 痛處，瘡口

例句 My throat is sore.
/我喉嚨痛。

1829 ☐☐☐
sorry
[`sɑrɪ]

圈 難過的，惋惜的；對不起，抱歉的

例句 I am sorry you are ill.
/你生病了我很難過。

辨析 I'm sorry, Excuse me
(1) I'm sorry 指心中感到抱歉、難過。
(2) Excuse me 多用於麻煩或打擾別人時。

注意 作主詞補語時，表示「懊悔的，遺憾的」

1830 ☐☐☐
sort
[sɔrt]

名 種類，品種；類型；排序

例句 What sort of meat do you like best?
/你最喜歡吃哪一種肉？

片語 a sort of 一種 ‖ all sorts of 各種各樣的

1831 ☐☐☐
sort
[sɔrt]

動 [及物] 分類，整理

片語 sort out ①整理 ②挑出

例句 We must sort out the good apples from the bad ones.
/我們必須把好蘋果與壞蘋果分開。

1832 ☐☐☐
soul
[sol]

名 靈魂，心靈；人

例句 Christians believe that the soul lives forever.
/基督徒相信靈魂永生。

片語 heart and soul 全心全意

1833 sound
[saʊnd]
動 [不及物] 聽起來
名 聲，聲音

例句 His idea sounds good.
／他的主意聽起來不錯。

用法 sound 可作連系動詞，後跟形容詞作主詞補語。

1834 soup
[sup]
名 湯

例句 Will you have some soup before the meat course?
／主菜前先來一點湯好嗎？

用法 一般情況下，表示「喝湯」用 eat soup；但若強調不使用湯匙而用杯子喝湯時，用 drink soup。

eat soup   drink soup

1835 sour
[ˋsaʊr]
形 酸的，酸味的；餿的，酸臭的

例句 Lemon is sour. ／檸檬是酸的。

1836 source
[sors]
名 源（泉），發源地；來源，出處

例句 We followed the river back to discover its source.
／我們溯河而上尋找它的源頭。

1837 south
[saʊθ]
名 南，南方
副 向南　形〔作限定詞〕南方的，向南的

例句 The town is to the south of the mountains.
／這個城鎮在山的南邊。

反義 north 名 北，北方　副 向北方　形 北方的

1838 southern
[ˋsʌðɚn]
形 南方的，南部的

例句 He spoke English with a southern accent.
／他講英語帶有南方口音。

反義 northern 形 北部的

1839 soy-sauce
[ˋsɔɪˏsɔs]
名 醬油

例句 Do we need some soy-sauce and vinegar?
／ 我們需要些醬油和醋嗎？

A B C D E F G H I J K L M N O P Q R S T U V W X Y Z

1840 □□□
space
[spes]

名 空間；太空；空地；間隙，間隔

98

巧記 圖解 space 的一詞多義：

空地

太空 間隔

行間的空白

例句 Put it in the space between the table and the wall.
／把它放在桌子和牆之間的空隙裡。

1841 □□□
spaghetti
[spə`gɛtɪ]

名 義大利麵

例句 The boy ate a dish of spaghetti.
／那個男孩吃了一盤義大利麵。

1842 □□□
speak
[spik]

動 (spoke, spoken) 說，說話；講（某種語言）

例句 They speak English in Australia.
／他們在澳洲講英語。

片語 speak about/of 談論 ‖ speak highly of 高度讚揚 ‖ speak out ①大膽地說 ②大聲說

1843 □□□
speaker
[`spikə-]

名 發言者，演講者；擴音器

例句 He is a good speaker.
／他是個出色的演說家。

1844 □□□
special
[`spɛʃəl]

形 特別的；專門的
名 特色菜

例句 Are you doing anything special for Christmas?
／你在耶誕節那天有什麼特別的活動嗎？

1845 □□□
speech
[spitʃ]

名 講話，發言；演說

例句 The President made a speech.
／總統發表了演說。

第五週

1846 ☐☐☐ **speed**
[spid]

图 速度
動 (sped, sped) 加速

片語 at a speed of 以…速度 ‖ at full speed 全速 ‖ speed up 加速
例句 She sped up and overtook them.
／她加快速度超過了他們。

1847 ☐☐☐ **spell**
[spɛl]

動 [及物] (spelt, spelt) 拼寫；用字母拼

例句 He spelt the word wrongly.
／他把那個字拼錯了。

1848 ☐☐☐ **spelling**
[`spɛlɪŋ]

图 拼寫，拼寫能力；拼法

例句 What is the spelling of the word?
／這個字怎麼拼？

1849 ☐☐☐ **spend**
[spɛnd]

動 [及物] (spent, spent) 度過；花費 (金錢、時間等)

例句 It's nice of you to spend so much time showing me around your school.
／你真是太好了，花那麼多時間帶我參觀你的學校。

辨析 spend, pay, cost, take

花費	人 +spend+ 時間 / 金錢 +(in) doing/on+ 物
	人 +pay+ 金錢 +for+ 物
	事 / 物 +cost+ 人 + 時間 / 金錢
	It+takes+ 人 + 時間 +to do

1850 ☐☐☐ **spider**
[`spaɪdɚ]

图 蜘蛛

例句 There is a spider's web in the corner.
／牆角有一張蜘蛛網。

1851 ☐☐☐ **spirit**
[`spɪrɪt]

图 精神

例句 The spirit is willing but the flesh is weak.
／〔諺〕心有餘而力不足。

1852 □□□ **spoon**
[spun]

名 匙，湯匙；一匙的量

例句 He stirred his coffee with a spoon.
／他用湯匙攪拌咖啡。

1853 □□□ **sport**
[sport]

名 體育運動，運動

例句 I'm not interested in sport.
／我對運動沒興趣。

1854 □□□ **spot**
[spɑt]

名 斑點，污點
動 [及物] 認出，發現；玷污；點綴

例句 The ink has spotted my clean shirt.
／墨水把我乾淨的襯衫弄髒了。
片語 on the spot ①在現場，到場 ②立即，當場

1855 □□□ **spread**
[sprɛd]

動 名 (spread, spread) 展開；伸開

例句 The bird spread its wings and flew away.
／那隻鳥張開翅膀飛走了。

1856 □□□ **spring**
[sprɪŋ]

名 春天；泉水；彈簧

例句 The weather gets warmer in spring.
／春天天氣逐漸變暖。

1857 □□□ **square**
[skwɛr]

名 正方形；廣場；平方
形 正方形的；平方的

例句 The city covers ten square miles.
／這個城市占地 10 平方英里。
片語 Tian'anmen Square in Beijing 北京天安門廣場

1858 □□□ **stage**
[stedʒ]

名 階段，時期；舞臺

例句 The actors left the stage at the end of the play.
／劇終時演員們離開舞臺。
片語 bring/put...on the stage 上演… ‖ set the stage for ①佈置…的舞臺 ②為…作準備

1859 🔳🔳🔳
stair
[stɛr]

🔊 99

图 樓梯；(階梯的)一階

例句 She hurried up the stairs to her room.
／她匆匆上樓到她的房間去。

1860 🔳🔳🔳
stamp
[stæmp]

图 郵票；印章；蓋章；跺腳聲
動 蓋章；跺腳

巧記 多義：stamp 意為「郵票」，為何又作「跺腳」講？
內在聯繫：郵票，印花 → 印章 → 蓋章 → 跺腳

「跺腳」在動作上不正類似「蓋章」嗎？

例句 I'd like to collect stamps because they are interesting.
／我想收集郵票因為它們有趣。

1861 🔳🔳🔳
stand
[stænd]

動 [及物] (stood, stood) 忍受
動 [不及物] 站 图 看臺

片語 stand against 反對 ‖ stand by 袖手旁觀，站在旁邊 ‖ stand for ①象徵
②支持 ‖ stand in line 排隊 ‖ stand up 起立，站起來

例句 Which team do you stand for?
／你支持哪一隊？

1862 🔳🔳🔳
standard
[ˋstændəd]

图 標準，規格
形 標準的

例句 The girl speaks standard English.
／那女孩說一口標準的英語。

1863 🔳🔳🔳
star
[stɑr]

图 星星，恆星；星形，星號；明星

巧記 圖解 star 的一詞多義：

fixed star　　star　　super star
恆星　　　　星號　　超級巨星

例句 His wish to become a football star has come true.
／他想當足球明星的願望實現了。

1864 start [stɑrt]
- 動 出發；開始
- 名 開始，開端，出發

例句 We shall have to start at 5:30 a. m.
／我們最好在早上 5：30 出發。

片語 start off 動身，出發 ‖ start out 啟程，出發 ‖ starting/finishing line 起跑 / 終點線 ‖ to start with ①首先 ②起初

同義 begin 動 開始

1865 state [stet]
- 名 狀態；國家；州

片語 in a/an...state 處於…狀態

例句 Her grandmother is in a good state of health.
／她奶奶的健康狀況良好。

1866 station [`steʃən]
- 名 所；車站；局

例句 This train stops at every station.
／這列火車每站都停。

1867 stationery [`steʃənˌɛrɪ]
- 名 文具

例句 I bought a ruler in the stationery shop.
／我在文具店買了一把尺。

1868 stay [ste]
- 動 [不及物] 名 停留；暫住；保持

片語 stay at home 待在家裡 ‖ stay out 待在戶外 ‖ stay up 熬夜

例句 Don't stay up so often. It's bad for your health.
／不要這麼常熬夜，這對你的健康有害。

1869 steak [stek]
- 名 牛排，肉排

例句 Two steaks, please.
／請來兩塊牛排。

1870 steal [stil]
- 動 (stole, stolen) 偷，竊取

例句 Someone stole my bike.
／有人把我的腳踏車偷走了。

1871 ☐☐☐ **steam**
[stim]

名 水蒸氣，蒸汽
動 [不及物] 發出蒸汽 動 [及物] 蒸，煮

巧記 圖解水的三態：

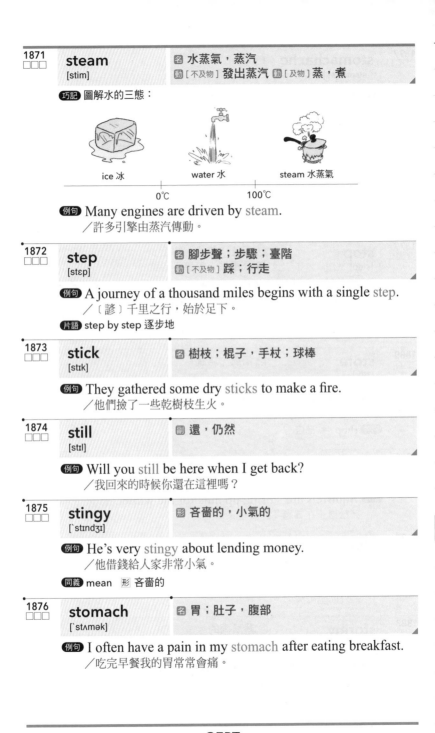

ice 冰 　　　 water 水 　　　 steam 水蒸氣
　　　 0℃ 　　　 100℃

例句 Many engines are driven by steam.
／許多引擎由蒸汽傳動。

1872 ☐☐☐ **step**
[stɛp]

名 腳步聲；步驟；臺階
動 [不及物] 踩；行走

例句 A journey of a thousand miles begins with a single step.
／〔諺〕千里之行，始於足下。

片語 step by step 逐步地

1873 ☐☐☐ **stick**
[stɪk]

名 樹枝；棍子，手杖；球棒

例句 They gathered some dry sticks to make a fire.
／他們撿了一些乾樹枝生火。

1874 ☐☐☐ **still**
[stɪl]

副 還，仍然

例句 Will you still be here when I get back?
／我回來的時候你還在這裡嗎？

1875 ☐☐☐ **stingy**
[`stɪndʒɪ]

形 吝嗇的，小氣的

例句 He's very stingy about lending money.
／他借錢給人家非常小氣。

同義 mean 形 吝嗇的

1876 ☐☐☐ **stomach**
[`stʌmək]

名 胃；肚子，腹部

例句 I often have a pain in my stomach after eating breakfast.
／吃完早餐我的胃常常會痛。

1877 ☐☐☐ **stomachache**
[ˋstʌməkˌek]

图 胃痛

例句 I've got a terrible stomachache.
／我胃痛得很厲害。

Group 4

1878 ☐☐☐ **stone**
[ston]

图 石頭，石材；寶石

100

例句 Most of the houses are built of stone.
／這些房子大部分是用石頭蓋的。

1879 ☐☐☐ **stop**
[stɑp]

動 阻止；停止，終止
图 公車站；停車；句號

片語 stop to do sth. 停下來做另一件事 ‖ stop doing sth. 停止正在做的事情
‖ stop sb. (from) doing sth. 阻止某人做某事

例句 The heavy snow stopped him from coming to our party.
／那場大雪阻止他前來參加我們的宴會。

1880 ☐☐☐ **store**
[stor]

图 商店，店鋪

例句 She bought a coat in the store.
／她在這家店買了一件外套。

同義 shop 图 商店

1881 ☐☐☐ **store**
[stor]

動［及物］貯存，貯藏

例句 Squirrels are storing up nuts for the winter.
／松鼠正在為過冬貯藏堅果。

1882 ☐☐☐ **storm**
[stɔrm]

图 風暴，暴風雨

例句 There was a big storm outside.
／外面風雨交加。

1883 ☐☐☐ **stormy**
[ˋstɔrmɪ]

形 暴風雨的

例句 The sky was starting to look stormy.
／開始變天了，看來暴風雨將至。

1884 ☐☐☐ **story** [ˋstorɪ]　　🔤 故事，傳說；經歷，閱歷

例句 Tom's father is telling him about the story of *Alice's Adventures in Wonderland.*
／湯姆的父親在給他講關於愛麗絲夢遊仙境的故事。

片語 tell a story 講故事

1885 ☐☐☐ **stove** [stov]　　🔤 爐子，火爐，暖爐

例句 She put the kettle on the stove. ／她把水壺放到火爐上。

1886 ☐☐☐ **straight** [stret]　　🔤 直的，筆直的　🔤 徑直地

例句 The smoke rose straight upward.
／煙筆直地往上冒。

1887 ☐☐☐ **strange** [strendʒ]　　🔤 奇怪的；陌生的

例句 The city is strange to me.
／我對這個城市感到陌生。

反義 familiar 🔤 熟悉的

1888 ☐☐☐ **stranger** [ˋstrendʒɚ]　　🔤 陌生人；新手

例句 Don't talk to strangers.
／不要跟陌生人說話。

1889 ☐☐☐ **straw** [strɔ]　　🔤 吸管；稻草，麥稈

例句 The boy was drinking orange juice through a straw.
／那男孩正在用吸管喝柳橙汁。

1890 ☐☐☐ **strawberry** [ˋstrɔˌbɛrɪ]　　🔤 草莓

例句 She likes strawberries very much.
／她很喜歡草莓。

1891 ☐☐☐ **stream** [strim]　　🔤 小河，溪流；流，一股，一串，潮流

例句 He was swimming against the stream.
／他在逆流而上。

A B C D E F G H I J K L M N O P Q R **S** T U V W X Y Z

1892 ☐☐☐

street
[strit]

名 道路，街道；(...Street)…街 (=ST.)

例句 This is the chief street in the town. ／這是城裡的主幹道。

辨析 street, road, sidewalk, path, way
(1) street 指兩側有建築物、商店的市內「道路」。
(2) road 車輛通過之「大馬路」，若有人行道 (sidewalk) 時則指「車道」。
(3) sidewalk 指和車道相對的「人行道」。
(4) path 指「小路，小徑」。
(5) way 指抽象意義的「路」。

1893 ☐☐☐

stress
[strɛs]

名 壓力，緊張
動 [及物] 強調，著重；重讀

例句 Continued stress causes illness. ／持續緊張會引發疾病。

片語 under the stress 在某種壓力下

1894 ☐☐☐

strike
[straɪk]

動 [不及物] (struck, struck) 襲擊，侵襲；罷工；敲打
動 [及物] 打動；敲打；侵襲；打擊；攻擊 名 罷工

例句 The enemy struck at dawn. ／敵人在拂曉時進攻。

片語 be on strike 在罷工 ‖ go on strike 舉行罷工

辨析 strike, beat, hit (擊打)
(1) strike 常指「猛地一擊」，如敲鑼。
(2) beat 指連續地打，如打鼓。
(3) hit 側重指「擊中」，有時也指「打一下」，如鐘敲幾點。

1895 ☐☐☐

strong
[strɔŋ]

形 強壯的，堅固的，結實的；(國家等)
強大的

例句 He's a strong man. ／他是個強壯的人。

反義 weak 形 虛弱的，不強壯的；不牢固的

注意 作限定詞時，表示「堅強的、堅定的」

1896 ☐☐☐

struggle
[ˋstrʌgl]

名 動 [不及物] 鬥爭，搏鬥；奮鬥，努力；競爭，
對抗

例句 The struggle between the two teams was hard.
／這兩個隊之間的競爭很激烈。

片語 struggle against 跟…競爭

GEPT
Elementary

Week 6

第六週

1897
☐☐☐

student
[ˈstjudn̩t]

名 學生

(例句) The teacher asked the students to keep quiet.
／老師要求學生們保持安靜。

1898
☐☐☐

study
[ˈstʌdɪ]

名 學習；研究；書房
動 學習；研究

(例句) I have studied the problem carefully.
／我已經對那個問題仔細地研究過了。

(辨析) learn, study
(1) learn 是普通用語，指「初學」或在老師的指導下「學習」，其目的是為了獲得基礎知識或技能，它還有「學會；瞭解」之義。
(2) study 常指較深入地學習或研究，含有「鑽研」之義，著重於「學習」這一活動或過程。

1899
☐☐☐

stupid
[ˈstjupɪd]

形 愚蠢的，笨的

(例句) How stupid of him to ask such a question!
／他問這樣的問題，真蠢！

(反義) silly 形 傻的，愚蠢的

1900
☐☐☐

style
[staɪl]

名 風格；式樣，類型；流行式樣，時尚

(例句) Books for children should have a clear and easy style.
／童書的風格應該要簡明。

(片語) in style 流行的，時髦的⟷ out of style 過時的

1901
☐☐☐

subject
[ˈsʌbdʒɪkt]

名 學科；科目；主題，話題；主詞

(例句) Let me have your thoughts on the subject.
／讓我聽聽你對這個話題的看法。

1902
☐☐☐

subway
[ˈsʌbˌwe]

名 〔美〕地鐵 (=underground=metro)；地下道

(巧記) sub-(=under)+way
(例句) He went to the other side of the street through the subway.
／他從地下道走到街道對面。

(同義) tube 名 〔英〕地鐵

1903 succeed
[sək`sid]
動 [不及物] 成功

例句 They succeeded in collecting a lot of money for the poor.
／他們成功地為窮人募到許多錢。

用法 succeed 是不及物動詞，其後通常接「in+ 名詞或動詞 -ing 形式」，不接動詞不定式。

反義 fail 動 [不及物] 失敗

1904 success
[sək`sɛs]
名 成功；成就

例句 I wish you success with your studies.
／祝福你學業有成。

反義 failure 名 失敗

1905 successful
[sək`sɛsfəl]
形 成功的；有成就的

例句 He became a successful actor.
／他成為一名成功的演員。

片語 be successful in (doing) sth. 在 (做)…成功

1906 such
[sʌtʃ]
形 這樣的，如此的
代 這樣的人 (事物)

例句 Can you believe that in such a rich country there should be so many poor people?
／你能相信在這麼富有的國家有這麼多窮人嗎？

用法 such 一般用來修飾名詞，當名詞前有 many, much, few, little 等表示數量的詞時，前面用 so 而不用 such。

1907 sudden
[`sʌdn̩]
形 突然的，意外的
名 突然

例句 His death was very sudden.
／他死得很突然。

1908 suddenly
[`sʌdnlɪ]
副 突然，忽然，出其不意地

例句 Suddenly the doorbell rang.
／門鈴突然響了。

1909 sugar
[`ʃʊgɚ]
名 糖；甜言蜜語；寶貝，親愛的，甜心

例句 Do you have sugar in your tea? ／你有在茶裡放糖嗎？

1910 □□□ **suggest** [sə`dʒɛst]　　動 [及物] 建議，提議；暗示，表示

例句 Jane's pale face suggested that she was ill, and her parents suggested that she (should) have a medical examination.
／珍蒼白的臉色顯示她生病了，她父母建議她作健康檢查。

用法 作「建議」講時，suggest 後常接動詞 -ing 形式而不接動詞不定式作受詞；後接 that 從句時，從句中的述語動詞須用虛擬語氣。作「暗示」講時，其後 that 從句中的述語動詞須用陳述語氣。

同義 advise 動 建議

1911 □□□ **suit** [sut]　　名 套裝；訴訟，控告

例句 Millie is wearing a white suit.
／米莉穿著一身白色套裝。

1912 □□□ **suit** [sut]　　動 [及物] 滿足 (某人) 需要，合 (某人) 心意；(衣服等) 合身；有利於

例句 It suits me to start work at a later time.
／晚一點再開始工作正合我意。

片語 be suited for/to... 適合做… ‖ suit sb. (fine) ① 〔口〕(很) 合某人的意 ②對某人 (很) 合適

1913 □□□ **summer** [`sʌmɚ]　　名 夏天，夏季

例句 It's very hot here in summer.
／這裡夏天很熱。

1914 □□□ **sun** [sʌn]　　名 (the ～) 太陽；陽光

片語 in the sun 在陽光下 ‖ under the sun 在天底下，在天地間，在這個世界上
例句 The children are playing in the sun.
／孩子們正在陽光下玩耍。

用法 sun, moon, earth 等表示獨一無二的名詞前須加 the。

1915 □□□ **Sunday** [`sʌnde]　　名 星期日 (=Sun.)

例句 Let's make it Sunday.
／我們星期天來做吧！

1916 □□□

sunny
[`sʌnɪ]

形 陽光充足的；樂觀的，快活的

巧記 由 sun 雙寫 n 加形容詞尾碼 -y 構成。

例句 It's sunny today.
／今天陽光明媚。

1917 □□□

super
[`supɚ]

形 極好的，超級的
副 極，超級

例句 That's a super new car.
／那是一輛超新的車。

1918 □□□

supermarket
[`supɚ,markɪt]

名 超級市場，超市

巧記 super（超級的）+ market（市場）

例句 I go to the supermarket every week to buy something.
／我每星期都會去超市買點東西。

1919 □□□

supper
[`sʌpɚ]

名 晚飯，晚餐

例句 We had a good supper.
／我們吃了一頓豐盛的晚餐。

片語 have supper 吃晚飯 ‖ the Last Supper 最後的晚餐（指耶穌被釘在十字架前夕與 12 名門徒共進的晚餐）

同義 dinner 名 晚飯

1920 □□□

supply
[sə`plaɪ]

動 [及物] 供給，提供；（需求等）滿足
名 供給量，供應（量）

片語 be in short supply 短缺 ‖ supply sth. to/for sb.(=supply sb. with sth.) 提供某物給某人

例句 We supplied them with money and clothes.
／我們提供他們金錢和服裝。

辨析 provide, supply
(1) provide 指「事先準備好」必需品來供應。
(2) supply 指「補給不足」的人員或設備。

1921 □□□

support
[sə`port]

動 [及物] 支持；贊助
名 支持；支援

例句 We couldn't win the match without their support.
／沒有他們的支持，我們就贏不了這場比賽。

片語 in support of 為了支持…

1922
☐☐☐
sure
[ʃʊr]

形 確定的，有把握的
副 當然；的確

片語 be sure of... 對…有把握 ‖ be sure that 確定，確信 ‖ make sure 確定，確認

例句 You need to take notes at the meeting, so make sure to bring a pen and some paper with you.
／你需要在會議上做筆記，因此先確認有帶筆和紙。

1923
☐☐☐
surf
[sɝf]

名 拍岸浪
動 衝浪；上網，瀏覽網頁

例句 I was surfing the Net looking for information on Indian music.
／我上網查詢印度音樂的資料。

片語 go surfing 去衝浪

1924
☐☐☐
surface
[`sɝfɪs]

名 面；表面；外表

片語 on the surface 表面上 (的)，外表上 (的)

例句 Dead leaves floated on the surface of the water.
／枯葉漂浮在水面上。

1925
☐☐☐
surprise
[sə`praɪz]

動 [及物] 名 驚奇，驚訝

片語 in surprise 驚訝地 ‖ to one's surprise 令某人驚訝的是

例句 To my surprise, he didn't get hurt when he fell from the tree.
／使我驚奇的是，他從樹上摔下來竟沒有受傷。

1926
☐☐☐
surprised
[sə`praɪzd]

形 吃驚的，驚奇的，驚訝的

例句 I was somewhat surprised.
／我有點吃驚。

※ To my surprise, my father wasn't surprised at the surprising news.
使我感到驚奇的是，我父親對那個令人吃驚的消息並不感到吃驚。

▲ surprise 是名詞「驚奇，驚訝」，某人對某事感到驚奇，用 surprised，而事物本身令人驚訝，則用 surprising。

1927
☐☐☐
survive
[sə`vaɪv]

動 [不及物] 活下來，倖存下來
動 [及物] 從…中逃出

例句 He didn't survive long after the accident.
／事故之後他沒活多久。

用法 survive 本身已表示「倖存，倖免於」，因而不要再加多餘的 in 或 from。

1928 ☐☐☐ **swallow** [`swɑlo] 名 燕子

例句 A swallow is a kind of bird.
／燕子是一種鳥。

1929 ☐☐☐ **swan** [swɑn] 名 天鵝

例句 The swan swam gracefully in the pond of the park.
／天鵝在公園池塘裡優雅地游著。

1930 ☐☐☐ **sweater** [`swɛtɚ] 名 運動衣，套頭的毛衣

例句 She is wearing a red sweater today.
／她今天穿一件紅色毛衣。

1931 ☐☐☐ **sweep** [swip] 動 [及物] (swept, swept) 掃，打掃，掃除
動 [不及物] 掃除，掃

例句 She swept the floor after supper.
／晚飯後她打掃了地板。
片語 sweep away 掃去 ‖ sweep off 拂去，掃去

1932 ☐☐☐ **sweet** [swit] 形 甜的，甜味的
名 糖果

例句 Do you like sweet food?
／你喜歡甜食嗎？
片語 the sweets and bitters of life 人生的苦樂
同義 candy 名 糖果

1933 ☐☐☐ **swim** [swɪm] 動 (swam, swum) 游泳，遊動

例句 Do you like swimming?
／你喜歡游泳嗎？

1934 ☐☐☐ **swimsuit** [`swɪmsut] 名 游泳衣，泳裝

例句 I wanted to get a new swimsuit.
／我想買件新泳衣。

1935 swing [swɪŋ]
103

動 (swung, swung)(使) 擺動，(使) 搖擺；(使) 旋轉
名 盪鞦韆

例句 The monkey was swinging in the tree.
／猴子在樹上盪來盪去。

1936 symbol [ˋsɪmbl̩]

名 象徵，標誌；符號

例句 This sign ÷ is the symbol for division.
／ ÷ 是除法的符號。

辨析 symbol, mark
(1) symbol 指作為象徵或表達某種深邃意義的特殊事物。
(2) mark 指在其他事物上留下的清晰可見的印痕或先天固有的標誌。

1937 system [ˋsɪstəm]

名 系統，體系；制度，體制

例句 The system has crashed.
／系統當機了。

1938 table [ˋtebl̩]

名 桌子；表格

例句 Father doesn't allow us to talk at the table, but he allows us to talk at the table after meals.
／父親不准我們吃飯時說話，但他允許我們飯後坐在桌旁說話。

1939 Taichung [ˋtaɪˋtʃuŋ]

名 台中

例句 How far is the distance from Taichung to Kaohsiung?
／從台中到高雄距離多遠？

1940 tail [tel]

名 (動物的) 尾巴；(飛機的) 尾部；末尾部分

例句 The dog ran away with its tail between its legs.
／那條狗夾著尾巴逃跑了。

1941 Tainan [ˋtaɪˋnæn]

名 台南

例句 I used to live in Tainan but now I live in Taipei.
／我住過台南，但現在住台北。

第六週

1942 ☐☐☐

Taiwan
[`taɪ`wɑn]

名 臺灣

例句 There are many scenic spots in Taiwan.
／臺灣有很多風景秀麗的景點。

1943 ☐☐☐

Taiwanese
[ˌtaɪwə`niz]

名 臺灣人
形 臺灣的；臺灣人的

例句 As many as one million Taiwanese live and work on the mainland.
／多達百萬的臺灣人在大陸生活和工作。

1944 ☐☐☐

take
[tek]

動 [及物] (took, taken) 拿走；取；就座；就職；花費；乘 (車等)

片語 take away 拿走 ‖ take off ①脫下 ②起飛 ‖ take out 取出 ‖ take place 舉行；發生 ‖ take up ①佔用 ②開始從事

例句 The plane will take off fromTaipei Songshan Airport and land in Tokyo.
／飛機將從台北松山機場起飛，在東京著陸。

辨析 happen, take place
(1) happen 常指偶然或突發事件的「發生」。
(2) take place 通常指經事先計畫或安排的事情「發生」。

take off 脫下　　take off 起飛

1945 ☐☐☐

talent
[`tælənt]

名 才能，天資，天賦；天才

例句 He had a talent for music.
／他有音樂天賦。

片語 be talented at... 在…方面有才能

1946 ☐☐☐

talk
[tɔk]

動 [不及物] 討論；談話，說話
名 演講；談話

片語 give a talk 作報告，演講 ‖ have a talk 談話，聊天 ‖ talk about 談論 ‖ talk with/to sb. 和某人交談

例句 They're talking to their teacher.
／他們正在和老師談話。

1947 ☐☐☐

talkative
[`tɔkətɪv]

形 多話的，愛說話的，健談的

例句 He's not very talkative, is he?
／他不是太健談，是吧？

1948 □□□
tall
[tɔl]

形 高的，身材高的；有⋯高度的

例句 He is a tall boy.
／他是個高個子男孩。

辨析 tall, high
(1) tall 指從底到頂的距離，指人的身高只能用 tall，反義詞為 short。
(2) high 指從地面到最高點，指海拔高度只用 high，反義詞為 low。

1949 □□□
tangerine
[͵tændʒəˋrin]

名 橘子；橘色

例句 There is a tangerine there.
／那裡有一顆橘子。

同義 orange 名 柳橙 形 橘色的

1950 □□□
tank
[tæŋk]

名（儲存液體或氣體的）缸，箱，罐；坦克車

巧記 諧音：〔英〕tank 一音譯→〔漢〕坦克

例句 Look at the tank of my car.
／檢查一下我汽車的油箱。

1951 □□□
tape
[tep]

名 錄音帶；膠帶；帶子
動 [及物] 用錄音帶為⋯錄音（影）

例句 I have a tape of the song.
／我有這首歌的錄音帶。

1952 □□□
target
[ˋtargɪt]

名 標靶；目標
動 [及物] 瞄準；以⋯為目標

例句 The arrow missed the target.
／那支箭未射中標靶。

同義 aim 動 瞄準

1953 □□□
task
[tæsk]

名 工作，任務

例句 I was given the task of building a fire.
／我分配到生火的任務。

同義 job 名 工作

1954 ☐☐☐ **taste**
[test]

🔊104

名 味道
動 有…味道；品嚐

例句 The cookies taste good.
／這些餅乾嚐起來好極了。

用法 taste 意為「嘗起來」時，後跟形容詞作主詞補語。

1955 ☐☐☐ **taxi**
[ˈtæksɪ]

名 計程車 (=taxicab=cab)

例句 He called a taxi for me.
／他幫我叫了計程車。

片語 by taxi(=take a taxi) 搭計程車

1956 ☐☐☐ **tea**
[ti]

名 茶葉，茶水；一杯茶

例句 She offered tea to her guest.
／她端茶給他的客人。

片語 black tea 紅茶 ‖ green tea 綠茶 ‖ make (the) tea 泡茶，沏茶

1957 ☐☐☐ **teach**
[titʃ]

動 (taught, taught) 教；講授

例句 To teach a fish how to swim.
／〔諺〕班門弄斧。

1958 ☐☐☐ **teacher**
[ˈtitʃɚ]

名 教師，老師，教員

例句 His teacher is Miss Green.
／他的老師是格林小姐。

1959 ☐☐☐ **Teacher's Day**
[ˈtitʃɚsˌde]

名 教師節

例句 Teacher's Day is on September 28.
／教師節是在 9 月 28 日。

1960 ☐☐☐ **team**
[tim]

名 隊，組

例句 He is the captain of the basketball team.
／他是籃球隊的隊長。

1961 □□□
teapot
[ˈtiˌpɑt]

名 茶壺

例句 The teapot is very hot.
／那個茶壺很燙手。

1962 □□□
tear
[tɪr]

名 (常 pl.) 眼淚

例句 Her eyes are filled with tears.
／她眼睛裡都是淚水。
片語 in tears 哭泣，流淚

1963 □□□
tear
[tɛr]

動 (tore, torn) 撕開，撕裂

例句 His clothes were torn.
／他的衣服被撕破了。
片語 tear at 撕破，用力扯 ‖ tear down 拆掉，拆除 ‖ tear sth. off 撕下某物

1964 □□□
teenager
[ˈtinˌedʒɚ]

名 (13 ～ 19 歲的) 青少年

例句 Sandy is a very busy teenager.
／姍蒂是個非常忙碌的青少年。
注意 從 thir**teen** 到 nine**teen** 都含有 teen。

1965 □□□
telephone
[ˈtɛləˌfon]

名 電話機，電話
動 打電話 (=phone)

例句 The telephone rang when I was leaving.
／我要走的時候電話就響了。
片語 answer the telephone 接電話 ‖ talk on/over the telephone 通電話
同義 call 動 打電話

1966 □□□
television
[ˈtɛləˌvɪʒən]

名 電視 (機)(=TV)

例句 What's on television tonight?
／今晚有什麼電視節目？

1967 □□□
tell
[tɛl]

動 [及物](told, told) 告訴；講述

例句 He told the news to everybody he saw.
／他告訴每個遇到的人這個消息。
片語 tell sb. sth. 告訴某人某事 ‖ tell sb. (not) to do sth. 告訴某人 (不要) 做某事

辨析 speak, talk, say, tell

(1) speak 強調開口說話、發言的動作，跟某種語言作受詞時是及物動詞。

(2) talk 強調雙方談話。

(3) say 強調說話內容，不接「人」作受詞。

(4) tell 接雙受詞或複合受詞。

　※ After she spoke at the meeting, she talked with the students. She told them that what she said was very important. 在會上發完言之後，她跟學生們進行了交談，並告訴他們她所講的很重要。

1968 ☐☐☐
temperature
[ˋtɛmprətʃɚ]

名 溫度，氣溫；體溫

例句 The temperature will stay above zero in the daytime.
／白天氣溫將保持在零度以上。

片語 take sb.'s temperature 量某人的體溫

1969 ☐☐☐
temple
[ˋtɛmpl]

名 廟宇，神殿，寺院；太陽穴

例句 The ancient temple was destroyed in the flood.
／那座古老的寺廟被大水沖毀了。

1970 ☐☐☐
ten
[tɛn]

代 名 形 十，十個

例句 It was ten degrees below zero.
／氣溫是零下 10 度。

片語 in tens 每十個一組 ‖ ten to one 很可能，十之八九

1971 ☐☐☐
tennis
[ˋtɛnɪs]

名 網球

例句 They are playing tennis in the park.
／他們正在公園打網球。

1972 ☐☐☐
tent
[tɛnt]

名 帳篷

例句 He is taking down the tent.
／他正在拆帳篷。

1973 □□□

term
[tɝm]

名 學期；期限
動 [及物] 把…稱為

105

例句 The President is elected for a four-year term.
／總統當選後任期為四年。

片語 in terms of ①用…的話 ②按照，從…方面來說 ‖ in the long/short term 從長遠／眼前來看

1974 □□□

terrible
[ˋtɛrəbl]

形 可怕的；極壞的

例句 He's a terrible man when he's angry.
／他生氣的時候很可怕。

1975 □□□

terrific
[təˋrɪfɪk]

形 可怕的，嚇人的；巨大的；極度的；非常好的，了不起的

例句 That's a terrific idea!
／那真是個了不起的主意！

1976 □□□

test
[tɛst]

名 測驗，考試；（身體）檢查
動 [及物] 試驗，考驗，測試

例句 I've passed my driving test.
／我已經通過駕駛考試了。

辨析 test, examination, quiz
(1) test 指「測驗，考查」。
(2) examination 通常只指正式的「考試」，如期終考試、入學考試等。
(3) quiz 指「測驗」，特指事先無準備，隨時進行的問答或測驗，也指廣播或電視節目中的一般「知識競賽」。

1977 □□□

textbook
[ˋtɛkstˌbʊk]

名 教科書，課本

例句 She wrote a textbook on how to learn English.
／她編寫了一本如何學習英語的教科書。

1978 □□□

than
[ðæn]

連 比；除…外；與其…，寧願…；一…就
介 比

例句 I like summer better than winter.
／跟冬天比起來，我比較喜歡夏天。

片語 more...than... 與其說…倒不如說…，不是…而是…

注意 用在比較級之後引出表示對比的第二部分時，表示「比」的意思；用在 else, other 後面時表示「除…外」的意思；用在 rather, sooner 後面時表示「與其…，寧願…」之意。

1979
☐☐☐

thank
[θæŋk]

動 [及物] 謝謝；感謝
名 (pl.) 感謝；謝意

片語 thanks to 幸虧，由於
例句 Thanks to your help, I passed the exam.
／多虧了你的幫忙，我通過了考試。

1980
☐☐☐

Thanksgiving
[ˌθæŋksˈgɪvɪŋ]

名 感恩節

例句 We always eat turkey on Thanksgiving.
／我們總是在感恩節時吃火雞。

1981
☐☐☐

that
[ðæt]

代 那，那個
形 那，那個，那種

例句 That bicycle is mine.
／那輛腳踏車是我的。
片語 now that 既然，由於 ‖ That's all right. 不必客氣。

1982
☐☐☐

the
[ðə]

冠 這（那）個，這（那）些

例句 The Great Wall is the longest wall in the world.
／萬里長城是世界上最長的牆。
用法 (1) the 不能與 this, that 等指示代詞連用；不能與 each, every, no 等形
容詞連用；my, his, her 等人稱代詞的所有格連用。
(2) 與一般形容詞連用時，加在前面，但與 all, half 等連用時則加在後面。

1983
☐☐☐

theater
[ˈθɪətɚ]

名 戲院，劇院，劇場；(the ～) 戲劇

例句 My grandmother likes to go to the theater to see Beijing
Opera.
／我奶奶喜歡去劇場看京劇。

1984
☐☐☐

their
[ðɛr]

代 他們的，她們的，它們的

例句 I took their books by mistake.
／我錯拿了他們的書。

1985
☐☐☐

them
[ðɛm]

代 他們，她們，它們

例句 Both of them are wrong.
／他們兩個都錯了。

1986 □□□ **themselves**
[ðəmˋsɛlvz]

代〔反身代名詞〕他／她／它們自己；〔加強語氣〕他／她／它們親自

(例句) They fell and hurt themselves.
／他們自己摔倒受傷了。

1987 □□□ **then**
[ðɛn]

副（指過去）當時，（指將來）到那時；（指時間、空間、次序）後來，然後

(例句) We went to Taichung, and then went to Yunlin.
／我們到了台中，接著又到了雲林。
(片語) from then on 從那時起 ‖ now and then 有時

1988 □□□ **there**
[ðɛr]

副 在／往那裡；（～ be）有
代 有

(例句) Don't put the table there.
／不要把桌子放在那裡。
(片語) get there〔口〕達到目的，順利成功 ‖ over there 在那裡（指較遠）
(辨析) 圖解 here, there, over there:

1989 □□□ **therefore**
[ˈðɛrˌfor]

副 因此，所以

(例句) He was busy, and therefore he could not come.
／他很忙，所以不能來。

1990 □□□ **these**
[ðiz]

代 這些

(例句) These are my children.
／這些是我的孩子們。

1991 □□□ **they**
[ðe]

代 他／她／它們；（籠統地指）人們

(例句) They all speak English very well.
／他們的英語都說得很好。

1992 □□□

thick
[θɪk]

形 厚的，粗的；(液體、氣體等) 濃的

106

例句 The old man likes to eat thick soup.
／那個老人喜歡喝濃湯。

反義 thin 形 薄的，細的；稀的，淡的

1993 □□□

thief
[θif]

名 (pl.thieves) 小偷，竊賊

例句 The thief broke into the house.
／這個小偷強行進入房子。

1994 □□□

thin
[θɪn]

形 細的，薄的；瘦的；(液體、氣體等) 稀薄的

巧記 圖解 thin 的一詞多義：

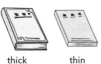

thick	thin	thick	thin
厚的	薄的	粗的	細的

例句 I want some thinner paper.
／我想要一些更薄的紙。

反義 fat 形 肥胖的；thick 形 厚的，粗的；濃的

1995 □□□

thing
[θɪŋ]

名 事情；東西，物品

例句 Are all the things in the car now?
／所有東西都在車上了嗎？

片語 above all things 最重要的是

1996 □□□

think
[θɪŋk]

動 (thought, thought) 想，思考；認為

例句 I don't think he will come.
／我不認為他會來。

用法 在 I think/suppose/believe/imagine... 句式中，如果從句有否定意義，
則否定詞應前移到主句，即否定轉移。

片語 think about 考慮 ∥ think of ①考慮 ②想出 ③認為

T

1997 ☐☐☐ **third** [θɝd]　　名 形 副（常 the ～）第三（個）

例句 I sleep on the third floor.
／我在三樓睡覺。

1998 ☐☐☐ **thirsty** [ˈθɝstɪ]　　形 口渴的；渴望的，渴求的

例句 We are thirsty for knowledge.
／我們渴求知識。

1999 ☐☐☐ **thirteen** [ˈθɝtin]　　數 代 名 形 十三，十三個

例句 Thirteen is believed to be an unlucky number.
／13 被認為是一個不吉利的數字。

2000 ☐☐☐ **thirty** [ˈθɝtɪ]　　數 代 名 形 三十，三十個

例句 Most likely she is over thirty.
／她很可能已經超過 30 歲。
片語 in one's thirties 在某人三十幾歲時 ‖ in the thirties 三〇年代

2001 ☐☐☐ **this** [ðɪs]　　代 這，這個
　　　　　　形 副（指較近的人或事物）這，這個

例句 This is my coat.
／這是我的外套。

2002 ☐☐☐ **those** [ðoz]　　代 那些，那
　　　　　　形 那些的，那個的

例句 Those are my two brothers.
／那是我的兩個弟弟。

2003 ☐☐☐ **though** [ðo]　　連 儘管，雖然
　　　　　　副 可是；然而

片語 as though 好像，仿佛 ‖ even though 即使，縱然
例句 Even though it is hard work, I enjoy it.
／即使這份工作很辛苦，但我喜歡它。

2004
thought 名 思考；思想；看法，想法
[θɔt]

例句 He spent several minutes in thought before deciding.
／他作決定前考慮了幾分鐘。

片語 at the thought of 一想到 ‖ be lost in thought 陷入沉思 ‖ Second thoughts are best.〔諺〕三思而後行。‖ without a second thought 不假思索地，立刻

2005
thousand 代 名 一千，一千個；(pl.) 許許多多，成千上萬
[ˋθaʊznd]

片語 thousands of 許多，成千上萬

例句 Because of the project, thousands of children have better lives.
／因為有了那項工程，成千上萬的孩子有了更好的生活。

注意 數字具體，thousand 用單數

2006
three 代 名 形 三，三個
[θri]

例句 I limit myself to three cups of beer a day.
／我限制自己一天喝三杯啤酒。

2007
throat 名 咽喉，喉嚨，嗓子
[θrot]

例句 He cleared his throat.
／他清了清喉嚨。

片語 cut one's own throat 自取滅亡

2008
through 介 副 通過，穿過
[θru]

例句 Light comes in through the window.
／光線從窗子穿透進來。

片語 get through ①通過 ②接通 (電話)

辨析 across, over, through
(1) across 強調從某個平面的一邊到另一邊。
(2) over 側重越過某種障礙物等。
(3) through 指從某個立體空間內穿過。

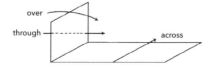

2009 □□□ **throughout**
[θru`aʊt]

介 遍及，遍布；貫穿，從頭到尾

例句 They searched throughout the town for the lost child.
／他們在鎮上到處找尋那個走失的孩子。
片語 throughout the country 遍及全國 ‖ throughout the day 整天

2010 □□□ **throw**
[θro]

動 (threw, thrown) 投，扔，拋，丟

例句 Don't throw stones at the dog!
／不要向那條狗丟石頭！
片語 throw away 扔掉 ‖ throw sth. to sb. 向某人扔某物

Ⓖroup 3

2011 □□□ **thumb**
[θʌm]

名 拇指

片語 all thumbs 笨手笨腳
例句 His fingers are all thumbs.
／他笨手笨腳的。

2012 □□□ **thunder**
[`θʌndɚ]

名 雷，雷聲；雷聲般
動 [不及物] 打雷，轟隆響

例句 I'm always afraid when it thunders.
／打雷時我總是很害怕。

2013 □□□ **Thursday**
[`θɝzde]

名 星期四 (=Thurs./Thur.)

例句 I went to Taipei on Thursday.
／我週四去了台北。

2014 □□□ **thus**
[ðʌs]

副 如此，這樣；因此，因而

例句 He studied hard, thus he got high marks.
／他用功讀書，因此得了高分。

2015 □□□ **ticket**
[`tɪkɪt]

名 票券，入場券；罰單；標籤

例句 Have you got an advance ticket?
／你拿到預售票了嗎？

2016 □□□ **tidy** [`taɪdɪ]
形 整齊的，整潔的，井然有序的
動 [及物] 整理，收拾

例句 Her room is tidy.
／她的房間很整齊。
片語 tidy away 收起，放好
反義 dirty 形 骯髒的；untidy 形 不整潔的，凌亂的

2017 □□□ **tie** [taɪ]
名 領帶；紐帶，聯繫

例句 He was wearing a red tie.
／他打了一條紅色領帶。

2018 □□□ **tie** [taɪ]
動 [及物] (tied, tied) 繫，紮，捆；把…打結，繫上

例句 Tie the tree to the top of the stick to keep it straight.
／把樹和木棍的頂端捆好，讓樹保持直立。
片語 tie together 綁在一起，使…連接 ∥ tie up 拴住，捆牢

2019 □□□ **tiger** [`taɪgɚ]
名 虎，老虎

例句 The tiger was beaten by the lion.
／老虎被獅子打敗了。

2020 □□□ **till** [tɪl]
介 連 直到 (…之時)(=until)

例句 He didn't give up smoking till he got ill.
／他直到生病才戒煙。
用法 till 用於肯定句，與延續性動詞連用；用在否定句中，與非延續性動詞連用 :Do not start till I give the word. 我還未下命令前不要出發。

2021 □□□ **time** [taɪm]
名 時間；次數；時代
動 [及物] 為…安排時間

例句 Time is money.
／〔諺〕時間就是金錢。
片語 all the time 一直，始終 ∥ at a time 曾經，每次 ∥ at any time 隨時 ∥ at the same time ①同時 ②然而 ∥ at times 有時 ∥ from time to time 有時，偶爾 ∥ have a good time 玩得高興 ∥ in time ①及時，還早 ②終於，最終 ∥ on time 準時 ∥ take (one's) time 從容進行，不慌不忙

2022 □□□ **tiny**
['taɪnɪ]

形 極小的，微小的，細小的

例句 This plant has tiny blue flowers.
／這株植物有微小的藍花。

2023 □□□ **tip**
[tɪp]

名 小費；訣竅，技巧
動 [及物] 給…小費

例句 I gave the guy a big tip.
／我給了那傢伙一大筆小費。

片語 from tip to toe 從頭到尾

2024 □□□ **tired**
[taɪrd]

形 累的，疲倦的；厭煩的

片語 be tired of sth. 對…厭倦或厭煩 ‖ be tired with/from sth. 由於某種原因感到疲倦

例句 You may be tired with reading, but you should not be tired of it.
／閱讀可能使你疲倦，但你不應該對閱讀感到厭煩。

2025 □□□ **title**
['taɪtl]

名 (書、畫、詩、曲等的)標題，題目；稱號，頭銜

例句 What's the title of your paper?
／你論文的題目是什麼？

2026 □□□ **to**
[tu]

介 到，向，往；到，直到

例句 Can you take it to the classroom?
／你能把它拿去教室嗎？

2027 □□□ **toast**
[tost]

名 烤麵包，吐司；敬酒，祝酒詞
動 [及物] 烘烤；為…乾杯

例句 Now, I'd like to propose a toast to our teacher.
／現在我提議舉杯敬我們的老師。

2028 □□□ **today**
[tə'de]

副 在今天，在今日；現在，目前
名 今天，今日；當今

例句 Young people of today have lots of things to do.
／現今的年輕人有許多事情要做。

2029 □□□
toe
[to]
名 腳趾

例句 He was dressed in white from head to toe.
／他從頭到腳穿了一身白色。
片語 on one's toes 踮著腳尖；警覺的

Ⓖroup 4

2030 □□□
🎵108
tofu
[ˋtofu]
名 豆腐 (=bean curd)

例句 Would you like some more tofu?
／你要再多一點豆腐嗎？

2031 □□□
together
[təˋgɛðɚ]
副 一起，共同

例句 Tie the two pieces of string together.
／把這兩根細繩繫在一起。
片語 all together 一起 ‖ get together 相聚 ‖ together with... 連同…，和…一起

2032 □□□
toilet
[ˋtɔɪlɪt]
名 廁所，洗手間；馬桶

例句 Where is the toilet?
／廁所在哪裡？

2033 □□□
tomato
[təˋmeto]
名 (pl.tomatoes) 番茄，蕃茄

例句 I'd like a glass of tomato juice.
／給我一杯蕃茄汁。

2034 □□□
tomorrow
[təˋmɔro]
副 在明天
名 明天，明日；未來

例句 Could you bring it to school tomorrow?
／你明天能把它帶來學校嗎？
片語 the day after tomorrow 後天

2035 □□□
tongue
[tʌŋ]
名 舌，舌頭；語言

例句 The dog is hanging out its tongue.
／那條狗伸出舌頭。
片語 lose one's tongue 有口難言 ‖ mother tongue (=mother language) 母語

2036
☐☐☐
tonight
[tə`naɪt]

副 在今夜，在今晚
名 今晚，今夜

例句 I'm going to a party tonight.
／我今晚會去參加聚會。

2037
☐☐☐
too
[tu]

副 也；太

片語 too...to 太…以致不能

例句 Lucy was too excited to say anything when she heard the good news.
／當露西聽到這個好消息時，興奮得說不出話來。

2038
☐☐☐
tool
[tul]

名 工具；方法，手段

例句 Computer is an important tool for the modern teacher.
／對現代老師來說，電腦是一種重要的工具。

2039
☐☐☐
tooth
[tuθ]

名 (pl. teeth) 牙齒，齒

例句 I clean my teeth twice a day. ／我每天刷兩次牙。

2040
☐☐☐
toothache
[`tuθ͵ek]

名 牙痛

例句 I've had a toothache all day. ／我的牙痛了一整天了。

2041
☐☐☐
toothbrush
[`tuθ͵brʌʃ]

名 牙刷

例句 Have you brought your toothbrush with you?
／你有帶牙刷來嗎？

2042
☐☐☐
top
[tɑp]

名 頂端，頂部；(物體的) 上面
形 最優良的 動 [及物] 幫…加蓋

片語 at the top of... 在…頂端 ‖ on the top of... 在…之上
例句 There is snow on the top of the mountain.
／那座山頂上有積雪。

反義 bottom 名 底部，下端
形 底部的

top 頂部

middle 中部

bottom 底部

第六週

2043 ☐☐☐ **topic**
['tɑpɪk]

名 話題，題目；議題

例句 This is a good topic.
／這是個不錯的話題。

2044 ☐☐☐ **total**
['totl]

形 總共，全部的
名 總數；合計 動 合計，總計

例句 What is the total population of London?
／倫敦的人口總數是多少？

片語 in total 合計，共計

2045 ☐☐☐ **touch**
[tʌtʃ]

動 [及物] 觸摸；接觸
名 接觸

片語 get in/into touch with... 與…建立聯繫 ‖ keep/be in touch with... 與…保持聯繫 ‖ lose touch with... 與…失去聯繫

例句 He still keeps in touch with his old friends.
／他仍和老朋友們保持著聯繫。

2046 ☐☐☐ **tour**
[tʊr]

名 旅行，旅遊
動 在…旅行；觀光

例句 We are planning a tour round China.
／我們正在計畫環遊中國。

2047 ☐☐☐ **toward(s)**
[tə'word(z)]

介 向，朝；對於；關於

例句 I couldn't see her face—she had her back toward me.
／我看不見她的臉——她背對著我。

辨析 toward(s), to
(1) toward(s) 強調方向。
(2) to 強調到達目的地。

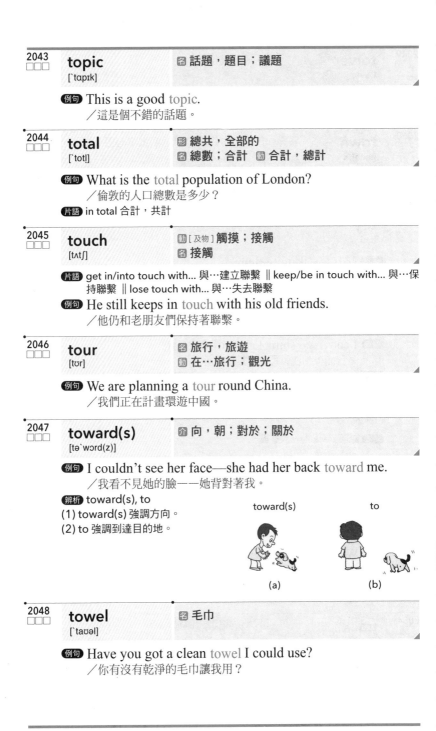

toward(s)　　　　to

(a)　　　　(b)

2048 ☐☐☐ **towel**
['taʊəl]

名 毛巾

例句 Have you got a clean towel I could use?
／你有沒有乾淨的毛巾讓我用？

Lesson3　Group 1

2049 ☐☐☐

tower
[ˋtaʊɚ]

名 塔，高樓

例句 The clock tower stands over 50 meters.
／這座鐘塔高度超過 50 公尺。

2050 ☐☐☐
town
[taʊn]

名 鎮，市鎮，城鎮；商業中心區，鬧區

例句 The small town is beautiful.
／這座小鎮很美。

2051 ☐☐☐
toy
[tɔɪ]

名 玩具

例句 This toy is quite funny.
／這個玩具相當有趣。

2052 ☐☐☐
trace
[tres]

動 [及物] 查出，找到；跟蹤；追溯
動 [不及物] 沿著…走 名 痕跡，蹤跡

例句 I can trace some letters of that date.
／我能查到注有那個日期的信件。

片語 a trace of 一絲，少許 ‖ trace back 追溯以往

2053 ☐☐☐
track
[træk]

名 (pl.) 軌跡，足跡，蹤跡；鐵軌；小道；跑道

巧記 圖解 track 的一詞多義：

track 車轍

track 鐵軌

track 跑道

例句 We saw his tracks in the snow.
／獵人追蹤那頭鹿。

片語 keep track of 跟蹤，記錄，保持聯繫 ‖ lose track of... 失去…的線索／聯繫

2054 ☐☐☐
track
[træk]

動 [及物] 追蹤，跟蹤

例句 The hunter tracked the deer.
／獵人追蹤那頭鹿。

第六週

2055 □□□
trade
[tred]

名 貿易，商業，交易
動 [及物] 交易

例句 Developing foreign trade is very important for our country.
／發展外貿對我國很重要。

2056 □□□
tradition
[trə`dɪʃən]

名 慣例，傳統，傳統的信仰（或風俗）

例句 By tradition, people play practical jokes on April 1.
／按照慣例，4 月 1 日人們可以惡作劇。

2057 □□□
traditional
[trə`dɪʃənl]

形 傳統的，慣例的；守舊的

例句 She is very traditional.
／她很傳統。

2058 □□□
traffic
[`træfɪk]

名 路上行駛的車輛，交通；交通運輸

例句 There's usually a lot of traffic at this time of day.
／通常每天這個時候交通都很繁忙。

2059 □□□
train
[tren]

名 列車，火車；（人、動物、車等的）列，行列

例句 We got on the train in Hsinchu.
／我們在新竹上了火車。

片語 by train 搭火車 ‖ catch/miss one's train 趕上 / 誤了火車

2060 □□□
train
[tren]

動 [及物] 培訓，訓練

例句 These dogs are trained to hunt.
／這些狗被訓練來狩獵。

2061 □□□
trap
[træp]

動 [及物] 設陷阱捕捉；使落入圈套
名 陷阱；圈套

例句 He trapped animals and sold their furs.
／他設陷阱捕捉動物並出售牠們的毛皮。

trap 陷阱

2062 ☐☐☐ **trash**
['træʃ']

名 垃圾，廢物；廢話

例句 Put out the trash, please.
／請把垃圾拿出去。

2063 ☐☐☐ **travel**
['trævl]

動 [不及物] 名 旅行，長途旅行

例句 I traveled from Hualien to Pingtung by bike.
／我騎自行車從花蓮到屏東旅行。

用法 travel 是「旅行」的統稱，是不可數名詞，其前不加冠詞；如果要談「某一次旅行」，則用 journey 或 trip 等。

2064 ☐☐☐ **treasure**
['trɛʒɚ]

名 財富；珠寶，寶藏
動 [及物] 珍重，珍惜

例句 He went to the island looking for treasure.
／他去小島尋寶。

2065 ☐☐☐ **treat**
[trit]

動 [及物] 對待；把…看作；處理；治療
名 招待

片語 treat...as... 把…看作…，把…當…看待
例句 They treated my idea as a joke.
／他們把我的意見當作笑話看。

2066 ☐☐☐ **treatment**
['tritmənt]

名 治療；療法；對待，處理，待遇

例句 He didn't expect such treatment in the company.
／他沒想到在公司會受到這樣的對待。

2067 ☐☐☐ **tree**
[tri]

名 樹，樹木

例句 They are planting trees now.
／他們現在正在種樹。

片語 family tree 族譜
辨析 in the tree, on the tree
(1) in the tree 在樹上 (指外來物，如鳥等)。
(2) on the tree 在樹上 (指長在樹上的，如蘋果等)。

2068
□□□

trial
[`traɪəl]

🔊110

名 審判，審問；試用，試驗；嘗試

例句 I've got a new car on trial.
／我正在試用一輛新汽車。

片語 be on trial ①受審 ②試驗中 ‖ by trial and error 反覆試驗，不斷摸索

2069
□□□

triangle
[`traɪˌæŋgl]

名 三角形

巧記 tri-(三) +angle (角)

例句 The three sides of this triangle are the same.
／這個三角形的三邊等長。

2070
□□□

trick
[trɪk]

名 詭計，騙局；惡作劇；訣竅，手法
動 [及物] 哄騙

例句 He got the money by a trick. ／他用詭計得到了那筆錢。
片語 play a trick on/upon sb. 捉弄某人
同義 cheat 動 欺騙

2071
□□□

trip
[trɪp]

名 (短途)旅行，遠足；行程，旅程

例句 The Palace Museum is only a short trip from here.
／故宮離這裡只有一小段路。

同義 journey 名 旅行；travel 名 旅行

2072
□□□

trouble
[`trʌbl]

名 困難，麻煩
動 [及物] 麻煩；使煩惱

片語 get into trouble 遇到麻煩 ‖ have trouble in doing sth. 做某事有困難
‖ out of trouble 擺脫困境

例句 I have great trouble in learning math and I'm so worried.
／我學數學遇到很大的困難，我很擔心。

2073
□□□

trousers
[`traʊzə-z]

名 (pl.) 褲子，長褲 (=pants)

片語 a pair of trousers 一條褲子
例句 I need a new pair of trousers for work.
／我上班需要一條新褲子。

2074
□□□

truck
[trʌk]

名 卡車，貨車；手推車

例句 He helped me load the furniture onto the truck.
／他幫我把傢俱搬到貨車上。

2075 ☐☐☐ **true**
[tru]

形 真的；真實的

片語 come true 實現，達到

例句 Scientists are working hard to make this dream come true.
／科學家正在努力工作來實現這個夢想。

辨析 true, real
(1) true 為「真的」，指符合實際情況的，反義詞是 false「假的」。
(2) real 為「真實的」，指非想像的，實際存在的，反義詞是 imaginary「想像的」。

2076 ☐☐☐ **trumpet**
[ˋtrʌmpɪt]

名 喇叭，小號

例句 He plays the trumpet very well.
／他小號吹得很好。

2077 ☐☐☐ **trust**
[trʌst]

名 信任，信賴
動 [及物] 相信，信任，信賴

例句 Children put their trust in their parents.
／孩子都相信自己的父母。

片語 trust in 相信，信仰
反義 distrust 名 動 不信任

2078 ☐☐☐ **truth**
[truθ]

名 事實，真相；真理

例句 The truth has come out.
／真相大白了。

片語 to tell the truth〔作插入語〕說實話

2079 ☐☐☐ **try**
[traɪ]

動 嘗試；努力
名 嘗試

例句 Have you tried this medicine?
／你試過這種藥嗎？

片語 have a try 試試看 ‖ try doing sth. 試著做某事 ‖ try on 試穿 ‖ try one's best 竭盡所能 ‖ try to do sth. 盡力做某事

2080 ☐☐☐ **T-shirt**
[ˋti͵ʃɝt]

名 短袖圓領衫，T 恤 (=tee-shirt)

例句 Today our teacher wears a T-shirt.
／我們老師今天穿 T 恤。

2081 □□□	**tub** [tʌb]	名 桶，木盆，盒；一盒的容量

例句 We ate a tub of ice cream.
／我們吃了一盒冰淇淋。

2082 □□□	**Tuesday** [ˈtjuzde]	名 星期二（=Tues./Tue.）

例句 The members meet at the club every Tuesday.
／會員們每星期二在俱樂部聚會。

2083 □□□	**tummy** [ˈtʌmɪ]	名（小孩）肚子

例句 He was up all night with a tummy ache.
／他肚子痛得徹夜未眠。

2084 □□□	**tunnel** [ˈtʌnl]	名 隧道，地道

例句 The train went into the tunnel.
／火車開進了隧道。

2085 □□□	**turkey** [ˈtɝkɪ]	名 火雞（肉）

例句 We bought a 20-pound turkey for Thanksgiving dinner.
／我們為了感恩節晚餐買一隻 20 磅重的火雞。

2086 □□□	**turn** [tɝn]	動 旋轉，轉動；翻轉；成為 名（依次輪流的）順序；轉彎

例句 We take turns to cook.
／我們輪流做飯。

片語 in turn 依次 ‖ turn down 調小（音量）‖ turn off 關掉←→ turn on 打開，擰開 ‖ turn over ①翻動 ②移交

Group 3

2087 □□□ track 111	**turtle** [ˈtɝtl]	名 烏龜，海龜

例句 If you turn over a turtle on its back, it will become helpless.
／如果你把烏龜翻過來，牠就無能為力了。

2088 ☐☐☐
TV
[`ti `vi]

名 電視 (機)(=television)

例句 We're going to buy a new color TV.
／我們要買一台新的彩色電視機。

2089 ☐☐☐
twelve
[twɛlv]

代名形 十二，十二個

例句 The clock began to strike twelve.
／鐘開始敲十二下。

2090 ☐☐☐
twenty
[`twɛntɪ]

代名形 二十，二十個

例句 Twenty people lost their lives in the accident.
／二十人在這次事故中喪生。

2091 ☐☐☐
twice
[twaɪs]

副 兩次；兩倍

例句 This room is twice as large as that one.
／這個房間是那間的兩倍大。

2092 ☐☐☐
two
[tu]

代名形 二，兩個 (的)

片語 by/in twos or threes 三三兩兩，零零落落 ‖ one or two days (=a day or two) 一兩天
例句 They are going to leave for Beijing in one or two days.
／他們這一兩天就要動身去北京。

2093 ☐☐☐
type
[taɪp]

動 打字

例句 Would you like me to type your composition for you?
／你願意讓我幫你把作文打字出來嗎？

2094 ☐☐☐
type
[taɪp]

名 類型，種類

例句 He grew a certain type of flower in the garden.
／他在花園裡種植了某種花。
辨析 type, kind, sort
(1) type 主要指「類型，樣式」。
(2) kind 表示「種類」，指性質相同的東西。
(3) sort 指「種類」基本相似的東西，講話時意思較含糊。

typhoon
[taɪˋfun]

名 颱風

巧記 諧音：〔英〕typhoon 一音譯→〔漢〕颱風

例句 The typhoon pulled up many trees by the roots.
／颱風把許多樹連根拔起。

---

ugly
[ˋʌglɪ]

形 醜的，醜陋的，難看的

例句 It has a very ugly face.
／它有一個難看的外表。

片語 ugly duckling 醜小鴨

反義 beautiful 形 美麗的；handsome 形 漂亮的，英俊的

---

umbrella
[ʌmˋbrɛlə]

名 傘，雨傘，遮陽傘；保護，庇護

例句 It's raining outside. Take your umbrella with you.
／外面在下雨，把你的雨傘帶著。

片語 under the umbrella of... 在…的保護下

---

uncle
[ˋʌŋkl̩]

名 伯伯，叔叔，舅舅，姑丈，姨丈

例句 He is living with his uncle.
／他和他叔叔一起住。

---

under
[ˋʌndɚ]

介〔表示位置〕在…下面；〔表示數量、標準等〕低於，少於；〔表示過程〕在…之中；在…情況下 副 在下面；更少（低、小）地

例句 If you are under 18 you are not allowed to drive a car.
／未滿 18 歲不准開車。

用法 有時漢語中說「下」，但英文中不能用 under：
〔譯〕他們坐在陽光下。
〔誤〕They sat under the sun.
〔正〕They sat in the sun.

---

underline
[ʌndɚˋlaɪn]

動 [及物] 在…底下畫線；強調，使突顯

例句 The report underlines the importance of pre-school education.
／這份報告強調學前教育的重要性。

2101 ☐☐☐
underpass
[`ʌndə‚pæs]
图 地下道；地道

例句 Keep the underpass clear.
／保持地下通道暢通。

2102 ☐☐☐
understand
[ʌndə`stænd]
動 [及物] (understood, understood) 懂；理解，了解

例句 I don't understand what you mean.
／我不了解你的意思。

同義 follow 動 [及物] 理解

2103 ☐☐☐
underwear
[`ʌndə‚wɛr]
图 內衣，貼身衣服

例句 She changes her underwear every day.
／她每天更換內衣。

2104 ☐☐☐
unhappy
[ʌn`hæpɪ]
形 不快樂的，傷心的；不悅的，不滿的；不幸的

例句 I had an unhappy time at school.
／我在學校裡過得不開心。

反義 happy 形 高興的，快樂的

2105 ☐☐☐
uniform
[`junə‚form]
图 制服，軍服
形 一致的，一律的，統一的

巧記 圖解 uniform 的構詞：

uniform〔uni (一) +form (式樣)；同一式樣→〕制服
例句 We all wear uniforms at school.
／我們在學校都穿制服。

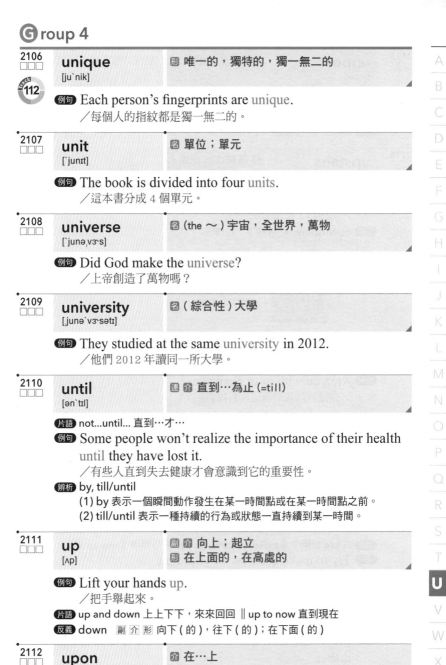

2106 ☐☐☐
112

unique
[ju`nik]

形 唯一的，獨特的，獨一無二的

例句 Each person's fingerprints are unique.
／每個人的指紋都是獨一無二的。

2107 ☐☐☐

unit
[`junɪt]

名 單位；單元

例句 The book is divided into four units.
／這本書分成 4 個單元。

2108 ☐☐☐

universe
[`junə,vɝs]

名 (the ～) 宇宙，全世界，萬物

例句 Did God make the universe?
／上帝創造了萬物嗎？

2109 ☐☐☐

university
[,junə`vɝsətɪ]

名 (綜合性) 大學

例句 They studied at the same university in 2012.
／他們 2012 年讀同一所大學。

2110 ☐☐☐

until
[ən`tɪl]

連 介 直到…為止 (=till)

片語 not...until... 直到…才…
例句 Some people won't realize the importance of their health until they have lost it.
／有些人直到失去健康才會意識到它的重要性。
辨析 by, till/until
(1) by 表示一個瞬間動作發生在某一時間點或在某一時間點之前。
(2) till/until 表示一種持續的行為或狀態一直持續到某一時間。

2111 ☐☐☐

up
[ʌp]

副 介 向上；起立
形 在上面的，在高處的

例句 Lift your hands up.
／把手舉起來。
片語 up and down 上上下下，來來回回 ‖ up to now 直到現在
反義 down　副 介 形 向下 (的)，往下 (的)；在下面 (的)

2112 ☐☐☐

upon
[ə`pɑn]

介 在…上

例句 He put a hand upon my shoulder.
／他把一隻手搭在我肩上。

U

2113 □□□
upper
[`ʌpɚ]
形〔up 的比較級〕上面的；較高的

例句 Please close the upper window.
／請把上面的窗戶關起來。

反義 lower 形 下面的，下方的

2114 □□□
upstairs
[`ʌp`stɛrz]
副 在樓上，往樓上
形（作限定詞）樓上的 名 樓上

例句 The upstairs of the house is new.
／這間房子的樓上是新的。

反義 downstairs 副 往樓下，在樓下

Jimmy

Tom

Jimmy is going downstairs.
吉米正在下樓

Tom is going upstairs.
湯姆正在上樓

2115 □□□
us
[ʌs]
代 我們

例句 Are you with us or against us?
／你是擁護我們還是反對我們呢？

2116 □□□
USA
[`ju`ɛs`e]
名 美國〔=United States (of America)〕

例句 Have you ever been to the USA?
／你去過美國嗎？

2117 □□□
use
[jus]
名 用途
動〔及物〕用，使用；利用

片語 in use 使用中 ‖ make good/full use of 充分利用 ‖ use up 用光，用完

例句 Try to make good use of your time.
／盡量充分利用時間。

2118 □□□
used
[juzd]
形 用過的，舊的；習慣於…

例句 Mr. White used to live in China, so he is used to Chinese dishes.
／懷特先生過去常常住在中國，所以習慣吃中國菜。

2119 used [just]
動 過去常常

例句 You used to smoke a pipe, didn't you?
／你過去常常抽煙斗對不對？

辨析 used to do sth., get/be used to (doing) sth.
(1) used to do sth. 意為「過去常常做某事」。
(2) get/be used to (doing) sth. 意為「習慣做某事」，to 為介系詞。

2120 useful [ˋjusfəl]
形 有益的，有用的

例句 The book is likely to be useful, only it's rather expensive.
／這本書可能很有用，只是它相當貴。

片語 be useful to sb. 對某人有用的
反義 useless 形 無用的

2121 user [ˋjuzɚ]
名 用戶，使用者

例句 The company is the biggest user of oil.
／該公司是最大的石油用戶。

2122 usual [ˋjuʒʊəl]
形 通常的；平常的

例句 Is it usual for you to come home so late?
／你常常這麼晚回家嗎？

片語 as usual 照例，照常，跟往常一樣
辨析 usual, common, ordinary
(1) usual 指在某地或某時間內所「常見的，普通的」，往往指常用的東西或常發生的事情，反義詞為 unusual。
(2) common 指為許多人或事物所共同具備因而「常見的，普通的」。
(3) ordinary 指由於與一般事物的性質或標準相同，因而顯得「平常的」，無奇特之處，反義詞為 special。

2123 usually [ˋjuʒʊəlɪ]
副 通常，經常

例句 She usually goes climbing on Saturdays.
／她星期六通常會去爬山。

2124 vacation [veˋkeʃən]
名 假期，休假
動 [不及物] 度假，休假

例句 Students sometimes take jobs during the vacations.
／學生們有時會在假期打工。

片語 on vacation 休假 ‖ take a vacation 放假

| 2125 ☐☐☐ **Valentine's Day** [ˋvælənˏtaɪnz de] 〔113〕 | 名 聖瓦倫丁節（情人節，2月14日） |

例句 I hate being alone on Valentine's Day.
／我討厭一個人過情人節。

| 2126 ☐☐☐ **valley** [ˋvælɪ] | 名 谷，山谷，溪谷；流域 |

例句 The hills above the valley are bare rock.
／溪谷上方的小山全是裸露的岩石。

| 2127 ☐☐☐ **value** [ˋvælju] | 名 價值；重要性；用途；價值觀 動 [及物] 評價，重視 |

例句 The winner will receive a prize to the value of ＄1,000.
／獲勝者將得到價值 1,000 美元的獎品。

片語 be of great value to... 對…有很大價值 ‖ put great value on sth. 對…非常看重 ‖ value for money 貨真價實

| 2128 ☐☐☐ **VCR** [ˏvisiˋar] | 名 錄影機 (=video cassette recorder)，錄影片段 |

例句 Don't forget to bring your VCR.
／別忘了帶你的錄影機。

| 2129 ☐☐☐ **vegetable** [ˋvɛdʒətəbl̩] | 名 蔬菜 形 植物的 |

例句 We grow a lot of different vegetables.
／我們種植許多不同的蔬菜。

| 2130 ☐☐☐ **vendor** [ˋvɛndɚ] | 名 小販；銷售商 |

例句 He bought a copy from a newspaper vendor.
／他在書報攤買了一份報紙。

| 2131 ☐☐☐ **very** [ˋvɛrɪ] | 副 很，非常 |

例句 I felt very tired when I got home.
／我回到家時覺得非常累。

用法 (1) very 不能修飾形容詞或副詞的比較級。
(2) very 不能修飾動詞。
(3) very 不修飾 asleep，awake，alone，alive 等形容詞。
(4) 一些不可分等級的形容詞，如 perfect，dead，ready，impossible，mistaken，wrong 等，一般不用 very 修飾，但可用 quite 修飾。

第六週

辨析 very, quite
(1) very 可修飾形容詞、副詞，但不能修飾動詞。
(2) quite 可修飾動詞、形容詞、副詞。

2132 ☐☐☐
very
[ˋvɛrɪ]
形 正是，恰好是

例句 This is the very dictionary I want.
／這正是我所需要的那本字典。

2133 ☐☐☐
vest
[vɛst]
名 背心，內衣

例句 This is a blue vest.
／這是一件藍色的背心。

2134 ☐☐☐
victory
[ˋvɪktərɪ]
名 勝利，成功

例句 They celebrated their victory.
／他們慶祝勝利。

反義 defeat 名 失敗

2135 ☐☐☐
video
[ˋvɪdɪ͵o]
名 錄影，錄影節目；錄影帶；影片
動 [及物] 錄(影)，錄製

例句 They showed a video of *Gone with the Wind*.
／他們放映了《亂世佳人》的影片。

片語 video camera 攝影機 ‖ video store 影音用品店 ‖ video tape 錄影帶

2136 ☐☐☐
view
[vju]
名 視線，眼界；景色；見解
動 [及物] 看待，考慮；觀察

例句 A ship came into view.
／一艘船出現在視線裡。

片語 in view ①在視線範圍內 ②考慮中，計畫中 ‖ in view of 考慮到
辨析 sight, scene, view
(1) sight「風景，名勝」，用複數形式指人文景觀。
(2) scene 普通名詞，指「一眼可以流覽的風景」，不限於自然景色。
(3) view 常指在遠處或高處以人的角度，看到的是景色的一部分。

2137 ☐☐☐
village
[ˋvɪlɪdʒ]
名 村，村莊；(the ～) 村民

例句 He lives at a village near the river.
／他住在那條河附近的一個村子裡。

2138 □□□
vinegar
[ˋvɪnɪgɚ]

图 醋

例句 The vinegar is an important flavoring in cooking.
／醋是烹調中一種重要的調味料。

2139 □□□
violin
[͵vaɪəˋlɪn]

图 小提琴

例句 Can you play the violin?
／你會拉小提琴嗎？

2140 □□□
visit
[ˋvɪzɪt]

動[及物] 图 參觀；拜訪，訪問

例句 The President visited five countries in Europe.
／總統在歐洲訪問了五個國家。

片語 give sb. a visit 訪問某人 ‖ pay a visit to sb. 拜訪某人

2141 □□□
visitor
[ˋvɪzɪtɚ]

图 來賓，訪問者，參觀者，遊客

例句 Visitors are asked not to take photographs.
／遊客不可以拍照。

辨析 guest, customer, passenger, visitor
(1) guest 旅社、飯店的「顧客」。
(2) customer 商店的「顧客」。
(3) passenger「乘客，旅客」。
(4) visitor「訪客」。

2142 □□□
vocabulary
[vəˋkæbjə͵lɛrɪ]

图 字彙，詞彙；單字集

例句 It's necessary to increase your vocabulary in studying
English.
／增加詞彙量對學英語來說是必要的。

2143 □□□
voice
[vɔɪs]

图 聲音，嗓音；意見，發言權

例句 The little girl has a sweet voice.
／這個小女孩有著甜美的嗓音。

片語 have (no) voice in... 對⋯(沒) 有發言權，對⋯(沒) 發表意見 ‖ in a low
voice 低聲地，小聲地 ‖ raise one's voice 提高嗓門

2144 □□□
volleyball
[`vɑlɪ,bɔl]
名 排球

(track 114)

片語 play volleyball 打排球 ‖ volleyball game 排球賽
例句 It's interesting to play volleyball on the sand beach.
／在沙灘上打排球很有趣。

2145 □□□
volume
[`vɑljəm]
名 卷，冊，書卷，容量，體積；音量

例句 The volume of this barrel is 27 cubic feet.
／這個木桶的容積為 27 立方英尺。

2146 □□□
vote
[vot]
動 投票，表決
名 選票，票；選舉

片語 vote down 否決 ‖ vote for/against 投票贊成 / 反對 ‖ vote in 選出 ‖ vote out 罷免 ‖ vote through 投票通過
例句 Did you vote for or against her?
／你投了她的贊成票還是反對票？

2147 □□□
voter
[`votɚ]
名 選民，投票人，選舉人

例句 A voter must necessarily be no younger than eighteen.
／投票人必須在 18 歲以上。

2148 □□□
waist
[west]
名 腰，腰部；（物體等）腰狀部分

例句 Betty has a 24-inch waist.
／貝蒂的腰圍是 24 英寸。

2149 □□□
wait
[wet]
動 等，等候，等待

例句 I missed the early bus and had to wait for the next one.
／我錯過了早班車，只好再等下一班。

2150 □□□
waiter
[`wetɚ]
名 （飯店、餐廳）男服務生

例句 Aren't there any waiters in this hotel?
／這家旅社沒有任何服務生嗎？

2151 □□□
waitress
[ˋwetrɪs]

图 (飯店、餐廳) 女服務生

例句 The waitress is bringing the soup.
／女服務生正在端湯過來。

2152 □□□
wake
[wek]

働 (woke, woken) 睡醒，喚醒

例句 The noise woke me up.
／噪音吵醒我了。

用法 表達「喚醒，覺醒」時，wake (up) 和 awake 較常用作不及物動詞，waken 和 awaken 較常用作及物動詞；waken (up) 較通俗，awake 和 awaken 較正式，常用於含比喻意味的情況。

2153 □□□
walk
[wɔk]

働 走，行走
图 步行，散步

例句 She walks to school every day.
／她每天走路上學。

片語 have/take a walk 散步 ‖ walk into 走進

2154 □□□
Walkman
[ˋwɔkmən]

图 隨身聽

例句 I always listen to the Walkman when I walk back home.
／我走路回家時總會聽隨身聽。

2155 □□□
wall
[wɔl]

图 牆壁，圍牆，城牆

例句 Some old towns have walls around them.
／有些古城周圍有城牆。

片語 drive a person to the wall 〔口〕把人逼到絕境

2156 □□□
wallet
[ˋwɑlɪt]

图 皮夾，錢包

例句 I lost my wallet in the park yesterday.
／我昨天在公園弄丟錢包了。

辨析 wallet, purse
(1) wallet 指 (男用的) 皮夾子。
(2) purse 通常是女用的皮夾子、帶扣的錢包。

wallet

purse

2157 □□□ **want**
[wɑnt]

勔 [及物] **想要，要；要求**

片語 want sb.to do sth. 想讓某人做某事

例句 Mother wants me to water the trees.
／母親要我幫樹澆水。

2158 □□□ **war**
[wɔr]

名 **戰爭；戰爭狀態；鬥爭，競爭**

例句 Many soldiers died in the war.
／許多士兵死於戰爭。

片語 be at war with... 和…處於戰爭狀態

2159 □□□ **warm**
[wɔrm]

形 **溫暖的，暖和的；熱情的；激烈的**
勔 [及物] **使溫暖，使暖和**

例句 We received a warm welcome.
／我們受到熱烈的歡迎。

反義 cool 形 涼的，涼爽的

2160 □□□ **was**
[wəz]

勔 [不及物] (be 的過去式) **是；成為**

例句 Our school was built in 1958.
／我們學校建於 1958 年。

2161 □□□ **wash**
[wɑʃ]

勔 **洗，洗滌，清洗；沖刷；洗澡**

例句 You should wash yourself at least once a week.
／你每個星期至少要洗一次澡。

片語 wash away 沖走，沖掉 ‖ wash down ①沖洗 ②吞下 ‖ wash out ①洗乾淨，洗掉 ②把…洗得褪色 ‖ wash up ①洗 (餐具) ②洗手和臉

2162 □□□ **washing machine**
[ˋwɑʃɪŋ məˋʃin]

名 **洗衣機**

例句 Tell me how to use the washing machine.
／請告訴我如何使用這台洗衣機。

2163 □□□ **waste**
[west]

勔 [及物] **浪費**
名 **浪費；廢料**

例句 Mother told me not to waste money.
／母親告訴我不要浪費錢。

A B C D E F G H I J K L M N O P Q R S T U V **W** X Y Z

2164 ☐☐☐

watch
[wɑtʃ]

图 手錶；守衛；注意，監視

115

例句 Could I borrow your watch, please?
／你的手錶可以借我嗎？

辨析 clock，watch
(1) clock 為固定放置的時鐘。
(2) watch 為可攜帶的錶。

clock   watch

2165 ☐☐☐

watch
[wɑtʃ]

動 觀看，注視；照顧，看護；留心，注意

例句 He is watching TV.
／他正在看電視。

片語 watch out/for 密切注意，留神，提防 ‖ watch over 守衛，看守，監視

辨析 watch, look
look at 與 watch 的區別在於：look at 是注意其受詞，而 watch 是注意其受詞的動作。
(a) I am looking at the boy. 我在注視這個男孩子。
(b) I am watching the boy. 我在注視這個男孩子 (的行動)。

| see a film | watch TV | look at the blackboard | watch a game | watch a patient |
| 看電影 | 看電視 | 看黑板 | 看比賽 | 看護病人 |

2166 ☐☐☐

water
[`wɔtɚ]

图 水；(一片) 水
動 [及物] 幫…澆水，幫…加水

巧記 圖解 water 的一詞多義：

water
图水   動澆水

例句 Have you watered the flowers?
／你澆花了嗎？

片語 by water 搭船，走水路 ‖ like fish out of water 感到生疏

2167 `☐☐☐`

waterfall
[ˋwɔtɚ͵fɔl]

名 瀑布

例句 The sound of the waterfall may be heard at a distance of two miles.
／在兩英哩外就能聽到瀑布聲。

2168 `☐☐☐`

watermelon
[ˋwɔtɚ͵mɛlən]

名 西瓜

例句 Watermelons are very popular in summer.
／西瓜在夏天非常受歡迎。

2169 `☐☐☐`

wave
[wev]

名 波，波浪；招手
動 揮手，招手

巧記 圖解 wave 的一詞多義：

waves 波浪

She's waving. 她在揮手。

例句 I showed my pass to the security guard and he waved me through.
／我向保全出示通行證，他揮揮手讓我通過。

2170 `☐☐☐`

way
[we]

名 路，路線；距離，路程；方法，手段；方面

片語 by the way 順便問一下 ‖ in a way 在某種程度上 ‖ in the way 妨礙，阻撓 ‖ on the way 在路上

例句 I couldn't get through the door because there was a big box in the way.
／我不能通過這扇門，因為有個大箱子擋住。

辨析 way, manner, method
(1) way「方法，手段」，普通用語。
(2) manner「方法，樣式」，較 way 莊重，意義極廣泛，兼有 mode, method 等的含義。
(3) method「方法」，指合乎邏輯的或系統的方法。

2171 `☐☐☐`

we
[wi]

代〔I 的複數〕我們

例句 We should leave now.
／我們得離開了。

2172 □□□ **weak**
[wik]

形 虛弱的；軟弱的，懦弱的

例句 He feels a bit weak.
／他覺得有點虛弱。

反義 strong 形 健壯的

2173 □□□ **weapon**
[ˈwɛpən]

名 武器，兵器

例句 The man is believed to be carrying a weapon.
／這名男子被認為攜帶了武器。

2174 □□□ **wear**
[wɛr]

動 [及物] (wore, worn) 穿，戴，佩帶
名 衣著，穿著，穿戴

例句 He wore glasses for reading.
／他閱讀時會戴上眼鏡。

辨析 put on, wear, dress
(1) put on 表示「穿，戴」的動作。
(2) wear 則表示「穿，戴」的狀態。
(3) dress 表示「穿」，其受詞是「人」，而不是「衣服」。

2175 □□□ **weather**
[ˈwɛðɚ]

名 天氣；氣候

例句 What fine weather it is today!
／今天天氣多好呀！

用法 問「天氣怎麼樣」一般說 What's the weather like...；weather 是不可數名詞，不能說 a weather。

辨析 weather, climate
(1) weather「天氣」，一般涉及範圍較小，持續時間較短，不可用不定冠詞修飾。
(2) climate「氣候」，波及範圍大，持續時間較長，是一個地區氣候的總情況，可用不定冠詞修飾。

2176 □□□ **wedding**
[ˈwɛdɪŋ]

名 婚禮，結婚；結婚紀念

例句 Their wedding will be held at nine tomorrow morning.
／他們的婚禮將在明天上午 9 點舉行。

bride
新娘

(bride) groom
新郎

wedding
婚禮

2177 □□□ **Wednesday** [ˋwɛnzde]　图 星期三（=Wed., Weds.）

例句 They left last Wednesday.
／他們上個星期三離開。

2178 □□□ **week** [wik]　图 星期

例句 See you next week.
／下星期見。

片語 by the week 按周計 ‖ week in week out 一周又一周

2179 □□□ **weekday** [ˋwikˌde]　图 工作日

例句 Weekdays are busy here.
／這裡工作日都很忙。

片語 on weekdays 在工作日

2180 □□□ **weekend** [ˋwikˋɛnd]　图 周末

例句 We spent a nice weekend in the countryside.
／我們在鄉下度過了一個愉快的周末。

片語 at/on weekends 在周末

2181 □□□ **weekly** [ˋwiklɪ]　圏 每周的，每星期的
圓 每周，一周一周地 图 周報，周刊

例句 We played chess two or three times weekly.
／我們每星期下兩到三次棋。

2182 □□□ **weight** [wet]　图 重量；體重

例句 What is the weight of this box?
／這個箱子多重？

2183 □□□ **welcome** [ˋwɛlkəm]　勔[及物] 图 歡迎
圏 受歡迎的

例句 You are always welcome at our house.
／隨時都歡迎你來我們家。

片語 welcome to... 歡迎來到… ‖ You are welcome! 不客氣！

W

Lesson **4**

2184 ☐☐☐
116

well
[wɛl]

形 健康的；令人滿意的；恰當的
副 滿意地，很好地

例句 Everything is going well with my studies.
／我的學業一切進展順利。

片語 as well 同樣地，也 ‖ as well as 既…又…，也 ‖ do well (in) (在某方面) 做得好

辨析 well, good
(1) well 既可作形容詞，也可作副詞，作形容詞時，意為「健康的，身體好的」。
(2) good 只有形容詞的詞性，意為「好的」。

同義 healthy 形 健康的

2185 ☐☐☐

west
[wɛst]

名 (the ～) 西，西部；(the W ～) 西方
形 西的，西方的 副 向西方

例句 Walk west two blocks.
／往西走兩個街區。

反義 east 形 東，東面，東部

2186 ☐☐☐

western
[ˈwɛstɚn]

形 西方的，向西的；西方國家的

例句 Many western countries raise a large number of beef cattle.
／許多西方國家飼養了大量的肉牛。

反義 eastern 形 東部的；來自東部的

2187 ☐☐☐

wet
[wɛt]

形 潮濕的，濕的；多雨的
動 [及物] (wetted, wetted;wet, wet) 弄濕，沾濕

例句 It must have rained last night, because the ground is wet.
／昨晚一定下過雨，因為地面是濕的。

反義 dry 形 乾燥的

2188 ☐☐☐

whale
[hwel]

名 鯨

例句 A whale is not a fish.
／鯨不是魚類。

2189 ☐☐☐

what
[hwɑt]

代〔疑問代詞〕什麼
形 什麼；〔用於感歎句中〕多麼

例句 What kind of music do you like?
／你喜歡什麼類型的音樂？

片語 what/how about... 怎麼樣，如何

第六週

辨析 what, how
(1) what 引導感歎句修飾名詞。
(2) how 引導感歎句修飾形容詞、副詞。

2190 □□□
whatever
[hwɑt`ɛvə·]

形 代 無論什麼，不管什麼；任何事物

例句 Whatever happens I'll be on your side.
／無論發生什麼事我都站在你這邊。

2191 □□□
wheel
[hwil]

名 輪子，車輪；方向盤，船舵

例句 The wheel is turning quickly.
／輪子轉得很快。

2192 □□□
when
[hwɛn]

副 什麼時候；在…時
連 在…時 代 什麼時候

例句 Amy was reading a book when I came in.
／我進來時艾咪正在看書。

片語 hardly...when 剛…就

2193 □□□
where
[hwɛr]

副 哪裡，什麼地方
連 在哪裡，在…的地方 代 哪裡

例句 Where do they live?
／他們住在哪裡？

2194 □□□
whether
[`hwɛðə·]

連 是否

例句 I'm not sure whether there are living things on other
planets or not.
／我不確定其他星球上是否有生命。

2195 □□□
which
[hwɪtʃ]

代 連 形 哪一個（些）

例句 Which of these books did you read?
／這些書中你看過哪幾本？

辨析 which, what
(1) which 指在已知人或物中進行選擇，可被 of 短語修飾。
(2) what 指在未知範圍的情況下進行選擇，不可被 of 短語修飾。

2196 ☐☐☐

while
[hwaɪl]

連 當…的時候，和…同時；而，然而

例句 Tom is good at drawing while John does well in playing football.
／湯姆擅長畫畫，而約翰則擅長踢足球。

2197 ☐☐☐

while
[hwaɪl]

名 一段時間，一會兒

例句 Where have you been all this while?
／這一段時間你在哪裡？

片語 after a while 過了一會兒 ‖ in a short while 不久

2198 ☐☐☐

white
[hwaɪt]

形 白的，白色的；空白的
名 白色，雪白

例句 He was wearing a white shirt.
／他穿著白襯衫。

片語 as white as snow 雪白 ‖ call white black/call black white 顛倒黑白

反義 black 形 黑的，黑色的 名 黑色

2199 ☐☐☐

who
[hu]

代 連 誰

例句 Who is that woman in the red hat?
／戴紅色帽子的那個女人是誰？

2200 ☐☐☐

whole
[hol]

形 整體的，全部的；完整的
名 整體

例句 We ate the whole cake in about ten minutes.
／我們大約 10 分鐘內就把整個蛋糕吃完了。

片語 as a whole 作為一個整體，一般來說 ‖ on the whole 大體上，總的看來

2201 ☐☐☐

whom
[hum]

代 連 誰（賓格）；什麼人

例句 The woman whom you talked with at the school gate is our new math teacher.
／剛才在校門口跟你說話的女士是我們新的數學老師。

2202 ☐☐☐

whose
[huz]

代 連 誰的

例句 Whose picture is this?
／這是誰的畫？

2203 □□□

(117)

why
[hwaɪ]

副 連 為什麼
感 啊，咦

例句 Why were you absent yesterday?
／你昨天為什麼缺席了？

片語 Why not? 為什麼不… ‖ Why not do sth.?﹙表示詢問、建議﹚做某事好嗎？

注意 表示吃驚、異議、不耐煩等時，意思是「啊、哎呀」。

2204 □□□

wide
[waɪd]

形 寬的，寬闊的；廣大的 副 很大地

例句 Her eyes were wide with surprise.
／她驚訝地睜大眼睛。

反義 narrow 形 狹窄的

2205 □□□

widen
[ˋwaɪdn̩]

動﹝及物﹞加寬，放寬，擴大
動﹝不及物﹞變寬

巧記 wide(寬)+-en(使)

例句 His interests widen as his knowledge increases.
／隨著知識增長，他的興趣面擴大了。

2206 □□□

width
[wɪdθ]

名 寬度，廣度；寬闊，廣闊

巧記 wide (寬) +-th (…度)

例句 What is the width of this lake?
／這個湖的寬度是多少？

2207 □□□

wife
[waɪf]

名 (pl.wives) 妻子，太太，老婆

例句 I'm fortunate in having a good wife.
／我很幸運有個好妻子。

反義 husband 名 丈夫

2208 □□□

wild
[waɪld]

形 野生的；野蠻的；荒涼的，荒蕪的；狂熱的

例句 Some wild flowers are growing in a corner of the garden.
／花園的角落長出一些野花。

片語 be wild about... 熱衷於…，狂熱崇拜… ‖ go wild 狂怒，狂喜，狂熱

2209 □□□

will
[wɪl]

動 助 將，會；願

例句 He will telephone you at six o'clock tonight.
／他今晚六點將會打電話給你。

A B C D E F G H I J K L M N O P Q R S T U V W X Y Z

2210 □□□ **willing**
[ˋwɪlɪŋ]

形 自願的，願意的，樂意的

例句 He is a willing helper.
／他是個樂於助人的人。

片語 be willing to do 願意去做

2211 □□□ **win**
[wɪn]

動 [不及物] (won, won) 贏，勝，得勝
動 [及物] 贏得；打勝 名 勝利，比贏

例句 You're sure to win.
／你一定會獲勝的。

片語 win a game 贏一局 ‖ win back 贏回

辨析 win, beat, defeat (戰勝，打敗)
(1) win 和 beat 都表示「戰勝」，但 win 後只接事或物，因為 win 的受詞不是競爭對手，而是比賽、戰鬥、獎品等。
(2) beat, defeat 後只接人。

 win the match
贏得比賽

 beat sb. (in the match)
（比賽中）贏了某人

反義 lose 動 輸掉（比賽、戰爭等）

2212 □□□ **wind**
[wɪnd]

名 風；氣息，呼吸

例句 A warm gentle wind is blowing from the east.
／和煦的微風從東邊吹來。

片語 against the wind 逆風 ‖ before/down the wind 順風 ‖ in the wind 即將發生

2213 □□□ **window**
[ˋwɪndo]

名 窗，窗戶，櫥窗；（電腦）視窗

例句 Mary opened the window after getting up in the morning.
／早上起床後，瑪麗打開了窗戶。

2214 □□□ **windy**
[ˋwɪndɪ]

形 有風的，多風的

例句 It's rather windy today.
／今天風很大。

2215 ☐☐☐
wine
[waɪn]

名 葡萄酒;酒,水果酒

例句 We use only the best brand of wine.
／我們只用最佳品牌的酒。

注意 「酒,水果酒」之意時,表示用植物或除葡萄以外的水果釀制的酒。

2216 ☐☐☐
wing
[wɪŋ]

名 翅;翅膀;機翼

例句 The wings of a crow can never cover up the sun.
／〔諺〕烏鴉的翅膀遮不住太陽。／別想要隻手遮天。

片語 take wing ①起飛 ②逃走 ‖ under the wing(s) of... 在…的庇護下

2217 ☐☐☐
winner
[ˋwɪnɚ]

名 獲勝者,優勝者,贏家

例句 The winner got a gold medal.
／優勝者獲得一枚金牌。

反義 loser 名 失敗者

2218 ☐☐☐
winter
[ˋwɪntɚ]

名 冬季,冬天

例句 It can be quite cold here in winter.
／這裡的冬天相當冷。

2219 ☐☐☐
wise
[waɪz]

形 有智慧的;聰明的;明智的

例句 A wise man thinks before he acts.
／〔諺〕智者先思而後行。

辨析 wise, clever
(1) wise 指一個人有智慧,有遠見;也可指由於知識、經驗豐富及良好的判斷能力而正確對待或處理人和事,常用於正式的場合。
(2) clever 指人或動物的腦子靈活;指做成的事物時,常含有巧妙的意思,該詞用得最廣。

2220 ☐☐☐
wish
[wɪʃ]

名 願望;祝福
動 [及物] 希望,想要;祝福,願

例句 I wish you a happy New Year.
／祝你新年快樂。

片語 with best wishes〔信末結束語〕祝好 ‖ wish (sb.) to do sth. 希望(某人)做…

辨析 wish, expect, hope
(1) wish 意為「希望，但願」，用以表示祝願，後接受詞從句時，從句中表示不能實現的或與事實相反的事情時，從句的動詞常用虛擬語氣。
(2) expect 表示預期某事即將發生。
(3) hope 意為「希望」，表示對願望的實現抱有一定的信心，這種希望往往是可以實現的。

2221 □□□

with
[wɪð]

介〔表示一起〕和；〔表示所有〕有，具有；〔表示工具、手段〕用

例句 The girl with long hair is my classmate.
／那個有長頭髮的女生是我同學。

辨析 with, in (用)
(1) with 指用工具。
(2) in 指用語言、寫字材料。

write with a pen
用鋼筆寫

with in ink
用墨水寫

write

Group 2

2222 □□□
118

within
[wɪˋðɪn]

介 在⋯內；不超出
副 在裡面；在內心裡

例句 I could hear sounds from within the building.
／我能聽見那棟房子裡傳出來的聲音。

反義 outside 介 副 在外面，在戶外

2223 □□□

without
[wɪˋðaʊt]

介 沒有，無

例句 We shouldn't go to school without breakfast. It's bad for our health.
／我們不能沒吃早餐就去上學，那樣對我們的健康不好。

2224 □□□

wok
[wɑk]

名 炒菜鍋

例句 You need to buy a new wok.
／你需要買一個新的炒菜鍋。

2225 □□□

wolf
[wʊlf]

名 (pl.wolves) 狼

例句 Wolves kill sheep and sometimes even attack men.
／狼會吃羊，有時候甚至攻擊人。

片語 a wolf in sheep's clothing 披著羊皮的狼，偽善者
‖ cry wolf 謊報狼來了，誇張、扭曲事實，危言聳聽 (源於《伊索寓言》)

2226 □□□

woman
[ˈwʊmən]

图 (pl.women) 婦女，女子；女人，女性

例句 Woman lives longer than man in general.
／女性一般比男性長壽。

用法 (1) 由 man 和 woman 構成的複合詞變複數時，除了其後面的詞要變
複數外，man 和 woman 同時也要變複數：a man teacher—two
men teachers; a woman doctor—three women doctors。
(2) 在某些情況下，用 lady 比用 woman 較為客氣：指在場的女人常說
「This lady...」，而不用「This woman...」。

2227 □□□

wonder
[ˈwʌndɚ]

囫 納悶；想知道；感到奇怪
图 奇蹟；驚奇

巧記 圖解 wonder 的一詞多義：

例句 I wonder how he is getting on.
／我想知道他的近況。

2228 □□□

wonderful
[ˈwʌndɚfəl]

圈 奇異的，令人驚歎的；〔口〕精彩的，極好的

例句 What a wonderful present!
／多麼棒的禮物啊！

同義 great 圈 非常好的

2229 □□□

wood
[wʊd]

图 木頭，木材，木柴；(pl.) 樹林，森林

巧記 漢語裡，兩「木」成「林」，三「木」成「森」；英語裡，常用 wood 的
複數表示「樹林」。

例句 This bridge is made of wood.
／這座橋是用木頭建造的。

注意 oo 在該詞中，不符合讀音規則，發短音。

2230 □□□

wooden
[ˈwʊdṇ]

圈 木頭的，木製的

例句 That's not plastic—it's wooden.
／那不是塑膠的——是木頭的。

2231 ☐☐☐
word
[wɝd]
名 詞，單字；話語，言語

例句 Do you know what this word means?
／你知道這個字是什麼意思嗎？

片語 beyond words 無法用言語形容 ‖ have a word with... 與…談一談 ‖ have words with〔口〕與（某人）爭論 ‖ in a word 總而言之 ‖ in other words 也就是說，換句話說

have a word with
與…談一談

have words with
與（某人）爭論

2232 ☐☐☐
work
[wɝk]
名 工作；作業；職業；(pl.) 作品
動 [不及物] 工作；（機器）運轉；活動

例句 I have a lot of work to do.
／我有很多工作要做。

片語 in work 有工作↔ out of work 失業 ‖ off work 休假的 ‖ get off work 下班
同義 job 名 工作
辨析 job, work
(1) job 作「工作」講時，特指「雇用工作」，是可數名詞。
(2) work「工作，勞動」，指一般的工作，為普通用詞且不可數。

2233 ☐☐☐
worker
[`wɝkɚ]
名 工人，勞動者；工作者，人員

例句 How many workers are there on the farm?
／農場上有多少工人？

2234 ☐☐☐
world
[wɝld]
名 世界
形 遍及全世界的

例句 How many countries are there in the world?
／世界上有幾個國家？

片語 the World Health Organization (WHO) 世界衛生組織 ‖ world record 世界紀錄

2235 ☐☐☐
worry
[`wɝɪ]
動 （使）擔憂
名 憂慮；煩惱

例句 Don't worry!
／別擔心！

2236 □□□ **worth**
[wɝθ]

介 值錢；有…價值；值得
名 價值

片語 be (well) worth doing... (很) 值得做…
例句 I think his idea is worth considering.
／我認為他的建議值得考慮。

2237 □□□ **would**
[wʊd]

助 助〔will 的過去式，表過去將來〕將；〔表示意願〕願；〔表示推測〕大概；〔用於虛擬語氣〕願，要

例句 Would you please lend me a bicycle?
／請你借給我一輛腳踏車好嗎？
片語 would like 想，想要 ‖ would like sb. to do 想要某人做 ‖ would rather do 寧願，寧可

2238 □□□ **wound**
[wund]

名 創傷，傷口
動〔及物〕傷害，損傷

例句 It was a very serious wound, so we took him to the hospital.
／他傷勢很重，因此我們送他去醫院。

2239 □□□ **wrist**
[rɪst]

名 腕，腕關節

例句 He noticed expensive foreign-made watches on every wrist.
／他注意到每人腕上都戴了昂貴的外國製造的手錶。

2240 □□□ **write**
[raɪt]

動 (wrote, written) 寫；書寫，寫字；寫作

片語 write down 記下，寫下 ‖ write to sb. 寫信給某人
例句 My mother writes to me every month.
／我母親每個月都寫信給我。

Ⓖroup 3

2241 □□□ **writer**
['raɪtə-]

名 作者，作家

例句 Who is the most famous living English writer?
／誰是現在在世的英國最著名作家？

2242 wrong
[rɔŋ]

形 錯誤的；有毛病的
副 錯誤地；出毛病地 名 錯誤；壞事

例句 What's wrong with that child—why is she crying?
／那個孩子怎麼了——她為什麼哭？

反義 right 形 正確的

2243 yard
[jɑrd]

名 庭院，院子；碼；場地

例句 There are two apple trees in our front yard.
／我們家前面的院子裡有兩棵蘋果樹。

辨析 garden, yard
(1) garden 通常指栽植花草、樹木的庭園。
(2) yard 則指庭院或房屋周圍的空地。
※ Our house has a garden at the front and a yard at the back.
我們的房子前面有個花園，後面有個院子。

2244 yeah
[jɛə]

感 副〔口〕是的，嗯 (=yes)

巧記 yes 就源於「yeah(是)+so(這樣)」。
例句 "You got married, right?" "Yeah, that's it."
／「你結婚了，是吧？」「嗯，我結婚了。」

2245 year
[jɪr]

名 年；(pl.) 多年，長久；年紀，歲數

例句 It will take years of hard work to finish this project.
／完成這項計畫需要努力工作好幾年。

片語 all (the) year round 一年到頭 ‖ at this time of year 每年這個時候 ‖ by the year 按年計 ‖ from year to year 年復一年 ‖ ...years old …歲 (年齡)

2246 yearly
[ˈjɪrlɪ]

形 每年的，一年一度的
副 每年，一年一次地

例句 The exam is held yearly.
／這項考試每年舉辦一次。

2247 yellow
[ˈjɛlo]

名 黃色
形 黃色的；黃皮膚的

例句 Yellow is her favorite color.
／黃色是她最喜歡的顏色。

yes
[jɛs]

感 副 是，是的，好；(表示疑問或反問，念升調)
真的嗎

例句 "Someone came a while ago and asked for you." "Yes?"
／「剛才有人來找你。」「真的嗎？」

2249
□□□

yesterday
[ˋjɛstɚde]

名 昨天
副 在昨天

例句 It seems as if I had graduated only yesterday.
／彷彿我昨天才畢業似的。
片語 the day before yesterday 前天
用法 yesterday 作時間副詞時，前面不加介系詞 on 或 in。

2250
□□□

yet
[jɛt]

副 仍然
連 然而

例句 Don't give up! There is hope yet. ／別放棄！還有希望。
用法 (1) 在 though/although(雖然…但是…) 結構中，「但是」不能用 but，
而要用 yet。
(2) yet 用在疑問句中時，常放在句尾；在否定句中也可緊接在 not 後面；
還可用在完成時或一般現在時的句子中：Is my coat dry yet? 我的外
套乾了嗎？
辨析 already, yet
(1) already 一般用於肯定句，常與完成時和進行時連用。
(2) yet 一般用於否定句和疑問句，談論預期發生的事情。

2251
□□□

you
[ju]

代 你，你們；(任何) 人

例句 You never know what will happen.
／你不會知道即將發生什麼事。
用法 英語中，出於禮貌，一般單數第二、三人稱代詞居前，第一人稱代詞居後。
例如：You and I are good friends. 我和你是好朋友。

2252
□□□

young
[jʌŋ]

形 年輕的；青年的，有青春活力的
名 (the ～) 年輕人

例句 He is six years younger than his brother.
／他比他哥哥小六歲。
片語 young and old 老老少少

2253
□□□

your
[jʊɚ]

代 你的，你們的

例句 When you face the south, the east is on your left.
／當你面向南邊的時候，東邊就在你的左側。

2254 ☐☐☐ **yours** [jʊrz]

代 你的（東西），你們的（東西）

例句 This pen is mine, not yours.
／這枝筆是我的，不是你的。

2255 ☐☐☐ **yourself** [jʊɚˋsɛlf]

代 (pl.yourselves) 你自己

例句 You yourself told me the story.
／你自己講故事給我聽。

片語 all by yourself ①獨自，單獨 ②獨立地，靠自己

2256 ☐☐☐ **youth** [juθ]

名 青少年時期；青春，活力，朝氣；(pl.)〔總稱〕青年（男女）

例句 She spent her youth in India.
／她在印度度過了她的青少年時期。

片語 in one's youth 在某人年輕的時候

2257 ☐☐☐ **yummy** [ˋjʌmɪ]

形〔口〕很好吃的

例句 The cake is really yummy.
／這蛋糕真好吃。

2258 ☐☐☐ **zebra** [ˋzibrə]

名 斑馬

例句 The lion was running after a zebra.
／獅子在追趕斑馬。

片語 zebra crossing 人行道，斑馬線

2259 ☐☐☐ **zero** [ˋzɪro]

名 (pl. zeros 或 zeroes) 零；(氣溫、壓力等的)零度
形 沒有的

例句 The figure 100 has two zeros in it.
／數字 100 裡有兩個 0。

片語 above/below zero 零上／下

2260 ☐☐☐ **zoo** [zu]

名 (pl.zoos) 動物園

例句 He took his children to the zoo yesterday.
／他昨天帶孩子們去動物園。

MEMO

【英語大全 07】

字根字首巧記法！
中學英語單字大全

Shan Tian She

■著者
星火記憶研究所・馬德高◎著

■發行人
林德勝

■出版發行
山田社文化事業有限公司
地址　106 臺北市大安區安和路一段 112 巷 17 號 7 樓
電話　02-2755-7622
傳真　02-2700-1887

■郵政劃撥
19867160號　　大原文化事業有限公司

■總經銷
聯合發行股份有限公司
地址　新北市新店區寶橋路 235 巷 6 弄 6 號 2 樓
電話　02-2917-8022
傳真　02-2915-6275

■印刷
上鎰數位科技印刷有限公司

■法律顧問
林長振法律事務所　林長振律師

■出版日
2019年10月 初版

■定價
書+MP3　　新台幣350元

■ISBN
978-986-246-558-5